Attitudes toward Mental Patients

New Babylon

Studies in the social sciences

15

MOUTON · THE HAGUE · PARIS

Attitudes toward Mental Patients

a study across cultures

ALEXANDER ASKENASY

MOUTON · THE HAGUE · PARIS

Library of Congress Catalog Card Number: 72 - 93979

Printed in the Netherlands

Preface

The World Federation for Mental Health, as part of its efforts to increase international understanding of mental health and mental illness, sponsored a three-year research project to study attitudes related to the rehabilitation of former mental patients in cross-cultural perspective. The study was financed by the Vocational Rehabilitation Administration, U.S. Department of Health, Education and Welfare, and was also supported by the Research Institute for the Study of Man and the Postgraduate Center for Psychotherapy.

The project consisted of two complementary studies. The first dealt with the views of mental health personnel. The second, by Marisa Zavalloni and Alexander Askenasy, dealt with attitudes of the working public. The two studies are reported in this volume as, respectively, Parts I and II.

Part I, the expert study, investigates effects of cultural, hospital policy and occupational factors on the attitudes of mental health personnel toward mental illness, mental patients, and their rehabilitation. A pilot interview schedule was pretested on a sample of social workers in New York City. Based on that experience a revised interview schedule including a semantic differential section was developed and administered to a second sample of New York City social workers. From these pilot instruments the study's final questionnaire was designed. It was administered to more than one thousand members of the mental health occupations in an Eastern Border state, in Hawaii, and in the South of England.

Part II, the community study, utilized a second questionnaire developed for men and women in the general working population in England, Hawaii, and the Eastern United States. The community questionnaire was given to three samples including about 1,170 respondents ranging from unskilled workers to company management.

Mental illness is a human problem which reaches across national boundaries. It is hoped that this volume will contribute to a better understanding of attitudes toward mental illness, mental patients and their rehabilitation.

Acknowledgments

To Professor Otto Klineberg of the Sorbonne, Director of the International Center for Intergroup Relations, I am indebted in many ways. He introduced me to the challenges and intricacies of cross-cultural research in problems of mental health; he encouraged me to undertake this study and was always ready to give productive and pertinent advice throughout the investigation and the writing of this study. I am most grateful to Professor Richard Christie of Columbia University who gave generously of his time and counsel to this work. Dr. Joan Criswell of the Social and Rehabilitation Service provided wise and useful guidance. This study benefited from her valuable suggestions.

I thank Dr. Marisa Zavalloni of the École Pratique des Hautes Etudes and the International Center for Intergroup Relations for her stimulating and constructive criticism and for sharing with me her experience in international social research. Professors Herbert Hyman and Bruce Dohrenwend of Columbia University made helpful suggestions for the analysis of the findings. Professor Abraham Jacobs, Teachers College, Columbia University, provided expert knowledge on the problems involved in the vocational rehabilitation of mental patients. Dr. Frank Fremont-Smith and Dr. George Stevenson of the World Federation for Mental Health made pertinent suggestions based on their extensive experience with the problems of mental health and mental illness. Dr. E. L. Struening most generously gave me his time and advice based on his rich knowledge of research on attitudes of mental health personnel.

Dr. Kenneth Soddy, Scientific Advisor of the World Federation for Mental Health, made possible the English part of this study and was of invaluable help in familiarizing me with British conditions and issues. I am grateful to Miss Brete Huseth who contributed her skill and tact in collecting the English questionnaires and who provided helpful material on the British hospitals.

Professor Douglas Yamamura, of the University of Hawaii, was a most knowledgeable and helpful counselor. I am greatly indebted to Mrs. Sylvia Levy, Executive Director of the Mental Health Association of Hawaii, and to Merton Berger, by whose advice and familiarity with American mental health problems I profited greatly.

A study like the present one depends on the goodwill and cooperation of many persons. I am unfortunately unable to thank by name the superintendents and staffs and the members of mental health and community agencies who participated in this study. In spite of their already heavy workload, they generously contributed their time, their experience with and their views on the problems of mental illness and the rehabilitation of mental patients. Without their interest and cooperation this study would have been literally impossible. I am deeply grateful to all of them.

I appreciate the kind permission of the IBM Watson Scientific Computing Laboratory in New York to use its computing equipment in the analysis of the data. I owe thanks to Miss Elaine Rubinstein who was helpful in preparing the tables.

For Part II Dr. Zavalloni and I wish to thank Professor Suzanne Keller of Princeton University who was most helpful in revising part of the manuscript and who made many stimulating suggestions. Research Service Limited of London skillfully collected the English community questionnaires. We thank all our interviewers for their conscientious work. Limited space does not allow us to name all of them here. Mrs. Joseph P. Downing in the border state sample and Godfrey Chang in Hawaii, as chief interviewers, were indefatigable in tracking down respondents and in keeping accurate records. In order to preserve anonymity, we are unfortunately not able to thank by name the participating companies, their management and the respondents.

This project was supported by a grant from the Social and Rehabilitation Service (United States Department of Health, Education and Welfare), Mary E. Switzer, Director. The project received additional generous support from the Research Institute for the Study of Man, Dr. Vera Rubin, Director, from the Post-Graduate Center for Psychotherapy and from Smith, Kline and French Laboratories. The research has been conducted under the sponsorship of the World Federation for Mental Health: United States Committee, Inc., William T. Beaty, II, Executive Director. Mrs. George A. Stern, Vice-President of the Committee, was consistently helpful and greatly facilitated work on this project by her cooperation, energy and good advice. I gratefully acknowledge her support and that of Mr. Beaty.

Mary Raphael Humphrey of Columbia University gave much valuable help in the preparation of the book.

Contents

List of Tables

PART I

Mental health workers' attitudes toward mental illness and mental patients

CHAPTER 1

Introduction

MENTAL PATIENTS AND THEIR REHABILITATION

Mental patients pose a problem not only while they are acutely ill and hospitalized, but also after their cure and release from the mental hospital. The emphasis of the problem then shifts to the rehabilitation of the ex-patient into the community. There is considerable uncertainty as to what extent a former mental patient will be accepted by the community. The doubtful status of former mental patients is particularly critical in regard to their vocational rehabilitation. In the general public there have been traditionally distrustful and superstitious attitudes in regard to mental illness and mental patients. The ex-patient who is confronted by such attitudes may find it difficult to obtain employment commensurate with his training and abilities, and this difficulty may in turn have negative effects on his general readjustment.

In view of the above problems, it seemed worthwhile to investigate attitudes toward mental illness, mental patients, and their rehabilitation. One group who play a key role in the treatment and possible rehabilitation of mental patients are mental health personnel. They have been assumed to be especially experienced with and aware of the problems involved.

THE STUDY OF ATTITUDES TOWARD MENTAL PATIENTS

How can a search for attitudes help in an understanding of the situation of mental patients in a society? As Allport (1954) states, attitudes can be used as a 'meeting point' of psychological and sociological work. Thus, Thomas and Znaniecki (1918-1920) in their classic work on *The Polish peasant in Europe and America,* employed attitudes as a key concept to bring together individual and societal data.

The present study deals with samples of members of various mental health occupations in different cultural settings. Attitudes here were investigated in order to measure how they reflect the values of the cultural, socio-economic, occupational and institutional groups to which the holders of the attitudes belong.

Another function of attitudes is pointed out by Allport (1968, pp. 61-62):

> Without guiding attitudes the individual is confused and baffled. Some kind of preparation is essential before he can make a satisfactory observation, pass suitable judgment, or make any but the most primitive reflex type of response. Attitudes determine for each individual what he will see and hear, what he will think and what he will do. To borrow a phrase from William James, they 'engender meaning upon the world'; they draw lines about and segregate an otherwise chaotic environment; they are methods for finding our way about in an ambiguous universe.

Allport stresses here the structuring aspect of attitudes in situations of uncertainty. Mental patients appear to be particularly well suited as objects of guiding attitudes, as the causation and symptoms of their sufferings are not easily pinpointed but are often uncertain and ambiguous. Such uncertainty may be expected to be more characteristic of laymen than of experts in a given field. Even experts in psychiatry, however, do not agree on the etiology of psychoses and are very reserved in predicting the behavior of their patients and the chances of relapse of patients after they are released from mental hospitals. The public at large which has not been exposed to psychiatric training and experience is even vaguer and more puzzled in its perception of mental patients, the causation of their illness, and the prediction of the patients' future behavior.

In such a perceptually confusing area the conditions for the development of structuring attitudes exist. Traditionally, societies have developed specific labels for the mentally ill. These labels were often accompanied by superstitious explanations of the illnesses' causation and by norms for the behavior of the healthy community members toward the mentally ill. Until well into the nineteenth century, psychotics in North America were often ostracized, locked up in dirty cells and badly treated (Lewis, 1959, p. 8). In the course of time there have been notable improvements, but even at present the general public has carried over some traditional misconceptions about mental illness and is still receiving sensationalized, threatening and otherwise distorted information about mental disorders. (See, e.g., Nunnally, 1961.)

To understand better the place of popular attitudes toward mental patients, it may be worthwhile to consider the relationship between society and mental illness as was done, e.g., by Scheff (1963) and Szasz (1961). One view holds that 'Mental ill health is a symptom and index of the malfunctioning of society.' (Burgess, 1955, p. 16.)

The analysis by Parsons has been especially fruitful in tying the role of the ill person to the functioning of the wider society of which he is a member. Parsons discussed illness as 'aspects of the general social equilibrium of modern western society . . . "Deviant" behavior . . . is defined in sociological terms as failing in some way to fulfill the institutionally defined expectations of one or more of the roles in which the individual is implicated in society.' (Parsons, 1951, pp. 609-610.) Parsons sees alternative forms of deviant behavior for which society provides roles in the criminal, the hobo, or the member of an exotic religious sect. In Parsons' words, '. . . the phenomena of physical and mental illness and the counteraction are more intimately connected with the general equilibrium of the social system than is generally supposed.' (*Ibid.*, p. 617.)

'In the case of mental illness, on the other hand, the focus of disturbance is in the relations between the personality of the individual and the social system or systems in which he participates . . . A mentally ill person is then, in my view, a person who by definition cannot get along adequately with his fellows, who presents a problem to them directly on the behavioral level.' (Parsons, 1957, p. 109.)

Mental illness can become a threat to society's values; the mentally ill may exhibit forms of behavior which are directly in conflict with the culturally accepted rules and norms (see Foucault, 1965). How do different societies handle the problem of dealing with deviant behavior? As Parsons states, 'American societal values put a primary emphasis on achievement, and it is chiefly because mental illness hinders effective achievement that in our society it is defined as an undesirable state.' (*Ibid.*, p. 112.) Klineberg (1954, p. 399) discusses an Indian study of the relative infrequency of schizophrenia in Bombay mental hospitals. He concludes: 'It may mean that in India, where "escape from reality" in our sense is made possible through mystical religious experience, schizophrenia occurs with relatively less frequency because it is less needed.' Carstairs puts the situation as follows: 'It appears in fact that there is *no* clearcut criterion of what constitutes a psychiatric case. Whether a person is regarded as in need of medical treatment is always a function of his disturbance of behavior *and* of the attitude of his fellows in society.' (1959, p. 377.)

THE ATTITUDES OF MENTAL HEALTH PERSONNEL

One of the main arguments of the present study is that not only the public at large but also mental health personnel reflect the cultural values through their attitudes toward mental illness, mental patients, and their rehabilitation. In other words, it is argued that even mental health personnel are not free from popular misconceptions of mental illness and that they have not wholly taken over scientific and objective views of mental illness. It is held that while the attitudes of mental health personnel reflect the views of the wider culture, the professional views in turn can and do affect the views of the general community.

Research on the attitudes of mental health personnel has presupposed that their attitudes have some effect on the mental patients they work with. If there is to be any hope that in the future attitudes toward mental patients may be changed in a more favorable direction, it is necessary to know the current attitudes of these persons. (Treesh, Struening, Pratt, *et al.*, 1960.)

Since Pinel, psychiatrists have been concerned with the attitudes of mental hospital staff (Middleton, 1953), but there has been little objective measurement of their attitudes. In 1873, Isaac Ray wrote an article on the 'Ideal Characteristics of the Officers of a Hospital for the Insane,' but until recently, slight emphasis has been placed on the study of the outlook of mental health personnel. (Pratt, Scott, *et al.*, 1960, p. 26.)

FACTORS AFFECTING ATTITUDES OF MENTAL HEALTH PERSONNEL

Social class

Hollingshead and Redlich (1958) attempted to correlate social class with the incidence, development, diagnosis and treatment of mental illness in New Haven, Connecticut. As part of their overall study, they interviewed 17 psychiatrists on their attitudes toward mental patients and concluded that the psychiatrists preferred upper and middle class patients to lower class patients. (This study will be reviewed in Chapter 3.)

Occupations

The major work on the attitudes of mental hospital staffs has been done by Cohen and Struening (1959, 1960, 1962). In their study of more than 7,000 workers in 12 Veterans Administration neuropsychiatric hospitals, Cohen and Struening concluded that, within their sample, attitudes toward mental patients varied primarily with the occupation of the staff members. Their work will be discussed in detail in Chapter 2.

The various kinds of specialized personnel whose work involves the care, treatment and rehabilitation of mental patients may be combined into three major groups for the sake of brevity. (1) Psychiatrists and psychologists have the main responsibility for diagnosis and therapy. (2) The staff of aides and nurses plus the occupational and recreational therapists have the greatest amount of daily contact with patients in the hospital. (3) Social workers and vocational and rehabilitation counselors, as their primary functions, serve as links between mental patients and the community. Actually, the combination of the different occupations into three functional groups is a simplification, as Cohen and Struening have pointed out. The characteristics of the different occupations and their job functions will be discussed in some detail in Chapter 4.

Traditionally, in the mental hospital the job functions have been quite separate. Smith and Levinson (1957, p. 5) state, 'Few physicians have ever been aides, nor will the nurse become a physician. Each occupational level, therefore, tends to operate as a somewhat closed system. Its skills, values and attitudes are acquired within the occupation or profession and may be little known outside it.'

Even though the attendants or aides are the group with least psychiatric and general education, they are of special importance. As Schermerhorn (1955, p. 51) puts it, the patient's '. . . connection with the hospital culture is chiefly a function of his contacts with the attendant. For the average patient, the attendant is the hospital, or at least symbolizes its values. From the standpoint of the staff, however, the attendant least represents hospital values. In the hierarchy of administration, he is clearly at the bottom, with the doctors and superintendents at the top.'

Pratt (1961) among others, has spoken of the traditional mental hospital as enclosing a caste and class system. In this interpretation, staff and patients belong to different castes, while the staff, in turn, is divided into rigid class hierarchies. In recent mental hospital theory and in some applications, there have been new definitions of more overlapping and 'democratic' job functions, as will be discussed in the next section.

Implied in occupational membership are professional training and occupational functions and goals, both current and as they have historically developed. All of these factors may affect staff attitudes toward mental patients and mental illness. As the main argument of the present study deals with the interaction of various factors in their effects on attitudes toward mental patients and mental illness, it is held that the attitudes of different respondents are best understood not only in terms of their occupations, but also in reference to the socio-economic levels from which the different occupations recruit their members in a selective fashion.

Mental hospitals

Most of the work with mental patients is carried on within hospitals specialized for that purpose. The organization, functions and goals of mental hospitals have been undergoing re-evaluation in recent years, and a number of reforms of and alternatives to the traditional mental hospital have been proposed. Cohen and Struening (1962, p. 1) sum up the situation as follows:

> The past decade has witnessed several major shifts in the conception, care and treatment of hospitalized mental patients. There has been a move toward 'open' hospitals, milieu therapy, patient government, and patient work programs. This newer outlook is based on the general assumption that the well-being of mental patients is at least to some extent influenced by the social context. Derivatives from this assumption include the more specific hypotheses that mental patients are sensitive to and influenced by the attitudinal atmosphere created by hospital

employees, that the success of reintegrating former mental patients into society is affected by the attitudes of the general public toward mental illness.

A number of new hospital forms have been proposed. (For some overall discussions of the movement, the reader is referred to Arieti, 1959, 1966; Greenblatt, Levinson, and Williams, 1957; Pratt, Scott, *et al.*, 1960; Pratt, 1961, and Wechsler and Landy, 1960.)

The trend from the 'conservative' to the 'progressive' hospital may be seen in part as involving less emphasis on custodial care and more concern with therapy. As an example of this new tendency, one may mention the influential work of Maxwell Jones (1953, 1968) on *The therapeutic community.* This model was described by Linn (1959, p. 1831) as follows: 'In the therapeutic community the whole of the time which the patient spends in the hospital is thought as a treatment time, and everything that happens to the patient is part of the treatment program. Thus, the therapeutic community is to be found ultimately in a point of view which seeks to integrate every detail of mental-hospital life into a continuous program of treatment . . . the behavior of all personnel, without exception, is part of the program.' (See also Kraft, 1966; Polsky *et al.*, 1970.)

In contemporary mental hospitals, psychiatrists are seriously overburdened, and already the hospital staff fills some of the psychiatrists' therapeutic functions. The therapeutic community makes this dispersion of functions explicit. Rather than bewail the chronic shortage of psychiatrists in mental hospitals, this approach tries to maximize and to make purposeful the therapeutic functions of other staff groups. Among the innovations in mental hospital practices which have been advocated by the progressive school are open wards, increased patient self-government, therapy by a multidisciplinary 'psychiatric team,' such institutions as day hospitals (see Kramer, 1962), night hospitals, half-way houses (Fairweather *et al.*, 1969; Landy and Greenblatt, 1965), walk-in clinics (see Tannenbaum, 1966), foster family care (Morrissey, 1967), and use of para-professionals (e.g. Rappaport *et al.*, 1971). There is, above all, a concern with the hospital's atmosphere or 'social climate.' In addition to Maxwell Jones, one might mention here as some exponents of the new school, Hoenig and Hamilton (1969), Querido (1954), Stanton and Schwartz (1954) and Greenblatt (1957).

Gilbert and Levinson (1957a) have tried to correlate hospital policies with staff 'ideologies,' both of which they felt they could line up along a unidimensional continuum from 'custodialism' to 'humanism.' While this unidimensional approach may be useful for certain purposes, it has been criticized as being too simple for many others (Parsons, 1957, p. 111).

In all fairness, it should be pointed out that the custodial hospitals do not merely represent the absence of all that is laudable in mental hospitals nor do the reformed hospitals stand for all that is desirable. As Pratt, Scott, *et al.* (1960, pp. 23-24) phrase it, ' "Good" (but untested) ideas, reformist enthusiasm, interesting applications and practical developments are all to be found in the bandwagon support for the "open" approach to mental hospitals . . . The ideas sound so good, and in many ways for many patients may well prove to be therapeutic, that clinical personnel (particularly psychologists) tend to accept and proselytize without seeking verification or proof.' Furthermore, they state (p. 142), '*Tour de force* pressure for custodial-to-treatment transition often makes the gratuitous presumption of enlightened clinical attitudes throughout the staff with sometimes catastrophic results.' Not all 'custodial' practices are due to a negative perception of patients or to deliberate planning, but such practical factors as hospital overcrowding and understaffing play a regrettable but important role in determining hospital policies.

Socio-cultural factors

It is not sufficient to consider attitudes of mental health personnel only within the frame of institutional policies and of occupational or class membership. In Parsons' words (1957, p. 112), 'A hospital like any collectivity must be treated as a subsystem of a society. The value system of the collectivity then must be treated as a derivative of the values of the society as a whole.'

The values of the wider society are shared by the mental hospital staff to a greater or lesser extent and determine their attitudes. While the mental hospital is a sub-system of society, it also possesses special characteristics which distinguish it from other organizations in the society and which influence, e.g., the selection of the persons who work with mental patients.

If one sees the mental health personnel as members of a culture, then one might expect that cultural values may be reflected in their attitudes toward mental patients. A cross-cultural approach – even within the limited scope of the present study's American and English samples – might enlarge our knowledge of the factors involved.

Cultural relativism of the concept of mental illness was briefly discussed above (see also Ellenberger, 1960), and one may expect that various attitudes toward mental patients may also be affected by cultural traditions. Views on mental illness may be influenced not only by a culture's general development, but also by characteristic historical trends of specific sub-cultures such as that of psychiatry. Thus, in comparison between European and American psychiatry, it has been noted that in Europe genetics plays a stronger role (Ellenberger, 1955; Nigrin, 1959). Other differences were seen, e.g., in approaches to personality problems, which have been said to be more theoretical in Europe and more pragmatic in America, and in a greater European reliance on organic than on psychodynamic views (Mora, 1959).

It has been argued that a cross-cultural approach might widen and deepen the perspective and the understanding of American mental health problems. The present study will try to provide some empirical data for the questions which were raised in this section. Another question may be asked: What inferences can be drawn to the cultures from which the samples in this study were selected? Klineberg (1954, p. 378) states:

> What appear to be differences between two nations may turn out to be due to such factors as degree of urbanization, economic and industrial development, level of education, religion and other variables which cut across national lines. The answer to this criticism is that of course all these factors must be taken into account. We need studies of various religions within a nation, as well as of economic classes and other subgroups; we need a comparison of similar classes in different nations as well as of different classes within the same nation.

The present study can make no claims to approach a comprehensive coverage of the relevant social factors which may affect the attitudes of mental health workers in different societies. It will attempt to focus on certain regions, hospital sub-cultures, and occupational groupings which will be related to certain educational and economic characteristics. Differences in results among the Hawaiian, mainland American, and English samples will be examined in view of these factors.

Interaction of factors

In the preceding sections, occupation and social class membership, hospital policy and socio-cultural setting were discussed as factors which affect the attitudes of mental health personnel towards mental patients and mental illness. The individual respondent to the questionnaire in this study is then seen as being influenced by his membership in an occupational group with specific training, group norms and standards, as well as specific functions vis-à-vis mental patients. At the same time, he is employed by a particular institution with its own practices, policies and history. He also belongs to a certain socio-economic group within his society and has been exposed to a certain amount of general education. Furthermore, he may belong to an ethnic minority within his society. In a still wider sense, he can be seen as a citizen of a society with its particular history and traditions. All of these factors are seen as interacting and affecting the values and attitudes of a respondent.

QUESTIONS ABOUT ATTITUDES OF MENTAL HEALTH PERSONNEL

At this point it may be appropriate to raise some questions concerning attitudes of mental health personnel on which the present study may throw some light.

General questions

Do mental health personnel express preferences for certain types of mental patients? If yes, which types do they prefer, and what kinds of patients do they least like to work with? Are the views on mental illness and on the vocational rehabilitation of mental patients held by mental health personnel in accordance with current scientific knowledge and theory? What are the relations between the preferences of mental health workers and their factual knowledge, e.g., of ex-patients' chances for vocational success?

Social class

Hollingshead and Redlich found that a sample of psychiatrists in New Haven preferred to work with mental patients from a middle class background. Does this hold for other occupations? Does it hold in other locations in the United States and in England? Is there a general preference for one's own group or does preference cut across socio-economic groups? Are members of one's own socio-economic group felt to be easiest to work with? Do preferences for certain patients vary with the respondents' perception of their own class membership?

Occupation
Cohen and Struening showed that occupations are related to attitudes toward mental illness. Do Cohen and Struening's findings hold in other cultural settings? In which occupational groups are mental patients perceived most in accordance with current psychiatric thought? In which occupational groups do cultural factors most affect attitudes toward mental patients and mental illness?

Hospital
Do attitudes vary with hospital policy? If the policy is set at the top of the occupational hierarchy, how far down does it reach in the occupational ladder? For instance, does the nursing staff echo the views of the hospital administration?

Culture
(1) *Between hospitals (England vs. United States).* Do attitudes vary with the respondents' cultural settings? Which attitudes in particular do vary? How does culture affect attitudes relating to mental illness? Which occupational groups particularly reflect cultural values in their attitudes?

(2) *Within a hospital (Hawaii).* Are different cultural-ethnic backgrounds reflected in different attitudes toward mental illness and mental patients? Do attitudes toward mental patients of different ethnic origins vary with the respondents' own ethnic background? Do respondents find it easier to work with members of their own ethnic group? In Hawaii a general lack of negative attitudes toward other ethnic groups has been noted. Does this tolerance carry over to attitudes toward mental patients?

Interaction of factors
Is one of the above factors of predominant importance in determining attitudes toward mental illness and mental patients? If not, under what conditions do different variables play major roles? What are the relative influences of different factors on attitudes? In what ways do occupational, hospital, and cultural factors interact as they affect attitudes toward mental illness, mental patients and their rehabilitation?

SUMMARY

This chapter dealt first briefly with the problems of mental illness and of the rehabilitation of former mental patients. The following section was concerned with the role of attitudes in structuring the environment and attitudes toward mental illness and toward mental patients held by the general population. The next two sections dealt with the mental health personnel who are a part of this general population and various factors affecting their attitudes.

Finally, these factors were seen as interacting with one another, and a series of questions were asked, some of which it is hoped this study will help to answer.

CHAPTER 2

Review of the literature

Research on attitudes toward mental patients and mental illness is of relatively recent origin. The earliest study reported in the literature was conducted by Allen (1943). In this as in most subsequent studies, samples were drawn from the general population. Among these investigations, some of the better known ones were carried out by Crocetti, Spiro, and Siassi (1971), Cumming and Cumming (1957), Dohrenwend and Chin-Shong (1967), Lemkau and Crocetti (1962), Nunnally (1957; 1960), Pratt, Giannitrapani, and Khanna (1960), Shirley Star (1955; 1956; 1957), Woodward (1951).

In contrast to the body of work now existing on the general public's attitudes toward mental illness, only few studies exist on the attitudes of those directly working with mental patients. The present chapter is an attempt to summarize the literature in this field (see also Rabkin, 1972).

GILBERT AND LEVINSON

A pioneering study of considerable interest is that of Gilbert and Levinson (1957a). These authors set out to demonstrate congruences between mental hospital structure, staff 'ideology' and personality.

In order to describe hospital structures or policies, they assumed the existence of an unidimensional continuum from 'custodialism' to 'humanism' in mental hospitals which is matched by a corresponding continuum of staff ideologies. While the writers admit that these hospital forms are prototypes or 'ideal types' in Weber's sense (*ibid.*, p. 22), they assume that one grand dimension can account for the entire range of mental hospitals in between the two extremes.

Their model of a 'custodial' mental hospital resembles the traditional prison where 'inmates' are locked up. In such a hospital patients are seen as 'totally irrational, insensitive to others, unpredictable, and dangerous' (*ibid.*, p. 22). The staff is pessimistic, distrustful and cannot be expected to be of much help to most patients. The authors describe this prisonlike hospital as 'autocratic, involving as it does rigid status hierarchy, a unilateral downward flow of power, and a minimizing of communication within and across status lines' (*ibit.*).

The 'humanistic' orientations, on the other hand, are less one-sided. For one thing, they vary somewhat among themselves both in ecological bases from the 'large, architecturally horrendous, financially limited state hospital' to the small rich private hospital, as well as in theoretical positions. The 'humanistic' view is seen as stressing interpersonal and psychological sources of mental illness, at times neglecting somatic and hereditary factors. It is characterized by an occasionally unrealistic optimism about chances for recovery. It tries to 'democratize' the hospital, and follows modern ideas of a therapeutic community. Gilbert and Levinson explain their position: 'It is difficult to conduct a dispassionate inquiry into custodialism and humanism without idealizing the latter through contrast with the former. There is, of course, much evidence showing the therapeutic ineffectiveness, not to speak of the inhumanity and decadence, of the custodial system. Nevertheless, it is clear that the proponents of humanistic change are still groping their way in semi-darkness' (*ibid.*, p. 23). Staff ideologies follow a similar single dimension: 'We believe that the concepts of custodialism and humanism could meaningfully be applied not merely to hospital policies and to formal administrative philosophies, but as well to the orientations of individual hospital members toward mental illness and its treatment' (*ibid.*).

These ideologies are seen as attempts to rationalize and to justify existing hospital policies. In order to measure ideology, a Likert scale of 20 statements was developed of which 17 were considered as 'custodial' and 3 as 'humanistic.' The instrument was called 'Custodial Mental Illness Ideology' (CMI) scale. The 20 statements concerned the nature and causes of mental illness, patient-staff relations, etc. The scale was used to study ideology 'both as an individual and as a collective phenomenon' (*ibid.*, p. 33). An individual's ideology would be his CMI score. A collective ideology or 'modal ideology' would be the mean (not the modal) CMI score of a given group.

Finally, personality was measured by eight items from the F scale (see Adorno *et al.*, 1950). 'Modal personality refers to those ideology-relevant personality trends that are most common in each grouping' (Gilbert and Levinson, 1957a, p. 27). As the authors put it: 'One of our fundamental postulates is that an individual's ideological orientation is intimately bound up with his deeper-lying personality characteristics' (*ibid.,* p. 32). 'This aspect of the research was based on the hypothesis that the custodial orientation is one facet of an authoritarian personality, the humanistic orientation a facet of an equalitarian personality' (*ibid.,* p. 26).

The samples were chosen from three Massachusetts mental hospitals, a large (1,000 bed) state hospital, considered to be 'custodial', a Veterans Administration hospital of about the same size, seen as intermediate in policy, and a small (120 bed) active treatment state hospital, described as 'humanist.' In each hospital, samples of attendants, nurses, and psychiatrists were tested. The occupational groups were labeled with ranks in terms of 'custodialism' on the basis of education and job functions toward the patients so that *a priori* attendants were considered the most and psychiatrists the least custodial group. The total N was 335.

Hospitals and occupations were then put in a combined rank order of 'custodialism', in which occupation, being more permanent and more selective, overrode hospital membership. Each group's *a priori* rank order was then correlated with its mean CMI and F scores. Rank order correlations for the groups were, respectively, .92 (with CMI), .90 (with F score), and .81 (mean CMI with mean F scores). *Individual* CMI scores and group rank obtained a product-moment correlation (which, strictly speaking, assumes equal intervals between ranks) of .47. *Individual* F scores and group status membership correlate at .46. The authors conclude that hospital system and occupational status are related to ideology and personality. The relationships hold fairly well for group means, though individuals vary considerably within a given group, 'and the phenomenon of incongruence is as important as that of congruence' (*ibid.,* p. 33).

Like *The authoritarian personality* (Adorno *et al.,* 1950), the study reviewed here conceives of authoritarianism as being a deep-rooted permanent aspect of personality. Thus some criticisms raised against the earlier study can also be brought up here. Hyman and Sheatsley (1954) point out that differences in F scores 'could well be artifacts of an uncontrolled educational difference. That these personality traits do vary with education has been demonstrated in many representative samples of the adult population' (*ibid.,* p. 93). In the same work, Christie (1954) states that 'consistently high correlations between attitudinal dimensions and years of education, scores on intelligence tests (based largely on what is learned in school), and various other socio-economic criteria had been found' (*ibid.*, p. 167). He lists several studies which indicate negative relationships between education and F scale scores for educationally heterogeneous samples.

Gilbert and Levinson concluded that 'there is considerable evidence that the autocratic-democratic continuum of ideology is one aspect of a broader authoritarian-equalitarian continuum of personality' (Gilbert and Levinson, 1957a, p. 34). The individual CMI-F scales correlation of .71 for the sample may be less indicative of deeper personality traits than of the tendency of subjects to respond in similar fashion to similar scales. In this connection, it may be mentioned that 17 out of 20 items in the CMI scale asserted custodial views. Jackson and Messick (1958) feel that response style rather than content accounts primarily for the CMI-F correlation. They cite a study by Howard and Sommer (n.d.) who replicated Gilbert and Levinson's study with the Jackson-Messick reversed F scale (Jackson and Messick, 1957). The replicated study found that 'custodialism' on the CMI scale was correlated significantly with agreements to both the original and the reversed F scales.

One may appreciate the parsimonious appeal of the unidimensional approach used by the authors. Thus, they put different occupational groups from different hospitals into one combined ranked continuum of policy requirements. In a parallel fashion, staff ideology becomes one dimension between two extremes and in turn is analogous to 'personality' whose index is the F scale. All three dimensions become congruent in an authoritarian custodialism-equalitarian humanism axis.

The question may be raised whether a unidimensional approach can account for all the attitudes or whether some other factors might also be relevant. Thus, if cultural, socio-economic, and other factors were considered, personality and policy requirements might be seen as playing more limited roles in a wider perspective. For example, while there may be some ideological selfselection of hospital staffs if three hospitals exist in one state, in another state with only one mental hospital, the fact of proximity (and pay rates compared to other employers) may outweigh ideology in choice of hospital.

In spite of these questions, the writer wishes to stress the value of this imaginative pioneering study which has tried to correlate hospital policies with occupational and psychological factors. Gilbert and Levinson's study and the CMI scale have stimulated other research which will be discussed below.

Gilbert and Levinson (1957b), in a second study, seek to relate hospital aides' ideologies with their actions. That is, they try to correlate custodialism in ideology and authoritarianism in personality with custodialism in role performance. The latter was measured by a Custodial Role Performance (CRP) Inventory (*ibid.*, p. 199), on which nursing supervisors rated hospital aides.

Two samples were used. For a female sample of 16 aides, rank order correlations between the measures were .83 (CRP and CMI), .75 (CRP and F), and .80 (CMI and F). 'The findings in the case of the male aides are strikingly different. While the CMI-F correlation is about the same [i.e., .78] the correlation of CRP with CMI is only .31, and that between CRP and F is .21. [A correlation of .34 would be required to reach the 5% level of significance with a one-tailed test.] It is noteworthy that in both groups CRP correlates slightly better with CMI than with F; this was expected on the ground that ideology is a more proximate determinant of behavior than is personality' (*ibid.*, p. 206).

PINE AND LEVINSON

A study by Pine and Levinson (1957) sought to relate CMI score with role conception and personality syndromes. Ten aides, five with high and five with low CMI scores were selected. Each aide was given a two-hour interview. This consisted of (a) five TAT cards administered in standard fashion, (b) three TAT cards presented as hospital scenes (called Mental Illness TAT or MITAT) and two pictures from Caudill's series of mental hospital pictures, (c) a one-hour semi-structured discussion of the hospital and of mental illness. The aides were rated by two raters.

The type of results obtained by this clinical approach is suggested in the following quotations: 'In the case of custodial ideology, three aspects of personality were of special salience: (a) a tendency to idealize parents; (b) hostile feelings initially directed towards family members are warded off and permitted only diffuse and indirect expression; (c) anti-intraceptiveness' (*ibid.*, p. 217).

'The punitive orientation towards patients and the hostile criticism of individuals often found in custodial aides, seems to stem from a displacement of aggressive impulses that cannot be expressed against their original objects. The emphasis on aggressiveness in patients may also reflect a projection of aggressive impulses' (*ibid.*, p. 217). While the conclusions are stimulating and suggestive, it would appear that they would carry more general conviction if larger carefully chosen samples had been used and if the measurements were more objective.

CARSTAIRS AND HERON

Carstairs and Heron (1957) carried out a related study in an English mental hospital in London. They sought to investigate one aspect of 'the patients' social environment' (*ibid.*, p. 219) by inquiring into the 'social attitudes' of hospital personnel. A list of 38 statements was prepared. It consisted of the 20 CMI scale items, the 8 F scale items used by Gilbert and Levinson, 5 items from Eysenck's (1954) measure of 'tough-minded conservatism' and 5 additional items from Adorno *et al.*'s (1950) original F scale. The item list was presented to 210 male respondents in a London mental hospital.

On the CMI scores, the British investigators found that in all comparable occupational groups, the English sample was *more* 'custodial' than Gilbert and Levinson's Boston samples. However, the authors warn against a direct comparison. The responses were obtained in individual interviews, and the interviewer was known as a psychiatrist to his subjects. On the F scale items used by Gilbert and Levinson, the English respondents tended generally to score somewhat higher than their Bostonian counterparts.

The authors' discussion includes a critique of Gilbert and Levinson's approach. 'The CMI scale, while admittedly a crude instrument, was selected as the best measure known to us. Its limitations may be ascribed to the fact that the antithetical attitudes which it tries to assess are not unitary but complex phenomena . . . The CMI scale necessarily covers a variety of related topics on which unqualified agreement cannot be reached even theoretically. Sound psychiatric practice must always temper humanitarianism with social responsibility and therapeutic optimism with an awareness of the ultimate limitations imposed by the biological components of mental illness. Hence, a very low score on the CMI scale may indicate failure of judgment as well as humane sympathies, and an occasional custodial response might be variously interpreted as indicative of realism or of harshness in outlook' (*ibid.*, p. 226). 'The findings on social attitudes in the present study do not throw much light on the question of the degree to which an individual's personality structure determines his acceptance or rejection of an available ideology . . . Our findings are not sufficient in themselves to indicate whether any of these scales is in fact a measure of personality as distinguished from attitudes. It is for this reason that in the present paper these measures have been referred to as social attitude rather than as personality scales' (*ibid.*, p. 227).

The present reviewer feels that this sophisticated evaluation by Carstairs and Heron contributes to a better understanding of the CMI studies. It would be difficult to compare one English hospital, about which nothing further is reported, with three Boston hospitals and draw any general conclusions on British versus American mental hospital staffs.

NUNNALLY

Nunnally (1958) reports an interesting study in which he compared opinions of psychiatrists and psychologists concerning mental illness. By 'opinions,' the author meant verifiable knowledge, in contrast to subjective reactions or attitudes. Three thousand statements from miscellaneous sources were collected. A questionnaire of 240 items was constructed, condensed to 180 items, factor analyzed and reduced to 50 items. The final instrument was sent to 150 psychologists and 150 psychiatrists. The psychologists were drawn at random from the diplomates of the American Psychological Association, 75 being in the clinical field and 75 in the counseling and guidance field. The psychiatrists were members of the Group for the Advancement of Psychiatry. Eighty-six psychologists and 90 psychiatrists responded in time for the analysis. The sampling is open to the usual criticism of mailed questionnaires: a large percentage (more than 40%) of the sample did not respond, and it is impossible to say how their views might have changed the results. The author gives no account of how the non-respondents compared with the respondents in terms of age, sex, education, experience, etc. The psychiatrists can not be said to be representative of all American psychiatrists but only of members of the Group for the Advancement of Psychiatry (if they were drawn at random, which the author does not report). The psychological sample is not characteristic of all the psychologists who actually work with mental patients, and it would have been helpful to know what proportions of clinical and counseling psychologists did not answer. The results should be seen in the light of the sampling limitations.

The questionnaire asked not for agreement or disagreement with the statements, but rather 'whether each opinion was worthy of being advocated to the public, or used in programs of public information . . . In the strictest sense, the results of the study do not show what the experts believe but, more precisely, what they think the public should be told' (*ibid.*, p. 179). Later, a smaller group of presumably similar background was given the questionnaire with instructions to give 'agree' or 'disagree' answers. The responses corresponded so strongly with those of the main groups that Nunnally assumed these groups to have responded mainly in terms of their personal beliefs.

A comparison of mean responses showed the psychologists' and psychiatrists' replies to be very much alike. Also, the mean responses of clinical and counseling psychologists were very similar. The 22 items with the largest variance were factor analyzed. The strongest factor, concerning mostly optimal directiveness of psychotherapists, did not discriminate among professions. Factor II, dealing with causes of mental illness, showed psychologists on the average to endorse slightly more the effect of childhood experiences and personal history, psychiatrists to tend slightly toward an explanation in terms of the immediate environment. However, intraprofessional variation exceeded interprofessional variation by far. A third factor made up of items mixed in content was endorsed more strongly by psychologists. They were more skeptical than psychiatrists of organic explanations of mental illness like diet and physical exhaustion. One item dealing with psychiatric prognosis of mental illness was endorsed more by psychiatrists. In Nunnally's words this finding '. . . perhaps reflects more enthusiasm by some psychiatrists about their clinical prowess than would be granted by some psychologists' (*ibid.*, p. 182).

To summarize, Nunnally's study suggests that psychologists and psychiatrists in general did not differ on his instrument concerning mental health problems. The respondents constituted about 60% self selected from specific samples, and they cannot be said to represent all of their professional colleagues in the United States. Nevertheless, in the light of subsequent independent work (Cohen and Struening, 1959, 1960, 1962, 1963), the results may be roughly characteristic of the two professional groups.

MIDDLETON

One of the earliest reported studies on the attitudes of mental hospital employees was conducted in 1951 by Middleton (1953). The author, in a 2,400 bed state hospital in Texas, gave a questionnaire 'Prejudice Test' to 392 employees who volunteered. Two thirds of the subjects were ward attendants, the remaining third consisted of 23 laundry workers, 23 cooks, 18 dining room assistants and others in business, accounting, maintenance, technical and medical departments. The only further information given on the sample is that it includes no M.D.'s or psychologists.

The 'test' consisted of 39 statements concerning prejudice about mental illness. For the whole sample, 'prejudice' was correlated positively with age (.43 Pearson's r) and negatively with education (–.58) and IQ measured by the Revised Beta (–.75). Generally, attendants were just as prejudiced as non-attendants. The latter finding is not very conclusive due to the heterogeneity of the non-attendant group.

Middleton concludes that in the selection for employment, primary consideration should be paid to his findings on age, education and intelligence. 'Standards for employment should be set as high as the applying population will stand in order to get the groups with the best attitudes toward mental illness' (*ibid.*, p. 138). The conclusion appears somewhat open to question. The age factor in prejudice is confounded by length of employment in mental hospitals. On the average, the older subjects probably have worked longer with mental patients and conceivably may have received more custodial orientations than recent and younger employees. Also, different hiring standards may have been applied in past years. Over the years, persons with changing backgrounds may have sought employment in the hospital. It is possible that during their years of work in mental hospitals, employees tended to change from a well-intentioned to a more tough and 'prejudiced' view. All these possibilities imply that age is a doubtful criterion for employment on the basis of the evidence given. Education may be related to age, in that younger employees may be expected to have received somewhat more education. Intelligence in turn tends to be somewhat affected by education. It is not certain from the findings that all young applicants would be as unprejudiced as the currently employed young staff members. Intelligence and education may be related to job position and occupation rather that cut across different positions evenly.

Another conclusion states that all types of employees should be given periodic orientation and education courses to overcome prejudice by factual information. Such courses may do no harm and may even do some good, but their value cannot be clearly deduced from the results of the study. The Cummings' (1957) study, among other research, has thrown doubts on the efficacy of exposure to facts in overcoming prejudice against mental patients.

GIEDT

An unusual approach was employed by Giedt (1959). He argued that if mental illness is largely a disturbance of interpersonal relations, then such relations in a hospital ward would be important for treatment and should be investigated. He constructed a 60 item Likert-type scale containing some CMI items (see Gilbert and Levinson, 1957a), and statements on treatment, professional roles and work satisfaction. The questionnaire was given to twenty staff members who worked on three open wards. The subjects were 3 psychiatrists, 4 psychologists, 3 social workers, 4 nurses, 5 aides, and one patient work program supervisor. An index of similarity or dissimilarity in outlook was obtained by correlating (Pearson's r) each person's responses with all other persons' responses. Thus a matrix of intercorrelations was constructed. Higher correlations were graphically plotted for each ward, resulting in figures similar in appearance to sociograms. Such a graph is intended to show the ideological structure of a ward's staff.

Contrary to expectations, Giedt found average intercorrelations within wards (.30, .31 and .22) to be as low as the correlation between people working on separate wards (.30). On the other hand, within their own professions, subjects obtained higher relationships. Regardless of wards, psychiatrists were related at .47, psychologists and social workers at .42 each. Nurses, however, correlated only .25, and aides .22.

The author concluded that agreement among staff was more related to professional training and identification than to shared work experience on the same ward. Nurses and aides seemed to be exempt from the intra-professional attitude similarities. This may possibly be related to a less lengthy background of shared training. It may also be connected with some characteristics of the questionnaire which included, e.g., the issue of how much authority should be held by psychiatrists. On this issue, psychiatrists tended to take one side opposite to psychologists and social workers.

COHEN AND STRUENING

The most extensive study on attitudes of mental hospital personnel has been conducted by Cohen and Struening (1959; 1960; 1962; 1963). They criticized Gilbert and Levinson's CMI scale as being too *a priori* and set out to construct an empirical scale whose dimensions would not be predetermined but would emerge through factor analysis.

Two hundred opinion items were selected concerning causation, description, treatment, and prognosis of mental illness. Items were edited, balanced in terms of positive and negative content and reduced to 55. These were supplemented by 15 items from the Custodial Mental Illness Ideology (CMI) scale, the F scale, and Nunnally's (1961) work on popular conceptions of mental health. The resulting Likert scale was administered to staff samples of two veterans neuropsychiatric hospitals, one in the Northeast (N = 541) and one in the Midwest (N = 653).

Item intercorrelations were subjected to centroid factor analysis followed by quartimax rotation. Five dimensions resulted independently for both hospitals. In order of strength they were:

Factor A – Authoritarianism. This is identified with the F scale plus a view of mental patients as an inferior class needing coercive handling. Cohen and Struening believe it could be possible that for the authoritarian personality in the mental hospital, patients serve as a negatively stereotyped outgroup as do some minority groups in general society. Factor A accounts for roughly one half of the communal variance of the items.

B Benevolence – A kindly, paternalistic view towards patients whose origins lie in religion and humanism rather than science.

C Mental hygiene ideology – A positive orientation which embodies the tenets of modern mental health professionals and the mental hygiene movement whose Leitmotiv is mental illness is an illness like any other.

D Social restrictiveness – The central belief here is that the mentally ill are a threat to society, particularly the family, and must therefore be restricted in their functioning both during and after hospitalization.

E Interpersonal etiology – A circumscribed factor whose positive pole reflects the belief that mental illness arises from interpersonal experience, especially deprivation of parental love during childhood. (Cohen and Struening, 1962).

Each hospital sample was broken down by occupation, education, age and sex. For each demographic variable a one-way analysis of variance was performed according to each of the five factors. Occupational groups were significantly different in each hospital (excepting factor D in one hospital). Psychologists, psychiatrists and social workers were low on 'authoritarianism' (factor A) while aides and kitchen workers were high. On 'benevolence' (B) psychologists were at the low and nurses at the high end. In 'mental hygiene ideology' (C) aides and kitchen workers were weakest; psychologists, social workers, and in one hospital, psychiatrists strongest, thus presenting a reverse of scores on 'authoritarianism' (A). 'Social restrictiveness' (D) shows no great occupational variation though psychologists obtain the lowest scores and non-psychiatric physicians the highest. 'Interpersonal etiology' is most accepted by psychiatrists and psychologists, least by aides and kitchen workers. Cohen and Struening conclude that the variation of views among occupations reflects problems in communication among them and problems in patient care. Education is related to place in the occupational hierarchy as is reflected in the factorial scores of educational groups which closely parallel those of the occupational groups. 'Authoritarianism' decreases systematically with amount of education. The relationship between education and 'benevolence' is U-shaped with the highest scores in the high school graduate – some college group. This apex may be related to nurses' education and ideology. 'Social restrictiveness' appears to be unrelated to education as is 'interpersonal ideology' except for the group with postgraduate training.

Age and sex, when tested separately without control for occupation, show either no or weak relations with the factors. Weak but significant correlations were found between the female part of the sample and the factors of 'benevolence' and of 'social restrictiveness'. The authors believe that the high 'benevolence' scores may agree with the accepted cultural role of women and with the large portion of nurses in the female group.

Cohen and Struening (1963) subsequently condensed their scale to 51 items which were administered to the majority of staff members of ten additional Veterans Administration neuropsychiatric hospitals throughout the country. The sample population for all twelve VA hospitals amounted to 7,701 respondents.

Several occupational clusters emerged. A 'white collar' cluster consisted of dietitians, lab technicians, physical therapists, clerical workers, non-psychiatric physicians, dentists, and nurses (in order of increasing distance from the cluster centroid). The cluster is characterized by relatively low 'authoritarianism' and average scores on the other factor scales.

A second cluster is made up of 'blue collar workers,' i.e. maintenance personnel, kitchen workers and aides. They tend to be very high on 'authoritarianism,' high on 'social restrictiveness' and low on 'benevolence.' Within the cluster, aides score slightly below average on 'authoritarianism' and 'mental hygiene ideology' and above average on 'benevolence.'

Non-medical mental health professions, i.e., psychologists and social workers constitute the third cluster. The cluster mean scores are very low on 'authoritarianism' and 'social restrictiveness,' very high on 'mental hygiene ideology,' high on 'interpersonal etiology' and about average on 'benevolence.'

Psychiatrists do not fit any of the clusters. They come closest to the psychologists and social workers whom they slightly exceed in 'social restrictiveness,' 'authoritarianism,' and 'benevolence' while being weaker in 'mental hygiene ideology' and 'social restrictiveness.'

In reviewing their evidence, Cohen and Struening draw some conclusions:

> The cause of the increase in this authoritarian-restrictive ideology as one goes down the hierarchy is at least partly due to the social-educational class differences which the members of these groups brought with them to their first mental patient. It may well also be due to the differences in the nature of their responsibility, i.e., the aide may be the most coercive of the three because it is he who is charged with the immediate responsibility for maintaining order and security in the ward, and who is the one most frequently assaulted physically

and psychologically by a difficult patient. We are suggesting that the permissiveness of the psychiatrist (and even more so of the psychologist and social worker), no matter how effective in theory or even in the practice of the skilled professional, may simply be painfully non-functional for the aide, or even the nonspecialist nurse (*ibid.*, p. 10).

In the literature on attitudes of mental health workers, Cohen and Struening's study stands out by its extensive sampling and by the careful reasoning used in connecting methods, results and conclusions.

SUMMARY

This chapter reviewed the literature on attitudes of mental health personnel. Gilbert and Levinson in their pioneering work sought to demonstrate relationships between mental hospital structure or policy, staff 'ideology,' personality and role performance Carstairs and Heron did a somewhat similar study of social attitudes in an English hospital. Nunnally compared the opinions of psychiatrists and psychologists and showed them to be generally similar. Middleton gave a 'Prejudice Test' to mental hospital employees in Texas and found prejudice to increase with age and decrease with education. The views of Giedt's respondents were related more to occupation than to work on the same ward. Cohen and Struening have done the most extensive study on attitudes of mental hospital personnel. They showed opinions on mental illness to vary primarily with occupation.

CHAPTER 3

Instrument development

To obtain the relevant attitudes of workers in the mental health field, an instrument had to be developed. This instrument had to meet certain requirements:

INSTRUMENT REQUIREMENTS OR DESIDERATA

1. The instrument was to be comprehensible and capable of eliciting pertinent and accurate responses in different cultural settings, more specifically in the Eastern United States, in Hawaii, and in England. (It was hoped that the device might also be applicable to other settings if at a later time it would be deemed desirable to give it, or parts of it, to other groups.)

2. It was to be meaningful and capable of holding the interest of members of the various occupations involved: of psychiatrists and psychologists with years of postgraduate training as well as of hospital aides and attendants whose training might have lasted a few weeks or less and covered only matters of applied ward supervision.

3. The tool was to be equally comprehensible for employees with medical training, like nurses, and for others with specialization in non-medical fields, e.g., in social work. To be understandable to members of various specialties, it should be neither too difficult for many hospital attendants nor should it seem oversimplified or condescending to members of professions with long specialized training. It was therefore necessary to develop an instrument that could be understood and meaningfully filled in by respondents ranging from near the bottom to the top of the general educational ladder.

4. The tool was to be equally understandable to hospital personnel and to rehabilitation and social workers of the wider community.

5. The device was to be given to hundreds of persons in each of the hospitals sampled. As public mental hospitals tend to be understaffed and their employees to be overworked, the questionnaire should be as brief as possible while still obtaining the required information. In order to save both the employees' and the researchers' time, the instrument should be capable of group administration, thus minimizing the time required for introductory and explanatory statements and for answering procedural questions. The group administration technique would also expedite going through channels of the hospital hierarchy and enable the hospital leadership to arrange sessions for morning, afternoon and night shifts in such a way that the normal duties of the staff members would be least interfered with and that all staff members could be included in the sample while no wards or departments would be left critically understaffed at any time.

6. Certain potentially 'sensitive' background information would be desired for purposes of later analysis. This information would include such items of the respondents' background as their ethnicity, age, family income, father's education and occupation.

7. In order to get a full picture of the respondents' views and attitudes even on somewhat touchy and tabu matters like preferences among patients it should be ensured that unacceptable or unfashionable views could be expressed as well as generally acceptable attitudes.

8. The results of the survey should be, if possible, comparable with the findings of major work in the field of attitude research on mental health professionals.

9. The instrument should serve not only the purpose of gathering attitudinal responses but within the wider project should also obtain some information on subjects' knowledge in respect to vocational rehabilitation of former mental patients.

10. In addition to serving as an instrument for obtaining attitudinal statements of persons specializing in work with mental patients, the instrument was also seen as being a technique for the first stage of a larger project. A subsequent stage of the project would deal with the attitudes of members of the working lay community. It was deemed desirable to include items in the professional instrument which could be asked later in their original or in a modified form of community members.

INSTRUMENT DEVELOPMENT

Before starting with the collection of attitudes of cross-cultural, cross-occupational samples, it was decided to develop a pilot instrument for collecting attitudes from one occupational group. Due to the paucity of literature in the field under investigation, and in order to indicate the source of some of the ideas in the present study, the pilot research will be briefly summarized. As the group to be exposed to the pilot attitude inquiry, psychiatric social workers in metropolitan New York were chosen. It was felt that this occupational group would have some experience with both hospital treatment of mental patients and with community factors affecting their vocational rehabilitation. Metropolitan New York was chosen because of its easy accessibility and because one area along the East Coast was to be included in the final sample.

The purposes of the early interviews in New York were (1) the identification of topics which could evoke pertinent responses for investigation, (2) the selection of the most appropriate question forms, (3) the contraction of issues and question forms into a concise instrument. (4) At the same time, efforts were to be made to keep local idiosyncrasies and jargon out of the instrument so as to facilitate future cross-cultural and cross-occupational use. The scarcity of existing literature on the attitudes of social workers toward mental patients made it necessary to do first this exploratory work. Interview guides rather than questionnaires were to be used in the pilot studies in order to allow for maximum freedom in responses and to get an indication of the range of various issues and of alternate responses.

THE FIRST PILOT INSTRUMENT

A pilot interview schedule (1SW) was developed for a pre-test with psychiatric social workers in New York. The interview guide was designed to test the feasibility of various questions, primarily with social workers. This interview schedule inquired into:

(a) the attitudes of the respondents toward patients of various diagnostic categories, toward vocational rehabilitation and on cooperation with members of other professions;
(b) the respondents' training and experience in working with mental

patients, and their hospital or clinic caseloads;

(c) the respondents' knowledge of the behavioral attitudes toward mental patients and their vocational rehabilitation held by members of other professions, by co-workers, past and potential future employers, relatives, and community members;

(d) the respondents' own socio-economic and cultural background.

The first pilot instrument was 28 pages long and took about two hours to administer. Its usefulness consisted primarily in separating promising from unproductive questions and in identifying controversial topics for further inquiry. A review of the literature had not indicated the existence of previous data on the attitudes of social workers toward mental patients. Therefore, the pilot instrument was also used to collect some indications of existing dimensions in this attitudinal sphere.

THE SECOND PILOT INSTRUMENT

The results obtained with the first interview guide (1SW) were reviewed and critically evaluated. This experience provided a first rough indication of the productivity of various approaches, topics and questions. It was then possible to drop certain questions and topics, to condense and sharpen some items and to modify or elaborate other issues. Based on the findings of the first instrument, it became possible to change a number of open-ended items into a multiple choice or check off from. A revised interview schedule for social workers (2SW) resulted. This tool was designed to elicit attitudes of the respondents themselves as well as to gather their insights into and knowledge of attitudes and behavior of other persons related to the rehabilitation process. In addition, certain kinds of relevant factual information were asked for.

The interview schedule (2SW) could be broken down by content of questions as follows:

Question topics

1. *Factual data*
   a. Institutional setting and caseload information
   b. Personal and professional background information
2. *Attitude data*
   a. Attitudes and preferences of respondents
   b. Information on attitudes of others

(1) psychiatrists
(2) other social workers
(3) patients
(4) ex-employers
(5) ex-co-workers
(6) patients' families
(7) potential employers

The revised interview schedule 2SW was administered to 40 psychiatric social workers in the Metropolitan New York area representing different institutions dealing with mental patients, as follows:

15 in state mental hospitals
9 in out-patient clinics
7 in private mental hospitals
4 in psychiatric wards of private general hospitals
3 in Veterans Administration after-care clinics, and
2 in psychiatric wards of public general hospitals.

The revised and condensed instrument 2SW consisted of 11 pages, and took on the average somewhat less than an hour to be completed. The interviews were administered and reported by four graduate students in social work (Edelman, Hammouri, Maas and Tanenbaum, 1960).

These writers described the responses to the different items. They concluded in part that 'Social workers seemed to place strong emphasis on the effect of society's attitudes on the vocational rehabilitation of mental patients. However, there was little, if any, indication throughout the responses where the social workers considered the effect of their own attitudes on the rehabilitation process' (*ibid.*, p. 58).

The present writer cross-tabulated certain attitude items of the 2SW interview guide. It was found that social workers tended to prefer work with white collar over blue collar workers and with fee clients over non-fee clients. This finding was more pronounced for social workers with Master degrees than for those without such a degree. This finding also held more strongly among respondents who work in private institutions than among those working in public institutions. These findings are discussed more fully in Askenasy (1970).

The conclusion was reached that social workers in this sample tend to prefer patients relatively similar to themselves in socio-economic background.

THE SEMANTIC DIFFERENTIALS – A PILOT STUDY

Hollingshead and Redlich's attempt to correlate mental illness with social class was mentioned above in Chapter 1. Their work was focussed on the relationship between social class membership and the incidence, development, diagnosis and treatment of mental illness. Of special interest here is a minor substudy of their New Haven investigation in which seventeen psychiatrists were interviewed (Hollingshead and Redlich, 1958, pp. 344-351). This exploratory substudy sought to determine, among other things, whether the seventeen psychiatrists 'noticed differences in social class between themselves and their patients' and whether 'they liked their patients.'

> The attitudes of these psychiatrists were all expressed toward neurotic patients in ambulatory treatment. After these psychiatrists had expressed their views toward their patients to psychiatrists on our team, we rated the attitudes as 'like' or 'dislike.'
>
> The numerical ratings of 'likes' and 'dislikes' of patients in class I through class III in contrast to class IV and V patients are significantly different. The class I through III patients were the ones who were 'liked' and the class IV and V patients were 'disliked.' (*Ibid.*, p. 344.)

(Classes I, II, and III correspond roughly to the upper and middle classes and classes IV and V to the lower classes.)

Unfortunately, Hollingshead and Redlich present no quantitative data nor statistical computations to support their reported differences in the numerical ratings of 'like' and 'dislike' for patients from different classes. However, these authors do give a qualitative review of the psychiatrists' interviews. In their account of the 17 subsidiary interviews, they report certain characterizations attributed by psychiatrists to patients from different class backgrounds.

Class V (roughly lower class) patients were seen as showing 'dominant behavior patterns,' 'crude, vulgar language,' 'outbursts of violence,' 'passivity, and apathy,' 'endurance of poverty and economic insecurity,' 'inability to think in (the psychiatrists') terms,' 'dullness and stupidity,' and 'apathetic dependency' (*ibid.*). Patients of the lower classes (IV and V) in a more comprehensive sense were characterized in the interviews by their 'lack of education' (*ibid.*, p. 345), and by their failure to have 'learned to verbalize and symbolize in the same way higher class persons have. Neither have they learned to sublimate present needs for the realization of future goals' (*ibid.*, p. 348).

Communication between these patients and psychiatrists was seen as difficult (*ibid.*, p. 345), and lack of mutual understanding was reported (*ibid.*, p. 346). Lower status patients were said to make a 'tacit or overt demand for an authoritarian attitude on the part of the psychiatrist' (*ibid.*, p. 345). In the authors' words, 'we are aware that most class V patients fall, by and large, into the category of difficult patients' (*ibid.*, pp. 348-349).

A contrasting picture is presented by the upper and middle class patients, (classes I-III) at least as they are seen by the psychiatrists interviewed. These patients have a relatively higher education and the 'capacity (this varies from person to person) to think in symbolic terms' (*ibid.*, p. 346). 'In these classes (I and II) we find more definite attempts in the direction of sublimation' (*ibid.*, p. 348). Communication between the higher social strata and the psychiatrists is relatively easy (*ibid.*, p. 345). 'A good patient is a person who can cooperate with the therapist, one who understands his objectives, and what he is doing to attain them. A good patient is similar in cultural background to the good psychotherapist. The two can communicate with one another' (*ibid.*, p. 348).

Hollingshead and Redlich's report was derived from seventeen interviews with psychiatrists, presumably in the New Haven area. Two questions arise: (1) do comparable perceptions of mental patients from different socio-economic backgrounds hold among other professional groups, and (2) are they found outside of New Haven? It was decided to test these queries by designing an appropriate form to be included in the second pilot instrument for social workers.

It was felt that psychiatrists, due to their social and educational background, might be somewhat lacking in understanding of and empathy with lower class patients. On the other hand, social workers by their choice of occupation, by their training and experience might be expected to show considerably more understanding and sympathy, if not preference, for socially less favored patients. It was held that to test the social workers' preferences, a relatively disguised approach should be used so that the intent of the query would not be given away and the respondents would not be induced to reply with standard expressions. The method chosen was that of the Semantic Differential (see Osgood, Suci and Tannenbaum, 1957). This technique was selected as it is self-administered and can provide a fast and efficient way of getting at even those attitudes that respondents are reluctant to talk about. Data collected by this method are quantitative and easily comparable with those of other respondents or of other samples. The basic format of Osgood *et al.*'s technique was used, i.e., concepts were to be rated on lists of word pairs, each pair being separated by a seven point scale (seven dashes). Beyond this, no use was made of the specific adjective pairs developed by Osgood and his co-workers, nor were their theoretical interests pursued. The following concepts were to be rated:

'Mental Patient I Most Enjoy Working With,' and

'Mental Patient I Least Enjoy Working With.'

Thirty word pairs were made up to be used with the two concepts (see Table 1). The primary interest was with polar characteristics ascribed in Hollingshead and Redlich's work to upper and middle class (I-III) patients in contrast to lower class (IV-V) patients. An attempt was made to translate the accounts of these patients given by Hollingshead and Redlich into word pairs. The pairs ranged from the obvious ('poor ... well-to-do') to more veiled descriptions (e.g., 'verbal ... uncommunicative'). In addition, some medical ('manic ... depressive') and presumably neutral pairs were thrown in (e.g., 'old ... young') in order to disguise the purpose of the scales from the respondents. The interviewers were directed to hand the instrument to the respondent so that he could fill in the semantic differentials himself. Instructions to the respondents asked that the check mark be placed:

(a) on the dash next to a word if it was felt to be closely related to the patient being rated;
(b) on the dash one space removed from the word if it was felt to be somewhat related to the concept;
(c) on the dash two spaces removed from the word if it was felt to be slightly related to the concept; and
(d) on the central dash if no relationship between either word of a scale and the concept was seen.

For the analysis, each response was recorded as being placed on a scale of dashes, reading from left to right 1, 2, ... 7, with the midpoint at 4. An attempt was made to arrange the thirty scales in such a way that they would be distributed with about half of the *prima facie* more favorable words on the left and about half on the right side of the dashes. In this way it was tried to minimize the effects of a response set.

Table 1. *Mental patient I most enjoy working with – pilot study*

1.	Thoughtful	Carefree
2.	Excitable	Calm
3.	Trusing	Suspicious
4.	Unpredictable	Predictable
5.	Responsible	Irresponsible
6.	Changeable	Stable
7.	Outgoing	Self-centered
8.	Emotional	Unemotional
9.	Sociable	Unsociable
10.	Intelligent	Stupid
11.	Unreliable	Reliable
12.	Self-indulgent	Self-denying
13.	Old	Young
14.	Poor	Well-to-do
15.	Violent	Gentle
16.	Interested	Apathetic
17.	Understandable	Obscure
18.	Low education	High education
19.	Cooperative	Uncooperative
20.	Shiftless	Steady
21.	Religious	Irreligious
22.	Verbal	Uncommunicative
23.	Highly insightful	Without insight
24.	Flexible	Compulsive
25.	Manic	Depressive
26.	Delusional	Reality-oriented
27.	Aggressive	Submissive
28.	Independent	Dependent
29.	Rude	Polite
30.	Moral	Immoral

Mean scores were computed for the forty respondents. Table 2 shows the mean differences from the midpoint (4.0) for the forty social workers on the two semantic differentials 'mental patient I most enjoy working with' and 'mental patient I least enjoy working with.' An item analysis was performed for both semantic differentials. The first general finding was that social workers in fact have some preferences among mental patients. Only five scales were found to show no significant differences: (12) Self-indulgent – self-denying; (14) Poor – well-to-do; (21) Religious – irreligious; (25) Manic – depressive; and (30) Moral – immoral.

Table 2. *Mean differences from midpoint of ratings by social workers on two semantic differentials*

Mental patient I *most* enjoy working with	Mean distance from midpoint	Mental patient I *least* enjoy working with	Mean distance from midpoint
Interested	1.9	Stupid	2.0
Intelligent	1.9	Irresponsible	2.0
Reality-oriented	1.8	Uncooperative	2.0
Thoughtful	1.7	Apathetic	1.9
Verbal	1.6	Suspicious	1.8
Steady	1.5	Uncommunicative	1.8
Cooperative	1.5	Delusional	1.8
Responsible	1.5	Unreliable	1.7
Reliable	1.4	Violent	1.7
Emotional	1.4	Shiftless	1.7
Flexible	1.3	Compulsive	1.6
Understandable	1.3	Rude	1.5
Trusting	1.3	Unemotional	1.4
Highly insightful	1.1	Carefree	1.4
Young	1.0	Without insight	1.4
Sociable	1.0	Obscure	1.4
Outgoing	1.0	Self-centered	1.2
Gentle	.9	Unsociable	1.2
Polite	.9	Dependent	.9
Predictable	.9	Changeable	.9
High education	.8	Unpredictable	.9
Stable	.7	Excitable	.7
Independent	.7	Old	.5
Aggressive	.7	Self-indulgent	.4
Calm	.5	Low education	.4
Moral	.1	Immoral	.4
Well-to-do	.1	Submissive	.3
Manic, Depressive	.0	Well-to-do	.1
Self-indulgent, Self-denying	.0	Depressive	.1
Religious, Irreligious	.0	Religious, Irreligious	.0

A cursory inspection of the preferences and dislikes for patients shown on Table 2 indicated that the results seemed to be somewhat analogous to those of Hollingshead and Redlich's psychiatrists. The social workers, in line with their professional standards and teachings, expressed no preference for 'well-to-do' over 'poor' patients. When, however, class characteristics became less obvious, the social workers' class preferences were increasingly more pronounced. Class related characteristics here were those ascribed to the different class groupings by the seventeen New Haven psychiatrists. Thus, in mean difference from the midpoint, the 'mental patient I most enjoy working with' was 'well-to-do' (.1), had 'high education' (.8), was 'polite' (.9), 'highly insightful' (1.1), 'understandable' (1.3), 'verbal' (1.6), 'thoughtful' (1.7), and 'interested' (1.9). A trend appears to run from a denial of preference for obvious middle class attributes to an admission of preference for non-obvious ones, using Hollingshead and Redlich's psychiatrists' attitudes. For the semantic differential of the 'mental patient I least enjoy working with,' a roughly inverted trend seems to exist, in terms of mean distances from the midpoint ranging from 'stupid' (2.0) to 'well-to-do' (.1).

Still, the question remained whether the preferences expressed by the social workers referred actually to patients from different social backgrounds or whether their likes just applied to patients who happened, for any reason, to possess certain attributes. Thus it might be argued that social workers might well prefer verbal over uncommunicative patients without class connection being implied at all.

In order to test whether this interpretation was to be accepted, the same 30 word pairs were given to another sample to be rated for the concepts 'typical middle class person' and 'typical lower class person.' These two semantic differentials were given to nineteen graduate students at New York's New School for Social Research.

It was also expected that some adjectives which have a certain meaning in patient-client relationships may have no such meaning in defining a more abstract person.

Clear differences were found in preferences for the two concepts. An item analysis was performed which showed seventeen out of thirty word pairs obtained significant differences. Table 3 shows the mean differences from the midpoint of the nineteen graduate students' ratings.

Rank order correlation coefficients were determined for rank differences (a) between 'typical middle class person' and 'patient I most enjoy working with' and (b) between 'typical lower class person' and 'patient I least enjoy working with.' The Spearman Rho correlation coefficients were weak, presumably because patients for practicing social workers, and class-identified persons for students, are too diverse stimuli to produce similar ranks on semantic differentials. It was decided to test for the significance of differences in

Table 3. *Mean differences from midpoint of ratings by graduate students on two semantic differentials*

Typical middle class person	Mean distance from midpoint	Typical lower class person	Mean distance from midpoint
Responsible	2.1	Low education	2.1
Steady	1.8	Poor	1.8
Predictable	1.6	Excitable	1.7
Reliable	1.6	Emotional	1.7
Stable	1.5	Religious	1.6
Sociable	1.5	Sociable	1.5
Verbal	1.3	Carefree	1.2
Religious	1.1	Violent	1.2
Well-to-do	1.1	Without insight	.9
Compulsive	1.1	Dependent	.8
Polite	1.1	Outgoing	.8
High education	1.1	Self-indulgent	.7
Intelligent	1.1	Cooperative	.7
Understandable	1.1	Understandable	.6
Moral	1.1	Shiftless	.6
Thoughtful	1.0	Irresponsible	.6
Cooperative	1.0	Rude	.6
Reality-oriented	.8	Aggressive	.5
Gentle	.7	Stupid	.5
Dependent	.7	Apathetic	.4
Calm	.5	Irresponsible	.4
Self-denying	.5	Verbal	.4
Unemotional	.2	Manic	.4
Without insight	.2	Compulsive	.3
Suspicious	.1	Predictable	.3
Self-centered	.1	Unreliable	.2
Apathetic	.1	Suspicious	.2
Depressive	.1	Young	.1
Old	.1	Immoral	.1
Aggressive-submissive	.0	Delusional, Reality-oriented	.0

directionality between the two samples. The Chi square test was applied as follows: It was assumed that by chance alone one half of the mean scores for the 'most liked patient' would be on the same side of the midpoint as the mean scores of the corresponding scales of the 'typical middle class person.' If chance operated, the other half of the mean scores would be on opposite sides for the two samples. The same assumptions were made for the 'least liked patient' and the 'typical lower class person.'

A Chi square of 8.34 was obtained which is significant at the .01 level. Thus, in one case out of a hundred, results could be obtained by chance which would place on the same side (a) middle class persons with preferred patient ratings, and, respectively, (b) lower class persons with least liked patient ratings. The conclusion was reached that the forty social workers' preferences among their patients tend to coincide with the possession by these patients of characteristics attributed to middle class persons. At the same time, the patients whom these social workers least enjoy working with appear to be those who possess certain lower class characteristics. This conclusion came as something of a surprise when one considered that social workers tend to be a group which is self-selected on the basis of its interest in working with and helping persons who may be described as coming from the less favored socio-economic classes. It may be concluded that the middle class preference for mental patients which Hollingshead and Redlich found in their 17 interviews exists not only among psychiatrists working with neurotics, but can be extended at least to some New York social workers.

EFFORTS TO MEET INSTRUMENT REQUIREMENTS

The requirements for the final instrument were spelled out at the beginning of this chapter. The tool was to be administered to samples in an Eastern state, in Hawaii, and in England, each consisting of members of the different occupations working directly with present or former mental patients. The results of the pilot studies were carefully reviewed, and the experiences gathered were utilized in the design of the 'questionnaire for professionals in the mental health field' ('3P'). The following paragraphs try to specify the efforts made to meet the requirements set up for the instrument.

1. In order to make the questions equally comprehensible and relevant to the different sample settings, it was attempted to eliminate all localisms and regional slang. Next, counsel was sought from mental health experts in the three proposed settings. It was reported that all psychiatrists and many of the other major professionals in Hawaii were trained in the continental United States. Also, nurses, aides,

occupational and recreational therapists were said to receive essentially the same training and to use the same textbooks as their colleagues on the mainland. Therefore, it was felt that the same questionnaire could be administered to the Eastern and the Hawaiian samples. If Hawaiian respondents wanted to give spontaneous answers not provided in the form to a question, they were asked to 'write in' their choice.

In England, similarly, the writer sought advice from local mental health experts on question wording and on semantic distinctions from American usage. In order to minimize misunderstandings and to maximize the equivalence of British and American questions, some minor changes were made in the English form ('2E'). This form was preceded by a pilot instrument ('1E') which tried out the use of various question wordings and was given to an English sample of N = 50 respondents in an exploratory pre-test. Some Americanisms were changed to the corresponding British usage, e.g., the American 'Check one statement' became in England 'Tick one statement.' Parts of general instructions were slightly extended to explain the procedures to the British respondents who might not be as used to questionnaires as their American colleagues. Some technical terms were changed to fit British usage, e.g., American 'nurses and aides' became British 'nurses and nursing assistants,' and American 'vocational rehabilitation' became in England 'occupational resettlement.' In the final section which asked for the respondents' background, American terms were changed to British ones. This included categories of income, education, occupational level and religious group. Aside from these minor changes, the British and the American instruments were identical.

2. The inclusion in the sample of the whole range of the mental health occupations necessitated the use of language equally understandable to members of all occupations. It was attempted to reach this objective by excluding jargon and highly technical terms and by finding a common denominator which could be meaningful to even the less trained respondents without sounding naive to highly trained specialists. An effort was made to state specific issues in nontechnical language.

3. A similar dilemma was posed by the sample's wide range of general educational background. The attempt was made to find a relatively low common denominator so that the questions would be at least comprehensible to the whole sample. When it appeared

necessary, it was then explained to psychiatrists and to other highly trained specialists why the use of everyday language was required, and their indulgence was asked.

4. In order to make the items intelligible to both hospital and community mental health workers, an effort was made to avoid hospital terminology and to present the items in a way understandable to both groups.

5. To expedite the administration of the form to large numbers of employees, it was decided to use a self-administered questionnaire rather than an interview schedule (which had been used in the pilot stages.) During the pilot studies a number of question formulations had been used and alternative answers had been identified. It then became possible in the final instrument to change most questions from an open-ended to a multiple-choice form which included the various major alternatives. The final questionnaire included only two open-ended questions.

6. Background information questions of a 'sensitive' nature were placed at the end of the questionnaire and were surrounded as much as possible by less sensitive items of a similar format. Practically no difficulties were encountered in the collection of replies to these items.

7. Similar approaches were used in offering unpopular and unorthodox answers to a given attitude question. Special care was taken to allow respondents to express preferences among patients without feeling they were demonstrating prejudice.

8. To make data collected by the instrument comparable with major findings in the literature on attitudes of mental health workers, one section of the instrument was largely made up of items from the OMI (Opinions about Mental Illness) scale by Cohen and Struening described in Chapter 2. This scale has been used in the most extensive research to date with mental hospital personnel.

9. In order to fulfill the requirements of the wider project, a section was included with information questions about the vocational rehabilitation of former mental patients. Thus, the resulting instrument can be seen as a multi-purpose vehicle.

10. Persons with little education and technical training (primarily hospital attendants) and workers in the community outside of the hospital were included in the sample (see above, points 2, 3, and 4). For this reason, a good deal of shoptalk had already been removed and everyday language substituted. In the question formulation it

was further kept in mind that a subsequent instrument was to be developed for use with the lay community. Some items in the present (3P) instrument were phrased for direct applicability to laymen, others were formulated in such a manner that they could easily be modified for samples of the general population.

THE FINAL INSTRUMENT

The resulting instrument (3P) is attached as Appendix I. This 'questionnaire for professionals in the mental health field' consists of four major sections. A general introductory page with explanations and instructions precedes the questions.

The first section starts with an open-ended question on the respondent's view of the most urgent need in treating mental patients. A second open-ended question asks whether and why an ex-mental patient should or should not tell the employer about his hospitalization. The other items are of a multiple-choice form. This section (questions 1 through 31) deals with various attitudes and opinions about mental illness, mental patients, their hospitalization and their rehabilitation and with preferences for patients from different backgrounds. In this part, data were sought on specific issues involving mental patients.

Section two consists of two semantic differentials. The same instructions were given as in the second pilot study. As in that study discussed above, the respondents were asked to rate the 'mental patient I most enjoy working with' and the 'mental patient I least enjoy working with.' The original scales were used with a few changes. Four scales, which had turned out to be non-significant in the item analysis of the earlier instrument were omitted. These items were, '12. Self-indulgent . . . Self-denying,' '14. Poor . . . Well-to-do,' '20. Religious . . . Irreligious' and '25. Manic . . . Depressive.' Two scales were added with the expectation that they might show differences in the samples they were to be given to. The new items were: '13. City . . . Farm' and '20. Customary . . . Modern.' This changed the total to 28 scales for each concept to be rated.

Section three contains items from the 'opinions about mental illness' scale which are discussed below.

Cohen and Struening conducted the most extensive existing study on the opinions of mental hospital personnel about mental patients and mental illness. These writers developed by the Likert technique a 51-item scale labelled 'opinions about mental illness' (OMI). The OMI scale, Cohen and Struening's samples, and their factor analysis and findings were discussed above in Chapter 2.

It was stated earlier in the present chapter that one of the requirements for the construction of a new instrument was the fairly direct comparability of at least some of the data with the findings of existing major work in the area under investigation. Thanks to the kind permission of Dr. Struening, it was possible to include a number of the OMI scale items in the present questionnaire.

Due to the present project's purpose, the items from the OMI scale were selected with an emphasis on vocational rehabilitation of mental patients. About an equal number of what to mental health specialists may appear to be favorable and unfavorable statements on mental patients were arranged in random listing. A scale of 15 items was constructed which make up pages 10-11 of the questionnaire (see Appendix I). The items had been included in the Cohen and Struening factors as follows:

Factor A (authoritarianism) – Positively related: items 3 (it is easy to recognize someone who once had a serious mental illness), 5 (there is something about mental patients that makes it easy to tell them from normal people), and 12 (people with mental illness should never be treated in the same hospital as people with physical illness). Negatively related: item 11 (the patients of a mental hospital should have something to say about the way the hospital is run). This item was used in an earlier form of the OMI though excluded in the later condensed version.

Factor B (benevolence) – Positive: items 1 (mental illness is an illness like any other), and 7 (many mental patients are capable of skilled labor, even though in some ways they are very disturbed mentally). Negative: item 9 (to become a patient in a mental hospital is to become a failure in life).

Factor C (mental hygiene ideology) – Positive: items 2 (most patients in mental hospitals are not dangerous), and 6 (if our hospitals had enough well trained doctors, nurses, and aides, many of the patients would get well enough to live outside the hospital).

Factor D (social restrictiveness) – Positive: items 4 (although patients discharged from mental hospitals may seem all right they should not be allowed to marry), and 13 (although some mental patients seem all right, it is dangerous to forget for a moment that they are mentally ill). Negative: items 8 (people who were once patients in mental hospitals are no more dangerous than the average citizen), and 10 (most women who were once patients in a mental hospital could be trusted as baby sitters).

Item 14 (sex delinquents should be severely punished) was not derived from the OMI scale. This item would appear *a priori* to be probably relatively closest to 'social restrictiveness,' as measured by factor D. As the authors of the OMI scale use them, factors D and A ('authoritarianism') are logically related. While factor A deals more with the perception of patients, factor D is more concerned with how they should be treated, i.e., with a dimension of 'social restrictiveness.'

Item 15 (professionals who work with mental patients should try to raise a patient's opinion about himself) also was not a part of the OMI questionnaire. It would appear to be logically closest to factor B (benevolence). Item 15, as is indicated below, was later dropped from the analysis for being too variable. The remaining 14 items, because of their content, were called the 'rehabilitation scale.'

Section four of the instrument consists of questions about the respondent. They include the usual democraphic data and seek to obtain some specific information about his socio-economic, occupational and ethnic background which could prove useful in explaining differences in the results.

The final instrument (3P) consists of 14 pages and requires about twenty to forty-five minutes for completion. The length of time required to fill in the questions varied inversely with the respondent's education.

SUMMARY

The present chapter is the first of two chapters to deal with the methodology of the study. This chapter focussed on the data collection instruments. In order to obtain the pertinent attitudes of mental health workers, an instrument had to be developed which had to meet certain criteria which were listed. Two pilot instruments were designed. In the absence of an extensive body of pertinent literature, some relevant results of a pilot study were discussed. It was found that social workers tended to prefer work with patients who possessed characteristics attributed to middle class persons. The lessons of the early instruments were incorporated in the final questionnaire.

This final questionnaire consisted of four major sections. The first section contained multiple choice and open-ended questions about mental illness, mental patients, their hospitalization and their rehabilitation. The second section consisted of two semantic differentials about the 'mental patient I most (or least) enjoy working with'. The third section contained items from Cohen and Struening's 'Opinions about Mental Illness' (OMI) scale selected for their bearing on vocational rehabilitation. The last section used demographic questions. The instrument is attached as 'questionnaire for professionals in the mental health field' in Appendix I.

CHAPTER 4

The samples

SAMPLING AREAS

The sampling task involved several goals:

(1) In order to obtain cultural variation, samples were to be selected from the continental United States, Hawaii and England.

(2) To study the effects of institution policy, sample members were to be drawn from both relatively 'progressive' and relatively 'conservative' mental hospitals.

(3) The attitudes of members of the different mental health occupations were to be obtained.

The first given area was the State of Hawaii. According to the United States Bureau of the Census, its population in 1960 was 633,774. In 1960, the ethnic distribution was 32% Japanese, 32% Caucasian, 16% Hawaiian and part-Hawaiian,* 10% Filipino, 6% Chinese; and 4% of other ethnic origin (including .8% Negroes). The population is centered on the Island of Oahu, particularly in Honolulu which claims 47% of Hawaii's population. 27% live in other urban and suburban areas and 26% in small towns (less than 2,500 persons) and in rural districts. The 'neighbor islands' surrounding Oahu are largely agricultural. The main sources of the state's income are sugar, tourism and pineapples. The mental hospital studied has a patient population of about 1,200.

The second sample area was to be an East coast state roughly comparable to Hawaii in size and urban-rural distribution of its population, in land area, and in possession of one mental hospital of similar size. The choice fell on a state on the border between Northeast and South. This state's population in 1960 was nearly

* The two terms include all persons who possess any Hawaiian ancestor.

450,000. The state's area covers about 2,000 square miles, making it one of the smallest in the nation. About 14% of the population are Negroes. Roughly two-thirds of the population live in urban areas. The population is centered in one county, which contains the state's largest city of nearly 100,000 inhabitants. The other counties are largely agricultural. Leading products in 1960 were chemicals, followed by poultry and eggs, other food products and textiles. The state's mental hospital lies at the outskirts of the main city and houses 1,400 patients.

The third sampling area was England. As no political units comparable in size to American states exist there, two mental hospitals in adjoining counties were chosen from a list of mental hospitals. Hospital X is located in a 'catchment area' (area served by the hospital) of 900 square miles in south-eastern England on the outskirts of Colchester, a town of 65,000 people about fifty miles from London. The catchment area is populated by about 550,000 persons of whom 70% live in urban districts and 30% in rural sections. The area's income derives about one-half from agriculture and one-half from industry (electrical engineering, printing, textiles). There are hardly any foreign born and racial minority members. Severalls Hospital, which in this text and the tables is referred to as hospital X, has a population of about 1,460 patients.

The other British institution is Fulbourn Hospital, Cambridge, known in this study as hospital Y. Its catchment area covers part of a county also served by hospital X and several adjoining counties. The catchment area is 1,350 square miles and contains a population of 376,000, of whom about 28% live in urban and 72% in rural regions. The area's income derives primarily from agriculture, secondarily from industry (electronics) and from Cambridge University. However, the hospital does not serve the University. Students who suffer from psychiatric disorders are served by University facilities or by their home sources. Hospital Y has about 940 patients.

HOSPITAL CHARACTERISTICS

The English hospitals

At first, some thought was given to using in England one open-door hospital and one with closed wards. However, in recent years, British mental hospitals have generally opened their wards. Still, there are said to exist among British mental hospitals large differences in their degree of 'progressiveness' versus 'conservatism.' Different hospitals vary greatly, e.g., in the extent of democratic responsibility given to patients, in integration with the community and in the population's cooperation to rehabilitate patients in the catchment area served by the hospital. Of the institutions selected, X was said to be fairly 'conservative' until shortly before the study was conducted, while Y has had a reputation for its progressive outlook.

Hospital X, the more old-fashioned institution, was opened in 1913. Its site was chosen reputedly because the town offered cheap water. Until a few years ago, the hospital was said to be strongly set against any innovations and to use the old 'custodial' approach. During World War II, it was reported that rationing of food and clothing improved the patients' living by setting up higher standards. The former medical superintendent (until 1959) was said to be primarily interested in maintaining the status quo, although in the last few years some hospital administrators with modern views joined the staff.

In 1960, a new superintendent was appointed. He tried immediately to introduce a number of strong reforms. He was successful in implementing some policy changes, like the opening of wards to unrestricted visiting from 9 a.m. to 9 p.m. and returning geriatric patients of one ward to their families after one month in the hospital. The superintendent wrote a book on institutional neurosis* (Barton, 1966) and lectured and traveled extensively. Wards were opened, and a number of patients began to work during the day in the community or for pay on a production line in the hospital.

On the other hand, hospital X's staff was largely hired under the old administration (before 1960). Among the psychiatrists in particular, there was a good deal of opposition to the new superintendent's reforms. In his efforts to make quick changes, he failed to win the cooperation of many old staffers. At the time of the field study (early in 1961) the nursing staff at hospital X seemed to be cooperative with the new system in general, although it could not be said to have assumed the greater role in therapy and in decision-making called for in modern theories of the team approach. Little cooperation existed between the hospital and the surrounding com-

* A term connoting mental deterioration due to extended confinement in a mental hospital.

munity in respect to helping patients. Hospital X may be seen as an institution in transition from traditional to modern policies, with the conflict being most acute at the top of the hierarchy, especially among the psychiatrists.*

Hospital Y was opened in the 1850's and soon acquired a name for its humane treatment of patients, open doors, and varied recreational and social activities. By 1900, partly due to overcrowding, the doors were closed and the activity program reduced. In 1945, a new program of out-patient clinics was started. In 1953, a new superintendent took over and attempted to change the interpersonal structure throughout the hospital in accordance with 'therapeutic community' views. He attempted to interest the staff in the changes by asking at least the senior personnel to contribute to the decision-making process. Patient committees in the various wards decide on matters like parties, outings, and on actions to be taken about ward members who cause some trouble. Patients are encouraged from the time of admission to join work parties, and they advance to more complex work as soon as they are capable of it. Male patients visit female wards and vice versa. Before leaving the hospital, patients go on weekend trips, etc.

In contrast to hospital X, at hospital Y the modern policies seem to have been taken over by the physicians as well as by the rank and file of the staff. The nursing personnel seems to take a great deal of responsibility for running the hospital. When the field study was conducted, early in 1961, morale appeared to be high, and the psychiatrists seemed to feel at home in the hospital's atmosphere. Active community groups help to rehabilitate mental patients. Hospital Y is said to have come relatively close to the concept of a therapeutic community.

The American hospitals

In contrast to the two British hospitals, the American sample areas included in the study are not adjoining but separated by a continent and part of an ocean as well as by history and the cultural back-

* Interesting insights into the difficulties of changing a hospital from traditional to more modern ways are found in Barton's own account, 'Diary of change at Severalls Hospital' (Wing and Brown, 1970). Additional information about Severalls is given in Brown *et al.* (1966) which compares patient careers at this and two other English hospitals for five years after admission.

ground of their inhabitants. Hospital B is located in one of the original thirteen American states while Hawaii is the state most recently admitted to the Union.

Hospital B is situated in a border state between the Southern and the Northeastern regions of the United States, outside of the state's largest city. While in the United Kingdom mental hospitals are under the jurisdiction of the central Ministry of Health, which appoints their superintendents, American public mental hospitals (except Veterans Administration hospitals) are generally under each state's jurisdiction. Thus, policies and appointments are determined to some extent by the state legislatures.

The hospital grounds of hospital B are well kept; there is an abundance of flowers and much gardening activity. The old buildings are spacious. Much emphasis is put on construction. An active building program is going on, and the hospital's pride is a new treatment center of four wards, built rather luxuriously like a hotel according to the latest ideas in mental hospital architecture. The hospital had some open wards, and gradually more are supposed to be opened. A hospital publication for patients and staff is distributed monthly. The state has an active mental health organization and many groups which help ex-mental patients.

The second American hospital is located on a Hawaiian island at the foot of a mountain range near the Pacific. Until recently, hospital H was rather small but with the increase in the state's population since World War II it has expanded rapidly. The hospital site is so attractive that realtors have repeatedly tried to buy it, but they have been unsuccessful so far. The hospital superintendent has held the position only a few years. He has been much interested in applying current theories of a therapeutic community to the hospital. During the writer's field work at the hospital, a leading advocate of these theories had been invited from Boston and was giving a series of lectures on the therapeutic community which were widely attended and discussed by hospital staff members, especially in the more highly trained occupational groups. The hospital director's declared aim was to keep patients in the institution for a minimum of time during which intensive treatment could be given. Then after a short stay, they would be sent home. The calculated risk was taken of having the discharged patient return soon during another acute stage of mental illness. However, it was felt worthwhile to take a chance and thus to keep patients from becoming chronic cases during prolonged hospitalization. During the conduct of the field study (fall 1960), the hospital was not yet a therapeutic community, but it had made, and continued to make considerable progress in this direction.

Practically, this was seen, for example, in the policy of moving patients as much as possible out of the mental hospital and into hospitals located on the patients' home islands. Previously, with the transport of the mentally ill to the mental hospital, the ties with his family and community on his home island were effectively broken and, according to current theory, his rehabilitation might have been jeopardized.

A number of senile patients and of those suffering from incurable organic conditions have been transferred out of the hospital into private 'convalescent homes.' The intent was here to free hospital staff and facilities for therapeutic functions and to leave the custodial functions to other specialized agencies. The hospital buildings are small and scattered over the hillside. While some limited building construction was going on, the hospital's policy was to decrease the size of the patient population and to increase the intensity of therapy provided. As in other state positions in Hawaii, no ethnic discrimination in hiring policies appeared to be in effect at the hospital.

A comparison of the annual reports for the fiscal year ending 1958 of the Hawaiian and border state hospitals showed that the latter institution had a somewhat larger proportion of senile patients. The mental health association of Hawaii is very active, and a number of agencies in the community help those suffering from mental illness. The state division of mental health helps ex-patients and provides on all islands clinics for diagnosis, treatment, and counseling.

Some inter-hospital comparisons

It may be appropriate at this point to present some statistical information by which the four hospitals can be compared. It was noted before that English mental hospitals have by now largely opened their doors. American public mental hospitals have adopted the open-ward system only more recently. Sample members were asked in question 42 of the instrument to indicate where they worked on an average day. The responses of attendants and nurses in the four hospitals are presented in:

Table 4. *Attendants and nurses working on open and closed wards on an average day (approximate percentages)*

Hospital	*Open wards*	*Closed wards*
B	20	80
Hawaii	40	60
X	88	12
Y	100	–

It is evident that there is a sharp break between the two countries in the proportion of staff working on open wards. It may be noted that within each country, the more 'conservative' hospital has a larger percentage of nursing personnel still working on closed wards than is the case in that country's more 'progressive' hospital.

Table 5. *Discharges rates of hospitals for selected years*

English hospitals: 1955

	Hosp. X	Hosp. Y
Total patient population treated during year	2,684	1,653
Full and/or conditional discharges	725	610
Proportion discharged of all patients treated during year	.27	.37

American hospitals: July 1, 1957 to June 30, 1958

	Hosp. B	Hosp. H
Total patient population treated during year	2,423	1,782
Full and/or conditional discharges	648	461
Proportion discharged of all patients treated during year	.27	.26

English hospital X: 1956 to 1960

	Year: 1956	1957	1958	1959	1960
Total patient population treated during year	2,701	2,829	2,776	2,728	2,654
Full and/or conditional discharges	732	830	908	1,056	1,114
Proportion discharged of all patients treated during year	.27	.29	.33	.35	.42

In order to compare the four hospitals meaningfully, it may be useful to consider not only their policies and progress made in opening wards. It is also possible to contrast their discharge rates. This is done in Table 5. Figures were available for all hospitals, though they differed in the periods covered. Of the two British institutions, the more 'progressive' one (Y) showed a higher discharge rate during 1955. For the English hospital X, data were available for each year from 1955 to 1960. They indicated a progressive trend toward higher patient turnover. No noticeable difference in discharge rates was found between the two American hospitals during the last year for which comparative data could be obtained.

OCCUPATIONAL CHARACTERISTICS

It was decided to give the questionnaire within the sample areas chosen to the members of the different occupational groups engaged in the treatment and rehabilitation of mental patients. Included in these occupational groups would be psychiatrists and other physicians, psychologists, social workers, occupational and recreational therapists, nurses, and aides and attendants, all working within the selected mental hospitals. In addition to hospital personnel, other groups included in the sample would be those working for the rehabilitation of mental patients in the area served by the hospital.

Table 6. *Occupational composition of the samples* (in percentages)
(Absolute numbers are presented in parentheses)

Hospital	X	B	H	Y	Total
Attendants	24 (82)	33 (67)	29 (95)	26 (43)	28 (287)
Nurses	60 (206)	30 (61)	28 (92)	53 (86)	43 (445)
Recreational and occupational therapists	4 (14)	8 (16)	4 (12)	5 (8)	5 (50)
Social workers, rehabilitation and employment counselors	7 (25)	19 (39)	29 (97)	6 (9)	16 (170)
Psychiatrists	5 (16)	6 (12)	6 (20)	10 (16)	6 (64)
Psychologists	0 (1)	4 (8)	4 (15)	0 (0)	2 (24)
Total	100 (344)	100 (203)	100 (331)	100 (162)	100 (1040)

Most of these persons working outside of the hospital would be social workers, and rehabilitation and employment counselors. The total sample was broken down by hospitals and by occupations of the respondents. The sample as it was used in the analysis is presented in Table 6. Table 7 divides the sample further by education. Finally, Table 8 divides the respondents according to their ethnic background.

Table 7. *Education of the samples* (in percentages)

	Hospital B						
	Total N	G.S.	S.H.S.	C.H.S.	S.C.	C.C.	N/A
Aides	67	17	28	22	21	6	6
Nurses	61	3	8	33	36	15	5
O. and R. therapists	16		13	25	19	43	
Soc. workers & counselors	39			5	5	87	3
Psychiatrists	12				8	92	
Psychologists	8					100	
Total	203	6	13	20	21	36	4

	Hospital H						
	Total N	G.S.	S.H.S.	C.H.S.	S.C.	C.C.	N/A
Aides	95	17	21	46	14		2
Nurses	92	1	1	29	43	26	
O. and R. therapists	12			25	17	58	
Soc. workers & counselors	97				3	97	
Psychiatrists	20					100	
Psychologists	15					100	
Total	331	5	7	22	17	48	1

Key (American samples)
G.S. – Grade School
S.H.S. – Some High School
C.H.S. – Completed High School
S.C. – Some College
C.C. – Completed College
N/A – No Answer

Table 7. *Education of the samples (cont'd.)* (in percentages)

	Hospital X Total N	E.S.	S.S.	S.A.S.	S.P.	S.U.	C.P.	C.U.	N/A
Aides	82	52	20	7	9	2	2	1	6
Nurses	206	45	30	3	10	1	10	2	
O. and R. therapists	14	21	10		21		49		
Soc. workers & counselors	25	8	28	8	28	4	16	8	
Psychiatrists	16						6	94	
Psychologists	1								100
Total	344	41	25	4	11	1	10	7	2

	Hospital Y Total N	E.S.	S.S.	S.A.S.	S.P.	S.U.	C.P.	C.U.	N/A
Aides	43	44	28	9		9	7		2
Nurses	86	34	34	7	10		14		1
O. and R. therapists	8		37				50	13	
Soc. workers & counselors	9		33				22	45	
Psychiatrists	16						6	94	
Psychologists	0								
Total	162	29	29	6	6	2	13	12	1

Key (English samples)

E.S. – Elementary or secondary modern school
S.S. – Secondary or grammar school to G.C.E. ordinary level
S.A.S. – Secondary or grammar school to G.C.E. advanced level
S.P. – Some professional or technical training
S.U. – Some university
C.P. – Completed professional or technical training
C.U. – Completed university
N/A – No answer

Table 8. *Ethnic background of mental health personnel* (in percentages)

	Hospital X					Hospital B				
	Total N	NE	O	W	N/A	Total N	NE	O	W	N/A
Aides	82	2	1	91	5	67	36		61	3
Nurses	206	3	3	92	2	61	10		85	5
O. and R. therapists	14			100		16	13	6	81	
Soc. workers & counselors	25			100		39	8		92	
Psychiatrists	16		13	81	6	12		8	92	
Psychologists	1			100		8	13		87	
Total	344	6	6	81	7	203	19	1	79	1

	Hospital H						Hospital Y				
	Total N	NE	O	W	HA	N/A	Total N	NE	O	W	N/A
Aides	95		62	24	9	5	43	2		96	2
Nurses	92	2	61	35		2	86			99	1
O. and R. therapists	12		60	40			8			100	
Soc. workers & counselors	97		76	22	1	1	9			100	
Psychiatrists	20		20	80			16			94	6
Psychologists	15			100			0				
Total	331	1	60	34	3	2	162	1		97	2

Key

NE – Negro
O – Oriental
W – White
HA – Hawaiian

Psychiatrists

A few words may be said here about the different occupational groups in the sample. The psychiatrists are the main professionals in the treatment of mental patients not only by virtue of their medical training and function but also as administrators of the hospital from the top level on down as far as the number of psychiatrists will permit. They are also the bearers of the responsibility vis-à-vis the community for the hospital, for its activities and for its patients. As Parsons points out:

From the sheer point of view of technical contribution to the therapeutic function – to say nothing of the other functions of the hospital – it is by no means easy to draw the lines between contributions which are inherently medical and those which are not. Only the narrowest of medical partisans would claim that the M.D. degree conferred a complete monopoly of relevant competence, and that absence of it excluded a person from any contribution. Factors other than the sheer technical competence of medical personnel would seem to determine in part the tremendous emphasis placed on the legitimating role of the physicain in the authority exercised by mental hospitals. This emphasis in effect says that physicians may avail themselves of the cooperation and assistance of other groups, professional and non-professional, but it is legitimate to hold the physician responsible for the outcome, and he delegates his responsibility at his own risk. The basis of this seems to lie essentially in the institutionalized confidence that the general population rests in the physician as both a competent and an ethically responsible custodian of the interest of individuals who may in any way be defined as ill. Given the potential explosiveness in so many directions of the phenomena of mental illness, this is a great protection for the hospital; it can always say that physicians are in the last analysis responsible. (Parsons, 1957, p. 122.)

However, all the various demands made of the hospital psychiatrist come at a price. In Parsons' words:

Psychiatrists are by and large the most expensive members of the hospital staff. Most large mental hospitals stand, for obvious reasons, in a state of budgetary deficiency. In such a situation there is an economically understandable trend to replace the services of psychiatrists with those of less expensive personnel – nurses, social workers, psychologists, and aides. At the same time, because of the symbolic importance of the psychiatrist's legitimating role, there is a tendency, within sub-units of the hospital, to put psychiatrists in positions with a large component of administrative responsibility, i.e., as heads of services, etc.

The outcome of all this is both a scarcity of psychiatric service and a deflection of what there is into administrative rather than operative functions. The result places the psychiatrists in a difficult position. They are held responsible for the operative conduct of the hospital's therapeutic function, but because they are spread so thin and have so little direct contact with patients, they are, to a large extent, not implementing this responsibility but are delegating it to nonpsychiatric personnel. (*Ibid.*, pp. 127-8.)

It might be added that due to the comparatively low income of state hospital psychiatrists in contrast to their colleagues in private practice, American state hospitals frequently have unfilled positions on their medical staffs. As a consequence, some hospital 'psychiatrists' may be general practioners with a minimum of psychiatric training, or they are physicians who received their training abroad and are not allowed to practice privately.

The original sample included seven non-psychiatric physicians in the American samples, six in Hawaii and one in hospital B. Cohen and Struening (1962; 1963) demonstrated the existence of different attitudes between psychiatrists and other medical doctors on their OMI scale. The latter physicians tended to get less 'desirable' scores on the OMI factors. Several checks of the responses of these two groups on OMI items in our questionnaire showed that the same attitudinal discrepancies existed in the present sample. It was therefore decided that psychiatrists and other physicians should not be put in the same category on these questions. The small number of non-psychiatric physicians precluded a separate statistical analysis of their responses.

Psychologists

Psychiatrists were found in the Cohen and Struening work to be more similar in their attitudes to psychologists than to non-psychiatric physicians. Again, several checks were made between responses of psychologists and of psychiatrists, and it was found that in the present study, too, the attitudes for the two groups were similar. As, however, virtually no psychologists worked in the British hospitals, it was decided to keep apart the two occupations. In this way, any differences which might be obtained in the results from the occupations in the two countries could not be attributable to different proportions of psychologists in groups combining psychologists and psychiatrists. Furthermore, Baker and Schulberg (1967) found psychologists to score higher than psychiatrists on a community mental health scale. Also, de Carozzo (1971) reported differences between psychologists and physicians at a psychiatric clinic on several measures of attitudes toward the mentally ill.

In Hawaii, most psychologists were young, recently appointed, research-oriented Ph.D.'s. In hospital B the Chief Psychologist also worked as a chaplain. Another hospital B psychologist was administrative assistant to the superintendent.

In England, only one psychologist was found in the two hospitals. While his activities included psychological testing as well as research, in the hospital his function was still seen as a recent innovation. In 1959, only one graduate training center for clinical psychology existed in England. (Magee, 1959, p. 41.)

Social workers

Social workers as a group constitute a link between the hospital and the community, or in terms of the patient, between his treatment and his post-release rehabilitation. 'The social worker, from the first, proved to be practically indispensable in investigating the home situation, in the problems of hospital patients and of the child-guidance field, and in interpreting the nature of the problem to the family as well as aiding in the readjustment of the improved patient in the community.' (Lewis, 1959, p. 14.)

In all hospitals sampled, there were shortages of social workers. Consequently, the workers could not possibly fulfill all the various functions of psychiatric social work but had to spread themselves thin over the vast patient load, giving much time to tasks like writing social case histories. One American hospital medical director wrote about British psychiatric social workers: 'The general impression gained was that less emphasis was placed on academic background for the profession than in the United States; that personality, willingness to help others, dedication, and on the job training, in addition to certification, made for good psychiatric social work; and that by and large, a creditable job was being done in this field in England.' (Magee, 1959, p. 39.) The majority of social workers in the samples were not members of the hospital staffs but worked in the communities for other agencies helping mental patients. In Hawaii fairly large groups of social workers were active on all major islands.

Rehabilitation and employment counselors

This group works predominantly outside of the hospitals. In the United States, the counselors, at least in theory, carry the main burden of vocational rehabilitation of ex-patients. They still share this function to some extent with social workers. American counselors come generally under the jurisdiction of the state departments of vocational rehabilitation. Senior counselors may have acquired most of their competence through extensive experience. More recently, counselors have been receiving specialized training in postgraduate programs sponsored by the federal Office of Vocational Rehabilitation.

In England, vocational rehabilitation is a function of the Ministry of Labour offices. Each company above a certain size has to hire a fixed percentage of handicapped persons. It has been reported that

British employers tend to fill their quotas with handicapped persons other than ex-mental patients.

As the functions of counselors and social workers tended to overlap, and as the number of counselors in the samples was small, it was decided to combine the two groups for some statistical purposes. The alternative would have been to exclude the rehabilitation and employment counselors from some of the statistical analyses.

Occupational ana recreational therapists

These therapists work in the hospitals, and their vocational and recreational activities with patients are seen as having therapeutic value. Occupational therapy has been broadly defined as 'any activity, mental or physical, definitely prescribed and guided to hasten recovery from disease or injury.' (Lewis, 1959, p. 14.) 'Activities ranging from music, games and arts and crafts to industrial or housekeeping tasks and education were utilized' as early as in the nineteenth century in some American mental hospitals (*ibid.*). In 1917, the Society for the Promotion of Occupational Therapy was formed.

> The ability to participate in recreation is necessary for emotional health. Many of the mentally ill have never developed the normal capacity for play. Skilled recreation workers are of vital importance in cultivating these essential techniques of living. Such workers have been taught the psychological implications of normal play. Play serves as a learning device and a mechanism for mastering emotional traumata. In addition, it furnishes the patient with a valuable group experience and helps in sublimation and psychological defense. A hospital recreation program should operate in close liaison with the psychiatrists not only for the guidance which the latter gives the recreational worker but for the data which the recreational worker can give the psychiatrist, thereby increasing his understanding of the total clinical picture. (Linn, 1959, p. 1833.)

In England, occupational therapists take theoretically a three-year professional (post-secondary school) course. In practice, educational levels vary considerably among both British and American occupational and recreational therapists. (See Table 7.)

Registered nurses

'In 1952 the American Nurses Association, the National League for Nursing, and the American Psychiatric Association agreed to and stated the principle that all who give nursing care to patients are nursing personnel.' (Peplau, 1959, p. 1843.)

In the United States, among the registered nurses, psychiatric nurses are the elite. They hold a bachelor's or even a master's degree. Staff nurses may have graduated from a two-year junior college program or a three-year diploma program of a hospital school of nursing. The psychiatric phase of their nurses' training may have ranged from 8 to 20 days in a two-year program to 12 to 20 weeks in the four-year program. (*Ibid.*, p. 1844.) Most nurses in mental hospitals have experienced only the basic course. Registered nurses hold important administrative positions ranging from being in charge of a ward to supervising all nursing staffs and activities in the broader sense, as does the 'director of nursing' (in England 'matron' on the female and 'chief male nurse' on the male side). Mental hospitals also carry on training programs for student nurses through specialized nursing instructors.

In England, mental nurses receive a training entirely different from general medical nurses. The former take a three-year training course in a mental hospital. In contrast to the American situation, English mental hospitals in general do not suffer from a shortage of qualified nurses. One American psychiatrist reports: 'There was an impressive number of trained mental nurses on the wards visited.' (Magee, 1959, p. 38.) Male nurses are as frequent as female ones in England. The Matron (top nurse) is in charge of general ward administration, housekeeping, training and at times even of purchases.

Non-professional nursing personnel

In the United States, the chronic shortage of registered nurses in state hospitals is compensated for by the utilization of practical nurses, temporary licensed practical nurses, hospital or psychiatric aides and attendants. Their designations vary among hospitals, as does their training. According to Peplau, in 1959, there were 'approximately 700,000 patients, 14,000 registered nurses, and 90,000 non-professional nursing workers in all psychiatric facilities' in the United States. (Peplau, 1959, p. 1845.) She continues,

> Obviously, the largest share of nursing in public psychiatric hospitals is currently rendered by practical nurses, psychiatric technicians, aides, and untrained attendants. Unquestionably, nursing personnel in these categories render yeoman service that is fundamentally useful, owing to native talent and sustained interest in the work rather than to educational preparation for the tasks involved. Schools of practical nursing now include a brief basic psychiatric experience;

psychiatric hospitals, on a wider basis than ever before, now offer pre-service, on-the-job, and/or in-service training for all categories of non-professional nursing personnel. . . . Nursing personnel in these categories require supervision by nurses who have had professional and advanced preparation in psychiatric nursing. The work of a practical nurse or psychiatric technician includes the following: providing bedside care, offering companionship and socializing activities which remotivate the patient toward recovery, carrying out simple medical-surgical procedures, and carrying out many of the routines required in a ward situation. (*Ibid.*, pp. 1845-6.)

According to Struening, American attendants and aides differ from registered nurses not only by education but also by coming generally from a lower class background while nurses tend to come from the lower middle or at least upper lower class.

This should not mislead one to underrate the importance of the aides and attendants. They have more day-to-day contact with patients than any other group of the hospital staff. Consequently, their influence on the patient and his recovery is considerable. As Parsons put it:

There is, however, one category of great importance – because of contact with patients – namely, the attendant. In terms of both qualifications and authority, his role is defined residually. He has responsibilities in the direct care and management of patients, and yet he has no professional qualifications and no special competence other than that derived from direct experience. His role is clearly of great importance and because of the cost of professional personnel, a good deal of responsibility tends to be left in his hands. Until recently, the role has often been defined mainly by practical exigencies rather than by any clear conception of positive function.

Selectivity in recruitment is likely to be more pronounced for aides than for other categories of non-professional personnel. It is rather special personalities who can tolerate spending most of their working time in intimate contact with mentally ill people without the stabilization of their motivations provided by a well-defined professional role. Fortunately, some of these problems are coming to be studied, but at present relatively little can be said about this vital area. The most important point seems to be that the mental hospital is dependent on a specially selected set of lower-order occupational personnel, drawn on an unknown basis from the local community in which the hospital is situated. (Parsons, 1957, p. 119.)

Parsons points out another aspect of aides' selection: 'It has been noted that a substantial proportion of hospital aides are former patients. This is probably a significant fact, indicating that there is a tendency for persons with the experience of mental illness to hang together. Also, discharged persons who would have difficulty finding employment in the general labor market are often taken care of this way.' (*Ibid.*, p. 120.)

For an attitude study, attendants as a group are also of interest, because of the various occupational groups listed they have been least exposed to psychiatric indoctrination and hence may be expected to retain most of the unsophisticated popular conceptions of mental illness and of the chances for its curability.

In England, male and female 'nursing assistants' fulfill a function comparable to that of American aides and attendants. (Bennett, 1959, p. 18.)

ADMINISTRATION OF QUESTIONNAIRES

The first field study was conducted in the Eastern state. The initial step was the clearance of the project and of the questionnaire with the superintendent of hospital B. Simultaneously, working relations were established with the Mental Health Association of the state.

The hospital superintendent appointed his administrative assistant to be his liaison with the project. The writer went with this liaison person to all the department heads in the hospital and arranged dates and locations for questionnaire administration to their staffs. A large number of group sessions were held to make sure that all clinical personnel of all shifts could fill in the questionnaires at a time relatively convenient to them.

Each session was started with a brief introduction of the project, of its purposes, and of the value of the information the staff could provide for comparing problems of mental illness in different societies and for gaining insight to help mental patients. Particular emphasis was placed on the anonymity of the questionnaire and on the importance of answering every item. The semantic differentials appeared to be novel and somewhat difficult to understand, especially to some attendants. The proper answering procedure for the scales was demonstrated. During the period of questionnaire administration, any questions could be asked and were answered in a fashion which endeavored not to suggest any particular answers.

Questionnaires were administered to all clinical personnel, with one exception. It was felt that little could be gained by giving the questionnaires to all attendants at the hospital and that a random sample of every fifth person would demonstrate the relevant attitudes of attendants in this hospital. Therefore, a random choice of 20% of the attendants was decided on. An alphabetical list of all attendants was obtained and every fifth name was selected for the sample. Subsequent crosschecks indicated that the attendants selected in this random fashion represented proportionally the distribution of attendants on the morning, afternoon and night shifts and in the different wards. Most of the relevant staff members completed their questionnaires in this fashion. A few persons were on leave or ill. Their number was reduced by subsequent administrations. Questionnaires and stamped self-addressed envelopes were left for those persons who were absent for a longer period. With the help of the state's Mental Health Association, relevant agencies were identified, some of whose staff members work with mental patients outside of the hospital. The pertinent staff members, mostly social workers and counselors, were then given the questionnaires in the same fashion as the hospital staff. All relevant agencies were cooperative with the field study.

In each of the four samples, less than five percent of the eligible respondents refused to answer the questionnaire or did not attend the group sessions for filling it out.

The border state field work techniques were followed closely in the other samples. One exception was that in the Hawaiian hospital, which had fewer attendants than hospital B, two-fifths (or 40%) of their number were selected at random from an alphabetical list.

From the above discussion, it will be apparent that the four hospital groups and the occupational subsamples were uneven in size. While it is more convenient to work with large homogeneous groups from which larger N's of any desirable size can be drawn, in the present study one had to take the personnel as they were, and their numbers varied among the hospitals.

The questionnaires were administered in hospital B in August, 1960. In Hawaii, they were collected during a four week period in October and November, 1960. In the two English hospitals, the data were gathered in February through April, 1961. As far as can be determined, no events during or a short time before the data collection had an effect upon the results.

In order to preclude the possibility of contamination of responses, several precautions were taken. The introductory page of the questionnaire stressed that there were no 'right' and 'wrong' answers to the questions, that all questionnaires would be anonymous and held confidential, that the purposes of the study were to learn what problems in the treatment of mental patients exist in different countries, that the sponsor wanted to learn from the experiences of the respondents, etc. The reader may see the introduction to the questionnaire in Appendix I. In addition, the spoken remarks preceding questionnaire administration again stressed these points. No indications were given as to the expectations or the interpretative plans of the research staff. It was emphasized that the study's interest was in collecting the experiences and views of the respondents, whatever they might be. Respondents were asked not to discuss the questionnaire with colleagues or other potential respondents. There is no evidence that the instructions were violated.

The samples, of course, are in no way assumed to stand for the entire populations of their states or catchment areas, but they should fairly represent the mental health personnel in these areas.

SUMMARY

Four samples were selected. They consisted of the professional and nursing staffs of two English and two American mental hospitals and of social workers and rehabilitation counselors serving the mental patients released from these hospitals. One of the American institutions was located in Hawaii and the other in a border state between the Northeastern and the Southern sections of the United States. In terms of hospital policies, one English (X) and the border state (B) hospitals were considered to be relatively 'conservative.' The Hawaiian (H) and the other British institution (Y) were judged to be comparatively 'progressive.' On the basis of available information and of personal impressions the hospitals were ranked in order of increasing 'progressivism' as follows: English X, border state B, Hawaii H, and English Y. Six occupational groups were compared: aides, nurses, occupational and recreational therapists, social workers and counselors, psychiatrists, and psychologists.

CHAPTER 5

The rehabilitation scale

The scale is presented as items 1 to 15 preceding question 32 of the questionnaire (see Appendix I). It was chosen for the initial discussion of results because thirteen of the fifteen items which make it up were taken over from Cohen and Struening's Opinions about Mental Illness (OMI) Scale. Their extensive work was discussed in Chapter 2, and the corresponding items in the present questionnaire form a connection with the work of Cohen and Struening and the literature in the field.

As the psychiatrists' cells in the population are quite small (see Table 9), some thought was given to the possibility of including non-psychiatric physicians in the same cells. However, Cohen and Struening's findings had suggested a clear-cut attitudinal break between psychiatrists and other physicians. In particular, psychiatrists were surpassed on 'authoritarianism' (Factor A) and 'social restrictiveness' (D) by the non-psychiatric physicians in the samples. On the other hand, psychiatrists were stronger in Factors B ('benevolence') and C ('mental hygiene ideology').

Table 9. *Respondents who completed the rehabilitation scale* (in absolute numbers)

	X	B	H	Y	Total
Attendants	73	71	94	37	275
Nurses	217	64	91	86	458
O. and R. therapists	14	16	12	7	49
Social workers and counselors	23	39	97	8	167
Psychiatrists	16	12	20	16	64
Psychologists	–	9	15	–	24
Total	343	211	329	154	1037

Some checks were conducted with the present data to test the comparability of psychiatrists and non-psychiatric physicians. The outcome suggested that the two groups were dissimilar in the expected directions, (e.g., non-psychiatrists were stronger in Factor I and weaker in Factor II). Because of their small number (seven for the entire sample) it was decided to exclude the non-psychiatric physicians from further analysis. This group consisted of six physicians in Hawaii, one in hospital B and none in the English hospitals.

One may ask why aides and nurses are not combined, as both of them work generally on wards and are in daily contact with the same patients. The merger of these two occupational groups would have some clear advantages. For one thing, it would roughly double the size of their cells in each hospital and thus increase their strength in statistical tests of significance. Secondly, it would create a functional block of what might be called 'ward personnel' or 'nursing personnel' vis-à-vis the various professional specialist groups.

Although nurses and aides share certain functions in the hospital, they tend to differ systematically in their general education, their specific medical training and their socio-economic standing. Cohen and Struening's study has shown that members of the two occupations tend to have relatively similar but still distinguishable responses to OMI scales. As the N's for both groups were the largest in the present sample, it was decided to analyze them separately.

The fifteen items used in the scale were selected because of their apparent relevance for the issue of vocational rehabilitation of mental patients. A discussion of the items chosen in the construction of the scale may be found above in Chapter 3.

FACTOR ANALYSIS

The 15-item scale was submitted to a factor analysis. The system which Struening developed for the factor analysis with the original OMI scales was used with the 15 items in the present questionnaire. In order to avoid distortions, all the questionnaires were excluded which had more than 3 unanswered items out of 15. At first, separate matrices for the samples in hospital B, Hawaii, and England hospital B and Hawaii results appeared to be slightly closer to each samples was constructed. The matrices consisted each of 15 x 15 product-moment correlation coefficients between the scale items.

Factor extraction was performed in accordance with Thurstone's complete centroid method. The original matrices for the three areas showed two strong factors and several weaker ones. (See Table 10.) (For a discussion of the techniques used, see Harmon, 1960.)

Table 10. *Percentages of common variance included in the two strongest factors*

Sample	Factor I	Factor II
Hospital B	42.99	19.78
Cumulative		62.77
Hawaii	49.16	17.55
Cumulative		66.71
England	48.00	18.99
Cumulative		66.99
Total	52.37	18.13
Cumulative		70.50

A comparison of the different samples showed that the factors formed were similarly structured in the three areas. Only those factors were rotated which had an item variable with a loading of .300 or more. Three factors reached this level and were rotated to an orthogonal, simple-structure solution by the quartimax method of Neuhaus and Wrigley (see Harmon, 1960). The scale items fell into fairly consistent clusters in the three samples. On first inspection, the hospital B and Hawaii results appeared to be slightly closer to each other than to the English results. In the different matrices, the strongest factor was made up of essentially the items from the OMI factors A (authoritarianism), D (social restrictiveness) and negative B (benevolence). The second strongest factor consisted of items from Cohen and Struening's factors B (benevolence), C (mental hygiene ideology), A- and D-. Two dimensions appeared to emerge, each combining about one-half of the items. Within the major dimension two A (authoritarianism) items were slightly apart from the other A and D items in the matrices and might have been considered in a third factor. The two items (numbers 3 and 5) stated that it is easy to distinguish mental patients from other persons. However, it was felt that not much would be gained by splitting off these two A items from the other A and D items. Psychologically, the relation of the two A questions to the D items is fairly close, factor A dealing with a negative perception of patients and factor D with negative views on the treatment of patients. Although empirically in the matrices the two items are only slightly apart from the main cluster of the first factor, they are clearly distinct and removed from the second factor items. If a third factor were made up of the two items, it could reach only low reliability. These two arguments seemed to justify a solution in which the items are considered as a part or sub-dimension of a 'discrimination' factor, as they are not sufficiently strong or distinct to warrant separate scoring. Because of these considerations, items of the main and the third factors were combined into one oblique Factor I. Subsequent computations found internal consistency for this factor to reach .654, which is at a fairly high level for a seven item scale.

Item 15 ('Professionals who work with mental patients should try to raise a patient's opinion about himself') was dropped from further analysis when it turned out to be highly variable. It may be recalled that this item was not part of the original OMI scale.

Tests of internal consistency were conducted for both factors and for the total scale. The following estimate of the Kuder-Richardson formula 20 was used:

$$r_{xx} = \frac{n\,\bar{r}_{ij}}{1 + (n-1)\,\bar{r}_{ij}}$$

The coefficients found were, for the fourteen item scale $r_{xx} = .707$; for Factor I, $r_{xx} = .654$; for Factor II, $r_{xx} = .592$.

DEFINITION OF THE FACTORS

Table 11 lists the seven individual items which make up Factor I, in order of their strength in factor loadings. For each item, its membership in the original OMI group of factors is indicated. Item 14 ('Sex delinquents should be severely punished') was not part of the OMI scale and is identified by a small letter 'd'. It appeared that this item would fit most logically in the 'social restrictiveness' factor D.

Table 12 gives the corresponding information for the seven items which constitute Factor II.

The question may be raised whether we are not dealing here indeed with opposite poles of the same factor. The two factors appear to some extent to be logical opposites ranging from, one might say, an 'anti-patient' to a 'pro-patient' point of view. Still there were reasons which seemed to justify a separate discussion of the two factors. First, within the common factor space the two factors appear to lie approximately at right angles and may be considered to be roughly orthogonal. Another consideration is the history of the items. Factor I is made up primarily of items from OMI factors A ('authoritarianism') and D ('social restrictiveness') while in Factor II the majority of items were labeled B ('benevolence') and C ('mental hygiene ideology').

Table 11. *Factor I – Qualitative differentiation: items and factor loadings*

Factor loading	*OMI factor*	*Item*	
.696	A	5)	There is something about mental patients that makes it easy to tell them from normal people.
.684	A	3)	It is easy to recognize someone who once had a serious mental illness.
.395	D	4)	Although patients discharged from mental hospitals may seem all right, they should not be allowed to marry.
.280	B–	9)	To become a patient in a mental hospital is to become a failure in life.
.232	A	12)	People with mental illness should never be treated in the same hospital as people with physical illness.
.208	D	13)	Although some mental patients seem all right, it is dangerous to forget for a moment that they are mentally ill.
.202	d	14)	Sex delinquents should be severely punished.

The question arose as to how the factors might be meaningfully labeled for purposes of easy reference. The use of combined OMI factor labels, e.g., 'authoritarianism-restrictiveness' for Factor I, seemed not desirable as only very few of the original OMI items are involved in the present scale and as these items form a biased sample of each OMI factor represented. Also, a term like 'authoritarianism' has been employed so extensively and variously in the literature, that it seemed preferable not to assign still another meaning to it.

Table 12. *Factor II – Trust and meliorism: items and factor loadings*

Factor loading	*OMI factor*	*Item*	
.492	D–	8)	People who were once in mental hospitals are no more dangerous than the average citizen.
.464	D–	10)	Most women who were once patients in a mental hospital could be trusted as baby sitters.
.434	C	2)	Most patients in mental hospitals are not dangerous.
.383	A–	11)	The patients of a mental hospital should have something to say about the way the hospital is run.
.380	B	7)	Many mental patients are capable of skilled labor, even though in some ways they are very disturbed mentally.
.367	B	1)	Mental illness is an illness like any other.
.365	C	6)	If our hospitals had enough well trained doctors, nurses, and aides, many of the patients would get well enough to live outside the hospital.

The items in Factor I were then reviewed in terms of their factor loadings and of any logical communalities. By a process of induction, a perceptual discrimination seemed to emerge as the main characteristic possessed in common by the items. The factor also seemed to involve a qualitative rejection of mental patients. The term 'qualitative differentiation' was thought to be a brief summation of these item characteristics.

Factor II items tend to state that mental patients are not dangerous, that they can be trusted, and that they may be expected to respond favorably to better treatment. The label 'trust and meliorism' was an attempt to condence verbally the general attributes which run more or less through the factor's items.

While it was thought useful to look at responses to the two factors separately, still they might be viewed in a combined fashion, with the Factor I items representing a negative view and the Factor II statements indicating a more favorable view of mental patients. Both factors could then be combined so that the total score would equal the Factor II score minus the Factor I score.

What would be an appropriate label for all 14 items? It may be recalled that the primary criterion for inclusion of an OMI item into the present scale was its presumed bearing on the issue of rehabilitation of the mentally ill. Furthermore, the presence of 'trust and meliorism' and the absence of 'qualitative differentiation' seemed to fit in with the outlook of those who stress the need to rehabilitate mental patients. Thus, the overall label chosen for the 14 items was 'rehabilitation scale.' On this scale, a high score is presumed to favor rehabilitation, and a low score implies little support for rehabilitation.

ANALYSES OF VARIANCE

In order to determine the relationships between scores and demographic variables, analyses of variance were performed (Edwards, 1954). At first, analyses for each hospital across occupational groups were conducted for whole scale scores, for Factors I and II, and then F ratios of the same score measures were determined for each occupation across hospitals. Later, a two way analysis of variance was performed by hospitals and by occupations. Correction formulas were utilized to compensate for unequal N's in the cells (Snedecor, 1956, pp. 385-386). The technique of harmonic mean estimates was employed.

Secondary analyses were performed where the results seemed to require more detailed classification.

It may be useful here to recapitulate the main outcomes of the original OMI investigation so as to provide a background for the present study's findings. From the results of the Cohen and Struening attitude study, which were discussed in some detail in Chapter 2, certain conclusions were drawn. Occupation, closely paralleled by education, was used as the main explanatory variable. 'Authoritarianism' (factor A) and 'social restrictiveness' (factor D) varied roughly in inverse fashion with occupation and education, aides obtaining the highest scores followed by nurses, psychiatrists, and finally psychologists. 'Benevolence' (factor B) and 'mental hygiene ideology' (factor C) tended to run in the opposite direction with the following exceptions. Benevolence, a kindly acceptance of patients based more on a religious or 'humanistic' spirit than on scientific or professional theories, was most pronounced among nurses, followed by social workers, psychiatrists, aides and psychologists. Factor C – 'mental hygiene ideology' decreased in strength from psychologists to social workers, psychiatrists, nurses and aides. The relationships between attitudes and education is thus not clearly rectilinear but, especially in factors B and C, tends to be curvilinear. Not only amount of education, measured by years of schooling, is effective but also the emphasis and ideals of different professions and their training. Thus, the nursing ideal of 'tender loving care' (TLC, to quote the abbreviation used by some nurses filling in the present study's questionnaire), appears to be reflected in the high 'benevolence' scores, while the 'mental hygiene ideology' scores are strongest among the nonmedical professionals and slightly weaker among psychiatrists.

Cohen and Struening (1962, 1963) also compared their results by hospital, by age and by sex. They found virtually no systematic differences relating these factors to attitudes.* Differences for age and sex might perhaps have been obtained if occupation or education had been controlled. In the sex division, only for 'benevolence' and 'social restrictiveness' were significant differences obtained; women were stronger in both factors. Presumably, nurses account largely for the difference in 'benevolence'. Several items which made up factor D contain statements about women which may explain the sex difference in responses.

EXPECTATIONS

At this point one may state several expectations about the results on the rehabilitation scale.

1. On the basis of Cohen and Struening's results, one may expect to find variations similar to theirs, due largely to the respondents'

* In subsequent work, Cohen and Struening (1964, 1965) found that 'authoritarianism' and 'benevolence' varied with hospital location for aides and nurses but not for higher occupational levels.

positions in the occupational-educational hierarchy. If the results indeed did indicate such variation, then Cohen and Struening's thesis would be substantiated to the extent of this cross-cultural application.

2. Cohen and Struening (1962, 1963) did not find systematic differences among their hospitals. This may be due to the fact that all of the hospitals in their sample were under the jurisdiction of the Veterans Administration, which may maintain relatively standardized policies throughout its national neuropsychiatric hospital system. The four hospitals investigated in the present study differ in terms of their 'conservatism' versus 'progressivism' (see above Chapter 4) with hospitals X and B being relatively more 'conservative' and Y and Hawaii being on the more 'progressive' side. No safe comparisons can be made about the relative 'conservatism' of the hospitals as the parameters which make up 'conservatism' and their relative weights are not determined. An *a priori* guess based on overall impressions might rank the hospitals, starting with the most 'progressive' institution, from Y to Hawaii, B and X (see Chapter 4). If the results indicate that attitudes vary strongly among hospitals in roughly this order, the hospitals' policies and atmospheres may be considered in the explanation.

3. Cohen and Struening's twelve hospitals were located in the continental United States. If the results should indicate systematic differences between the American and the English hospitals, an explanation in terms of cultural and historical factors may be considered. If on the other hand, the Hawaiian sample stands out from the other samples, its ethnic composition may be scrutinized for an explanation. Only one-third of the Hawaiian sample were Caucasians; most of the remainder came from an oriental background. (See Table 13.)

Table 13. *Rehabilitation scale: Hawaii – Numbers of oriental and white respondents*

	Oriental	White	Total
Aides	59	24	83
Nurses	55	31	86
O. & R. therapists	7	5	12
Social workers and counselors	73	22	95
Psychiatrists	5	15	20
Totals	199	97	296

THE TOTAL SCALE

As was described above, the total scale is made up of seven Factor I items and seven Factor II items in such a way that the theoretical range of the scores extends from 0 to 70, increasing with rehabilitation-mindedness. The mathematical midpoint of this possible distribution would be at 35. The actual group means for the different occupations in the four hospitals are shown in Table 14. F ratios and significance levels are given for six occupational groups across hospitals and for the four hospitals across occupations. The range of means within each row and each column is also indicated. Table 15 contains the standard deviations for the same twenty-two sample groups and the corresponding nine ranges of sigmas by hospitals and by occupations.

Table 14. *Rehabilitation scale: means*

	X	B	H	Y	F ratio	Sign.	Range of means
Aides	41.2	45.3	41.3	42.7	5.26	1%	4.1
Nurses	45.1	47.9	47.2	47.7	3.73	5%	2.8
O. and R. therapists	43.9	47.4	49.1	47.6	.59	NS	5.2
Social workers and counselors	49.1	49.9	50.2	51.1	.22	NS	2.0
Psychiatrists	47.2	50.2	54.6	55.8	3.91	5%	8.6
Psychologists	–	50.1	53.0	–			
F ratio	2.45	23.96	4.90	10.97			
Significance	5%	1%	1%	1%			
Range of means	7.9	4.9	13.3	13.1			

The first and perhaps most striking impression of Table 14 is that for all four hospitals independently the scores increase systematically with occupation from attendants to psychiatrists. The F ratios for all four hospitals are significant, as one would have expected on the basis of Cohen and Struening's continental American samples. It appears that occupation plays a systematic role in affecting attitude scores on OMI type scales in Hawaii and England as well as in the continental United States.

The question arises which, if any, exceptions exist within this general occupational-educational trend. Two exceptions are found. First, in all hospitals except X, the psychiatrists appear at the top of their respective groups. In hospital X, they fall below the social workers. The most direct explanation appears to be the policy split at the top level of hospital X described in Chapter 4. It may be recalled that in this hospital, within a year before the data were collected, a new superintendent had been appointed who tried to bring about some rapid innovations in a traditionally 'conservative' hospital. Resentment seemed to be strongest on the psychiatrists' level, with some of the physicians in open vocal opposition to the reformer and his reforms. One might expect that hospital policy is set at the top administrative level and gets attenuated as one descends the occupational ladder. In hospital X, the results may indicate that the new superintendent had not yet been successful in creating a new approach to mental patients, to the extent that the 14-item scale measured it. In all occupational groups, hospital X is at the bottom of the four hospital sample. One might feel that the social workers were conceivably influenced by the new spirit as their mean score exceeds the psychiatrists' mean. However, this may be the result of the abnormally low psychiatrists' mean, and even the social workers in sample X get a lower mean than their colleagues in the other three samples.

Table 15. *Rehabilitation scale: standard deviations*

	X	B	H	Y	F ratio	Sign.	Range of S.D.
Aides	7.07	7.11	7.45	6.14	5.26	1%	1.31
Nurses	8.61	7.33	7.59	6.80	3.73	5%	1.81
O. and R. therapists	13.84	8.97	5.28	9.44	.59	NS	8.56
Social workers and counselors	7.61	8.82	6.18	3.41	.22	NS	5.41
Psychiatrists	10.12	6.93	6.52	7.24	3.91	5%	3.60
Psychologists	–	7.46	5.11	–			
F ratio	2.45	23.96	4.90	10.97			
Significance	5%	1%	1%	1%			
Range of S.D.	6.77	2.04	2.31	6.03			

(Ranges exclude psychologists)

A glance at Table 15 suggests that sample X produced the two highest variances in the table and a generally wide dispersion of views. This may imply that while the new regime at hospital X had not yet succeeded in improving the average outlook to any large extent, it had at any rate created some diversity of opinions. The writer gained a strong impression of opposing factions, particularly among the physicians and nursing administrators, during his visits to the hospital. This factionalism may lie behind the large variance for the psychiatrists and possibly for some other groups as well. While hospital Y, the more 'progressive' English sample, exceeds hospital X in each occupational mean, it is surpassed by hospital X in the size of all occupational variances. The writer confesses that he anticipated some variation between the two hospitals due to their different policies and the new administration at hospital X, but his expectations were exceeded.

The second exception to the occupational trend of means is found among recreational and occupational therapists who fall below nurses especially in hospital X and non-significantly in two other hospitals. It will be noted that in three samples, these auxiliary therapists have the largest respective variances, suggesting intra-professional disagreements. Table 15 shows that this group obtained the highest of the ten ranges of S.D. The therapists at X show the highest single S.D. in Table 15. This may again reflect the divided ideologies of this hospital in a state of transition. For the whole occupational group, the irregular responses may reflect its newness as a profession and the present heterogeneity of training. As yet, no general standards of professional training exist and practitioners come from a variety of educational backgrounds. It is also possible that occupational therapists responded somewhat differently from recreational therapists to a scale which emphasizes vocational aspects of rehabilitation. Unfortunately, the occupational subsamples were relatively small (see Table 9) so that it would be somewhat tenuous to derive firm conclusions from the obtained data.

Across hospitals, the range of means is largest for the psychiatrists. (See Table 14.) This is due to the extraordinarily strong contrast of the two English samples. The psychiatric (and social worker) samples follow precisely the order of hospitals by 'progressiveness' as they were tentatively ranked above from general impressions. The finding seems to support the argument that hospital policy is most conspicuously represented at the top administrative level. In hospital X, the new superintendent's views are still the minority opinion, even among the psychiatrists in this relatively 'conservative' institution.

The smallest range of means is found among social workers across sample areas. This may indicate that regardless of area, the social workers and counselors tend to have some common professional principles which are relevant to the scale used. Perhaps a more direct reason is the scale's topic of rehabilitation which is the function of the social workers and counselors. This group is made up of persons who on the average spend the greater part of their time outside of the hospital. This may account for the relatively weak effect of hospital policy on this group's means.

It was noted above that for all English occupational groups the scale means are greater in the more 'progressive' hospital (Y). In the American hospitals, this situation obtains only in the higher educational groups. Aides and nurses in the more 'progressive' American institution (Hawaii) produce lower mean scores (and larger S.D.'s) than their colleagues in the more 'conservative' hospital B.

One possible explanation might be the ethnic composition of the Hawaiian sample. More than 60% of the Hawaiian aides and nurses are orientals. A sub-analysis of this cultural tradition hypothesis was conducted.

Table 16. *Rehabilitation scale: Hawaiian sample – oriental (O) and white (W) respondents: means*

	Total scale				Factor I				Factor II			
	O	W	F ratio	Sign.	O	W	F ratio	Sign.	O	W	F ratio	Sign.
Attendants	41.8	41.7	.01	N.S.	16.2	15.6	.22	N.S.	23.0	22.3	.39	N.S.
Nurses	45.1	51.2	13.92	1%	13.5	9.9	13.34	1%	23.7	26.0	5.75	5%
O. and R. therapists	48.6	49.8	.13	N.S.	12.6	10.2	.65	N.S.	26.1	25.0	.39	N.S.
Soc. workers and counselors	49.7	52.1	2.87	N.S.	9.9	8.6	2.21	N.S.	24.7	25.7	1.64	N.S.
Psychiatrists	54.4	54.6	.00	N.S.	7.0	7.0	.00	N.S.	26.4	26.6	.01	N.S.

The results of the sub-analysis by major ethnic groups in Hawaii are presented in Tables 16 and 17. As Table 16 indicates, among nurses, the white respondents get a significantly higher score, while among aides the ethnic differences are non-significant. (The same relationships also hold for Factors I and II.) It has been reported that among the Japanese, the nursing occupation is held in low esteem.

Table 17. *Rehabilitation scale: Hawaiian sample – oriental (O) and white (W) respondents: standard deviations*

	Total scale				Factor I				Factor II			
	O	W	F ratio	Sign.	O	W	F ratio	Sign.	O	W	F ratio	Sign.
Attendants	7.24	8.49	.01	N.S.	4.83	6.20	.22	N.S.	4.79	4.57	.39	N.S.
Nurses	7.11	7.20	13.92	1%	4.58	4.14	13.34	1%	4.31	4.45	5.75	5%
O. and R. therapists	6.16	3.60	.13	N.S.	5.68	2.23	.65	N.S.	3.09	2.45	.89	N.S.
Soc. workers and counselors	5.71	5.90	2,87	N.S.	3.56	3.86	2.21	N.S.	3.40	3.40	1.64	N.S.
Psychiatrists	4.22	7.12	.00	N.S.	3.29	3.67	.00	N.S.	2.87	4.08	.01	N.S.

Further data would be needed to explain the difference in attitude scores among the Hawaiian nurses group. Among Hawaiian aides, practically no difference was found to go with ethnicity. As mental hospital attendants are a highly self-selected group, it would be necessary to get additional information about their characteristics in Hawaii before a safe interpretation of their similarity in mean scores could be reached. Table 18 shows that in the two-way analysis of variance, the F ratio for ethnicity accounts for the greatest part of the variation in the total scale as well as in the two factor subscales, while interaction between occupation and ethnicity tends to account for the smallest part of the common variance.

Table 18. *Rehabilitation scale: Two-way analysis of variance: Hawaii – Oriental versus white respondents*

	Total scale		Factor I		Factor II	
	F ratio	Sign.	F ratio	Sign.	F ratio	Sign.
Ethnic group	11.92	1%	13.94	1%	3.08	N.S.
Occupation	2.59	5%	4.07	1%	.24	N.S.
Interaction	.84	N.S.	.68	N.S.	.74	N.S.

The cultural approach to the scale scores accounts for only some of the variation found. The American mean scores generally overlap with the British mean scores (see Table 14). The only exception to this finding are the occupational and recreational therapists who tend to score somewhat higher in the United States than in England. Training of American therapists may differ from that of their English colleagues. However, it has already been said that therapists show large variances and that their N's are quite small. Hence, the national difference among therapists may not be very meaningful. In both British hospitals, therapists showed the largest S.D.'s among occupational groups. Their bimodal educational background may be at least partly responsible. Table 7 shows that 36% of the English therapists had less than a complete secondary education while 64% had at least some college.

Aides and nurses show the smallest ranges of variances and fairly small ranges of means (see Tables 14 and 15). This may support the argument that institutional policies of 'conservatism' or 'progressivism' are most effective at the higher hospital levels and tend to be least effective on the ward level of aides and nurses.

When one compares the range of means by occupations for the four hospitals, it appears that the two more 'progressive' hospitals show wider ranges of means than do the two more 'conservative' hospitals. The reason for this distinction is not immediately apparent, but it may be that the roles of the various occupations are more differentiated in the 'progressive' than in the 'conservative' hospitals. For example, in the 'conservative' institutions attitudes of psychiatrists tend to be more like those of aides than is the case in 'progressive' hospitals. Aides in general are said to be least influenced by 'progressive' theories of psychiatric treatment and mental health. To the extent that the scale measures these theoretical views one might expect scores to reflect the absence of 'progressive' thinking among psychiatrists.

After the review of the rehabilitation scale scores, we can now look at the responses obtained on the two subscales.

FACTOR I: THE 'QUALITATIVE DIFFERENTIATION' SUBSCALE

Mean scores for the different hospitals and occupational groups, F ratios, significance levels, and ranges of means are presented in Table 19. Table 20 contains the standard deviations and their ranges for the same occupational and hospital samples. On this subscale, the theoretical range of scores was from 0 to 35, with the presumed neutral midpoint at 17.5. A high score means acceptance of the 'qualitative differentiation' outlook, while a low score indicates its rejection.

Table 19. *Factor I subscale: Qualitative differentiation – means*

	X	B	H	Y	F ratio	Sign.	Range of means
Aides	15.9	14.4	16.5	16.2	2.78	5%	2.1
Nurses	14.6	12.1	12.4	13.0	6.17	1%	2.5
O. and R. therapists	14.5	12.0	11.6	12.7	.59	NS	2.9
Social workers and counselors	11.1	9.3	9.7	10.1	.87	NS	1.7
Psychiatrists	12.1	9.8	7.0	5.9	5.91	1%	5.1
Psychologists	–	11.0	6.8	–			
F ratio	5.83	31.16	4.38	13.40			
Significance	1%	1%	1%	1%			
Range of means	4.8	5.1	9.5	10.3			

Table 20. *Factor I subscale: Qualitative differentiation – standard deviations*

	X	B	H	Y	F ratio	Sign.	Range of S.D.
Aides	4.44	4.76	5.43	4.64	2.78	5%	.99
Nurses	5.48	4.71	4.79	4.95	6.17	1%	.77
O. and R. therapists	6.94	6.20	4.72	5.17	.59	NS	2.22
Social workers and counselors	5.10	5.34	3.83	2.67	.87	NS	2.67
Psychiatrists	5.40	4.80	3.58	4.22	5.91	1%	1.82
Psychologists	–	4.22	3.53	–			
F ratio	5.83	31.16	4.38	13.40			
Significance	1%	1%	1%	1%			
Range of S.D.	2.50	1.49	1.85	2.50			

(Ranges exclude psychologists)

As was the case with the total scale, the mean scores of the Factor I subscale tends to 'improve' systematically with occupation from aides to psychiatrists. The F ratios by occupation are significant for each of the four hospitals. In the relatively more 'progressive' hospitals, the psychiatrists and psychologists have the lowest or 'best' scores on the Factor I subscale. In the more 'conservative' hospitals, on the other hand, the lowest or 'best' mean scores are reached by social workers, and psychiatrists drop behind these mean scores. This reversal is most pronounced in the English 'conservative' institution. The variation of the psychiatrists' views (their standard deviations) is largest for the two conservative hospitals, particularly the British one in which the split in opposing groups was noticed above. Again, as in the total scale, the occupational ranges of means for subscale I are wider in the 'progressive' than in the 'conservative' institutions whose staff attitudes appear to be relatively more homogeneous. Also, as in the fourteen-item scale, the subscale range of means across hospitals is largest for psychiatrists and smallest for social workers and counselors.

The psychiatrists' mean scores run in the sequence in which the hospitals had been ranked according to their 'progressiveness.' Again, as in the larger scale, attendants and nurses obtain 'poorer' mean scores in the Hawaiian than in the border state hospital. Of the two British hospitals the more 'progressive' one shows 'better' mean scores for all occupations with the exception of aides. As in the parent scale, among occupations the auxiliary therapists express the most diverse views, and among hospitals, the 'conservative' English institution tends to show the greatest variety of opinions.

In this English hospital, among the four institutions, all occupations save one show the most 'qualitative differentiation' in their mean scores. The exception is the hospitals' attendant group which is surpassed on Factor I by the Hawaiian and hospital Y aides. Again, the explanation may be sought in the relatively strong effect cultural factors have on mental health attitudes among the psychiatrically least trained respondents.* Within the Factor I subscale perceptual discrimination is the strongest aspect. As the literature on perception shows, man tends to organize his perceptual environment in some kind of meaningful order. In the absence of a sophisticated psychiatric understanding, aides, that is, the relatively least trained group, may tend to fill the vacuum by interpreting the strange phenomena of mental illness in terms of the nearest available explanation, which may be the traditions of folklore. In groups with strongly different cultural traditions, the differences may be reflected in attitudes toward mental patients. In the course of time, acculturation, education and new means of communication, like television, may be

* Table 16 shows that in Hawaii, oriental aides reached the highest mean score for Factor I, but white aides obtaines also a relatively high mean score.

expected gradually to minimize cultural differences in such attitudes.

As in the whole scale, the auxiliary therapists tended in the subscale to show large standard deviations. In most respects, then, the Factor I results paralleled those found in the parent scale.

FACTOR II: THE 'TRUST AND MELIORISM' SUBSCALE

This factor is positively related to the total scale, so that a high score on the subscale points in the same direction as a high overall score. As in the other subscale, the scores' theoretical range was from 0 to 35 with the neutral midpoint at 17.5. Table 21 presents the mean scores for the different hospitals and occupations, F ratios, significance levels, and ranges of means. Table 22 shows the standard deviations for the same groups, and the ranges of S.D.'s across occupations and across hospitals.

Table 21. *Factor II subscale: Trust and meliorism – means*

	X	B	H	Y	F ratio	Sign.	Range of means
Aides	22.2	24.6	22.8	23.9	4.18	1%	2.4
Nurses	24.7	25.0	24.6	25.7	1.87	NS	1.1
O. and R. therapists	23.4	24.4	25.7	25.3	.39	NS	2.3
Social workers and counselors	25.3	24.3	24.9	26.3	.68	NS	2.0
Psychiatrists	24.3	24.9	26.6	26.7	1.17	NS	2.4
Psychologists	–	26.1	24.8	–			
F ratio	3.68	.32	4.48	2.27			
Significance	1%	NS	1%	NS			
Range of means	3.1	.7	3.8	2.8			

Table 12 lists the items of the Factor II subscale. A glance at the table shows that this scale is made up of items from the original OMI factors, 'benevolence' (B) and 'mental hygiene ideology' (C), as well as some negative statements from the factors 'social restrictiveness' (D-) and 'authoritarianism' (A-). As responses among OMI factors varied somewhat with occupation, one might expect some corresponding variation in the responses to the present subscale. For example, the OMI Factor B ('benevolence') showed nurses to have the highest mean score. In 'mental hygiene ideology' (C), on the other hand, psychologists and social workers excelled.

Table 22. *Factor II subscale: Trust and meliorism – standard deviations*

	X	B	H	Y	F ratio	Sign.	Range of S.D.
Aides	4.68	4.36	4.59	4.00	4.18	1%	.68
Nurses	4.96	4.74	4.49	3.51	1.87	NS	1.45
O. and R. therapists	8.10	4.65	2.90	4.37	.39	NS	5.20
Social workers and counselors	4.68	4.53	3.57	2.77	.68	NS	1.91
Psychiatrists	5.87	3.01	3.81	3.67	1.17	NS	2.86
Psychologists	–	4.65	2.86	–			
F ratio	3.68	.32	4.48	2.27			
Significance	1%	NS	1%	NS			
Range of S.D.	3.42	1.73	1.69	1.23			
	(Ranges exclude psychologists)						

A look at Table 21 shows that on the 'trust and meliorism' subscale nurses obtained relatively high mean scores. Psychiatrists in the 'conservative' English hospital again scored poorly. Nurses and aides in Hawaii obtain weaker mean scores than their colleagues in the more 'conservative' hospital B. The psychiatrists follow again the hospital rank order from the English to the American 'progressive' hospital to the American and British 'conservative' hospitals.

As in the total scale, mean scores in subscale II show the 'progressive' English hospital consistently ahead of the 'conservative' British institution in all occupational groups. For the two hospitals in the United States, the same relation holds with the exception that aides and nurses, as noted, show less 'trust and meliorism' in Hawaii. Psychologists get higher scores on both factors in hospital B. (The two psychologists' groups were very briefly discussed in Chapter 4.) The conservative English institution generally shows low scores on Factor II combined with a wide range of means and the highest variances in all occupational groups. This seems to indicate that the present subscale is particularly sensitive to the tensions and conflicting outlooks characteristic of this institution. Hospital B, the other 'conservative', but less heterogeneous hospital, obtained a small range of means. The results of the 'trust and meliorism' subscale may be briefly summarized as showing generally the expected relations between hospitals together with less occupational unidimensionality, which may be due to the greater heterogeneity of the items which make up the subscale.

VIEWS ON THE EFFECT OF MORE WELL TRAINED DOCTORS, NURSES AND AIDES

A few examples will be given for the heterogeneity of items which constitute the Factor II subscale. Item 6 states, 'If our hospitals had enough well trained doctors, nurses and aides, many of the patients would get well enough to live outside the hospital.' This item has the lowest factor loading of the subscale items. It expresses a melioristic view, consonant with the OMI scale's 'mental hygiene ideology'. The meliorism, however, implies a certain criticism of existing conditions akin to the phrase, 'There's plenty of room for improvement.' At the same time, the blame for present conditions is not sought in oneself or in one's own behavior but rather in external circumstances; namely in a lack of enough trained personnel and possibly, by implication, in a lack of sufficient public support to finance the additional positions or higher salaries required to achieve the improvement.

The mean scores are indicated in Table 23. Individual items in the scale were scored as follows: Strongly agree, 1; Agree, 2; Not sure but probably agree, 3; Not sure but probably disagree, 4; Disagree, 5; Strongly disagree, 6. It will be noted that in all occupations, the British mean scores are more melioristic in the 'conservative' hospital, in direct contrast to that hospital staff's performance on the subscales and the whole scale. In fact, this is the only item in the whole scale in which the 'conservative' English hospital obtains consistently high scores in the 'positive' direction. It appears then that in the more 'conservative' hospital more room for improvement is expressed in the sense of the question, but an implied criticism of present shortcomings is passed on to outside factors.

Table 23 also indicates a strong tendency for American respondents to agree more strongly with item 6 than do British respondents. This cultural difference is strongest among psychiatrists. While the F ratios reach significance level only in 3 out of 9 cases, the trend suggests on the part of the American subsamples a greater faith in results that can be achieved by education and, perhaps implicitly, by bigger expenditures for hospital payrolls.

Table 23. *Rehabilitation scale – item 6: If our hospitals had enough well trained doctors, nurses and aides, many of the patients would get well enough to live outside the hospital*

	Means					
	X	B	H	Y	F ratio	Sign.
Aides	2.34	1.85	2.02	2.54	4.57	1%
Nurses	2.21	2.18	1.92	2.34	1.73	N.S.
O. and R. therapists	2.36	1.80	1.67	2.57	1.55	N.S.
Social workers and counselors	2.26	2.08	2.35	2.50	.61	N.S.
Psychiatrists	2.88	1.77	2.04	3.13	3.62	5%
F ratio	1.12	.99	2.47	1.10		
Significance	N.S.	N.S.	5%	N.S.		

SHOULD MENTAL PATIENTS HAVE SOMETHING TO SAY ABOUT THE WAY THE HOSPITAL IS RUN?

Item 11 proposes that 'The patients of a mental hospital should have something to say about the way the hospital is run.' Table 24 presents the results. In England, the more 'progressive' hospital in all occupations obtained more agreement. In the United States, however, hospital B's mean scores tend to be more in agreement with the item than the 'progressive' hospital's mean scores. It may be that greater emphasis on clear authority and order in the hospital exists in the Hawaiian group. (*Cf.* the discussion of Hawaiian preferences among patients below.) In all four hospitals nurses tend to agree much more with this item than attendants. To the aides, greater authority for the patients may seem to be an inefficient idea and perhaps even a threat to their own relative status.*

* Several t tests were performed. Significance tests between hospital B and Hawaiian aides and between hospital B and Hawaiian nurses were not significant. Tests between aides and nurses within the same hospital were significant in hospital B (5%), Hawaii (1%), and hospital Y (1%).

Table 24. *Rehabilitation scale – item 11: The patients of a mental hospital should have something to say about the way the hospital is run*

	Means					
	X	B	H	Y	F ratio	Sign.
Aides	3.75	3.54	3.66	2.84	3.26	5%
Nurses	2.88	2.93	3.10	2.19	7.50	1%
O. and R. therapists	3.21	3.13	3.67	2.29	1.27	N.S.
Social workers and counselors	2.87	3.33	3.32	2.75	1.22	N.S.
Psychiatrists	2.94	2.54	2.65	1.75	2.86	5%
F ratio	4.96	1.94	3.81	3.76		
Significance	1%	N.S.	1%	1%		

COULD MOST WOMEN WHO WERE ONCE PATIENTS IN A MENTAL HOSPITAL BE TRUSTED AS BABY SITTERS?

This assertion is made in item 10. Mean scores are shown in Table 25.

Table 25. *Rehabilitation scale – item 10: Most women who were once patients in a mental hospital could be trusted as baby sitters*

	Means					
	X	B	H	Y	F ratio	Sign.
Aides	3.67	3.15	3.40	3.59	2.15	N.S.
Nurses	3.09	2.87	3.27	2.98	1.61	N.S.
O. and R. therapists	3.00	2.80	3.33	2.57	.71	N.S.
Social workers and counselors	3.17	3.05	3.12	2.50	.81	N.S.
Psychiatrists	3.00	2.92	2.81	2.06	2.36	N.S.
F ratio	3.04	.52	1.61	6.93		
Significance	5%	N.S.	N.S.	1%		

As in item 11, the results in England can be explained in terms of the noted differences between the two hospitals. Among the American hospitals, however, Hawaii falls behind the more 'conservative' institution except on the psychiatrists' level. An explanation may be sought in some of the cultural views said to be traditional in a part of the

Hawaiian sample and concerning such matters as the role of children in the family.*

OTHER ITEMS

Responses to some other individual items are shown in Tables 26 and 27:

Item 3: 'It is easy to recognize someone who once had a serious mental illness'

Item 4: 'Although patients discharged from mental hospitals may seem all right, they should not be allowed to marry'

Item 5: 'There is something about mental patients that makes it easy to tell them from normal people'

Item 13: 'Although some mental patients seem all right, it is dangerous to forget for a moment that they are mentally ill.'

Table 26. *Rehabilitation scale – items 10 and 13: Percentage who agree*

	(Total number of respondents)			Most women who were once patients in a mental hospital could be trusted as baby sitters			Although some mental patients seem all right, it is dangerous to forget for a moment that they are mentally ill		
	B.	*Hawaii*	*England*	*B.*	*Hawaii*	*England*	*B.*	*Hawaii*	*England*
Aides	(67)	(95)	(125)	63	60	46	70	77	62
Nurses	(61)	(92)	(292)	74	67	71	59	66	68
O. and R. therapists	(16)	(12)	(22)	75	58	77	56	58	50
Social workers	(26)	(79)	(19)	69	72	68	31	29	37
Rehabilitation & employment counselors	(13)	(18)	–	69	61	–	31	44	–
Psychiatrists	(13)	(26)	(32)	69	81	84	23	19	12
Psychologists	(8)	(15)	–	100	80	–	38	7	–

* Two t tests were conducted. For Hawaiian versus hospital B aides, no significance was found. For Hawaiian versus B nurses, the difference was significant at the 5% level.

Table 27. *Rehabilitation scale – items 3, 4 and 5: Percentage who agree*

	It is easy to recognize someone who once had a serious mental illness			Although patients discharged from mental hospitals may seem all right, they should not be allowed to marry			There is something about mental patients that makes it easy to tell them from normal people		
	B.	*Hawaii*	*England*	*B.*	*Hawaii*	*England*	*B.*	*Hawaii*	*England*
Aides	46	47	45	28	24	35	39	60	47
Nurses	15	37	41	10	12	27	21	37	45
O. and R. therapists	31	42	23	13	8	18	31	33	46
Social workers	19	16	37	4	4		19	14	21
Rehabilitation & employment counselors	15	44	–	8		–	15	44	–
Psychiatrists	23	19	34	23	4	6	15	31	19
Psychologists	38	33	–		13	–	25	13	–

EXPECTATIONS AND FINDINGS

We may now review the three expectations at the beginning of this Chapter in the light of the findings.

Occupations

1. The dependence of attitudes toward mental illness on respondents' position in the occupational-educational hierarchy was confirmed for all four samples. Thus, the findings strongly suggest that attitudes tended to increase in the 'pro-rehabilitation' direction from aides at the bottom to psychiatrists and psychologists at the top.

To explain these findings, it was argued that aides had been least exposed to modern psychiatric theories and to views of the need for rehabilitation of mental patients. Their primary functions – and to some extent those of nurses – are taking care of the physical needs of patients and maintaining peace and order on the wards. In short, the customary functions of ward personnel may be described as being more 'custodial' than 'rehabilitating.' The group of social workers and counselors may be expected to be especially aware of problems facing the ex-patient who reenters the community, and their mean scores generally favor rehabilitation.

Psychiatrists are the most important and responsible group in the eyes of the community and hold administrative positions in addition to their therapeutic functions. While their pro-rehabilitation mean scores are sometimes exceeded by psychologists, who are less influenced by medical training and have been more exposed to the 'mental hygiene ideology,' psychiatrists are usually at or near the top in their hospital's ranking of 'rehabilitative' scores. Psychiatrists set a hospital's specific policies. On the total scale and on both subscales, the psychiatrists' outlook on rehabilitation follows exactly the predetermined rank order of the hospitals' 'progressivism'.

Hospitals

2. In addition to occupational effects, systematic differences among the different hospitals were also demonstrated. For example, in England employees of the more 'conservative' hospital generally got 'weaker' scores on the whole scale and on the two subscales, than did their colleagues at the more 'progressive' hospital. Among the two American hospitals, similar results were obtained. On all three measures, the range of means among the occupational groupings was largest for psychiatrists and tended to be smallest for social workers and counselors. These results may be due on the one hand to the policymaking power of psychiatrists within the hospital and, on the other hand, to the relatively large part of their time social workers spend outside of the hospital, so that the differential effects of various hospital policies may tend to be minimized.

Among the psychiatrists, largest variances were found for the doctors of the 'conservative' British hospital X which was described as being in a period of transition. For many years, X had a reputation as a relatively 'conservative' mental hospital. Within the year before the field study, a new superintendent had been appointed who tried to bring about a number of rapid reforms. Some members of the existing staff were apparently antagonized, including psychiatrists with different orientations. On the total scale and on both subscales, the respondents at X obtained the largest variances among hospitals in eleven out of fifteen cases. Only social workers and aides were exempt (in two cases each). The relatively limited contact of social workers and counselors with the hospital was mentioned above. Aides or nursing assistants were presumed to be least exposed to psychiatric theories and to indoctrination by specific hospital ideologies. The relatively 'weak' mean scores and the sizeable variances at X were interpreted as implying that while the new regime at X had not yet succeeded in 'improving' the average attitudes on rehabilitation to any large extent, it had created some diversity of opinions. Only in one item of the scale did all occupational groups at X obtain scores consistently strong in favor of rehabilitation. This item stated, 'If our hospitals had enough well-trained doctors, nurses and nursing assistants, many of the patients would get well enough to live outside the hospital.' This finding was thought to indicate primarily a feeling that there was 'room for improvement'.

Cultural factors

3. Finally, some differences were found which could be best explained in terms neither of occupation nor of hospital policy but in terms of cultural and historical factors. For example, American respondents of all occupations had greater faith in the beneficial effects of more well trained personnel than did their English counterparts (Item 6).

Some differences between Hawaiian sample members and border state respondents appeared to run opposite to the respective hospital policies and to be partly explained in terms of different cultural traditions. Among nurses such differences seemed to be especially strong.

The conclusion may be drawn that the rehabilitation scale shows attitudinal differences according to all three expectations, along occupational-educational, hospital policy, and cultural lines. Cohen and Struening's findings on attitudinal variation with occupations and with education were supported in general and supplemented in respect to variation of hospital and cultural settings.

Table 28. *Rehabilitation scale: Two-way analyses of variance*

	Total scale		Factor I		Factor II	
	F ratio	Sign.	F ratio	Sign.	F ratio	Sign.
Hospitals	18.03	1%	25.83	1%	3.03	5%
Occupations	4.87	1%	4.87	1%	2.32	5%
Interaction	1.15	N.S.	1.38	N.S.	.62	N.S.

A two-way analysis of variance was performed for the 14-item scale and for Factors I and II. Table 28 shows that the different hospitals accounted for most of the common variance, followed by occupations. Both dimensions, hospitals and occupations, were significant. Interaction between the two dimensions did not reach significance levels.

SUMMARY

Items were derived from Cohen and Struening's 'Opinions about Mental Illness' (OMI) scale, selected for their bearing on rehabilitation. The OMI-derived items made up a 'rehabilitation scale' which was statistically factor analyzed. Two subscales resulted. One subscale involved perceptual discrimination and concomitant rejection of mental patients and was labeled 'qualitative differentiation'. Items in the other subscale held that mental patients are not dangerous, can be trusted, and will respond favorably to improved treatment. This second subscale was said to express 'trust and meliorism'. Both subscales could be combined so that the total score would equal the Factor II score minus the Factor I score. The whole scale was labeled 'rehabilitation scale'. Statistical analyses of variance were performed for both subscales and for the whole 'rehabilitation scale'.

CHAPTER 6

The semantic differentials: The mental patients I most (and least) enjoy working with

The semantic differential scales were discussed, and their development was reviewed in Chapter 3. The concepts to be rated on 28 scales were, 'mental patient I *most* enjoy working with' and 'mental patient I *least* enjoy working with'. The scales and instructions for filling them in may be seen in Appendix I. In order not to have to deal with 28 items individually, it was decided to submit each semantic differential to factor analysis and thus to determine which items would tend to go together.

It will be recalled that the rehabilitation scale dealt with attitudes concerning mental illness and mental patients in *general,* as well as with their prospects for rehabilitation. The semantic differentials, in contrast, deal with *specific* characteristics of mental patients. The respondents were asked to express their preferences (and their dislikes) for certain attributes of mental patients with whom they had been working. The first question then might be whether mental health workers in the four areas express preferences and relative dislikes toward patients possessing various attributes. If the respondents do express such positive and negative choices, one could ask further into what clusters their liked (and disliked) patient characteristics would fall. How consistent are likes and dislikes? Do they form mirror images of each other? Are respondents more willing to express choice of a given characteristic than rejection of its opposite?

Here are some more questions that will be asked of the results. Does occupational membership account for variation in the respondents' preferences as it did in the respondents' attitudes measured by the rehabilitation scale? Do differences in the results vary with hospital policies in the fashion one may expect from that scale? And further, does cultural or ethnic background account for variation in the results? In the literature on the use of semantic differentials it has been reported that some concepts hold across cultures while many others do not.

Factor analysis

The semantic differentials were submitted to factor analysis in a way analogous to the method employed with the rehabilitation scale. For the semantic differential 'mental patient I most enjoy working with', a 28 x 28 product-moment correlation matrix was computed. Factors were extracted according to Thurstone's complete centroid method (see Harmon, 1960). There was an obvious two factor solution.

In the four sample areas the following percentages of the common variance were involved for these two dimensions (see Table 29). The same technique was used on the semantic differential for the 'mental patient I least enjoy working with'. The resultant factor space showed the 28 scale items arranged in four clusters very similar to those obtained for the 'most liked patient'. The same two factors were again identified. The two factors were then rotated to an orthogonal simple structure solution by the quartimax method of Wrigley and Neuhaus (see Harmon, 1960).

Table 29. *The two strongest factors for the semantic differential 'mental patient I most enjoy working with' (Percentages of common variance included)*

Sample	Factor I	Factor II
B	65	11
Hawaii	60	17
X	72	13
Y	51	16
All four samples	79	15

For the two factors on both semantic differentials, tests of internal consistency were performed.* The factor I scale for the 'patient I most enjoy working with' obtained an internal consistency index of r_{xx} = .921. For the least liked patient, factor I reached an index of r_{xx} = .947. These indices suggest that factor I is internally

* The following formula was used to estimate the Kuder-Richardson formula 20:

$$r_{xx} = \frac{n\,\bar{r}_{ij}}{1 + (n-1)\,\bar{r}_{ij}}$$

so consistent that not much variation would be expected among the individual items which make up the factor scale. In the case of the most liked patient, the coefficient of determination accounts for 85% of the variation, and for the least liked patient, 90% of the variation is so determined.

The same tests of internal consistency were performed for factor II. This factor showed considerably less consistency. For the preferred patient, r_{xx} was .524 and for the disliked patient .482.

Definition of the factors

In the factor spaces for the 'patient I most enjoy working with' and for the least liked patient, these two concepts roughly tend to form mirror images on each factor. Each factor formed two clusters on opposite sides of its dimension. These bipolarities are reflections of the bipolar nature of the scales used in the semantic differentials, and of the random assignment of words to the left and to the right side of a scale.

It seemed, therefore, appropriate to list the items which constitute each factor according to the strength of their factor loadings regardless of sign. This is done in Tables 30 and 31.

It may be seen that in both semantic differentials, the same 21 items make up factor I and the same seven items constitute factor II. A high score on factor I would indicate (on Table 30) that the most liked patient tends to be seen as cooperative, responsible, reliable, steady, etc. The high scoring word in each pair is indicated by italics and by the sign in front of the factor loading. On factor II (Table 30) a high score would indicate preferences for a patient who tends to be low in education, old, submissive, etc. Again, italics and signs indicate which of two words on a scale tend to go with a high score.

Table 31 presents the items and their factor loadings for the *least* liked patient. On factor I, a high score would show least liking for a patient who is uncooperative, shiftless, apathetic, etc., as indicated by italics. On factor II, a high score suggests relatively strong dislike of an aggressive, highly educated, young, etc., patient, again as marked by italics.

The factor analysis, which was performed with the responses of all four sub-samples, answers in the affirmative the question whether mental health workers express preferences and relative dislikes toward patients who possess various characteristics.

Some thought was given to the meaning of the two factors. Factor

Table 30. *Semantic differential – most liked patient: Items and factor loadings*

Factor loadings	*Item No.*	*Item*
		Factor I
(–).733	18)	*Cooperative** . . . Uncooperative
(–).709	5)	*Responsible* . . . Irresponsible
.699	11)	Unreliable . . . *Reliable*
.696	19)	Shiftless . . . *Steady*
(–).689	9)	*Sociable* . . . Unsociable
.683	14)	Violent . . . *Gentle*
(–).674	16)	*Understandable* . . . Obscure
.659	27)	Rude . . . *Polite*
.646	6)	Changeable . . . *Stable*
(–).644	3)	*Trusting* . . . Suspicious
(–).619	15)	*Interested* . . . Apathetic
.588	24)	Delusional . . . *Reality oriented*
(–).574	23)	*Flexible* . . . Compulsive
(–).572	28)	*Moral* . . . Immoral
.571	4)	Unpredictable . . . *Predictable*
(–).561	10)	*Intelligent* . . . Stupid
(–).548	21)	*Verbal* . . . Uncommunicative
.528	2)	Excitable . . . *Calm*
(–).526	22)	*Highly insightful* . . . Without insight
(–).445	7)	*Outgoing* . . . Self-centered
(–).205	1)	*Thoughtful* . . . Carefree
		Factor II
.428	17)	*Low education* . . . High education
.414	12)	*Old* . . . Young
(–).412	25)	Aggressive . . . *Submissive*
(–).369	13)	City . . . *Farm*
(–).336	26)	Independent . . . *Dependent*
.267	20)	*Customary* . . . Modern
(–).264	8)	Emotional . . . *Unemotional*

* The high scoring word in each pair is italicized.

II, consisting of seven scales, tends to include items which contrast old age, an old way of life and submissiveness with high education, youth, modernity and aggressiveness. In terms of patients, factor II seems to oppose the old, relatively less educated, old-fashioned,

Table 31. *Semantic differential – least liked patient: Items and factor loadings*

Factor loadings	*Item No.*	*Item*
		Factor I
.837	18)	Cooperative . . . *Uncooperative**
(–).818	19)	*Shiftless* . . . Steady
.791	15)	Interested . . . *Apathetic*
(–).788	11)	*Unreliable* . . . Reliable
.783	9)	Sociable . . . *Unsociable*
.778	3)	Trusting . . . *Suspicious*
.777	5)	Responsible . . . *Irresponsible*
.749	16)	Understandable . . . *Obscure*
(–).744	14)	*Violent* . . . Gentle
(–).742	27)	*Rude* . . . Polite
.698	28)	Moral . . . *Immoral*
.679	23)	Flexible . . . *Compulsive*
.671	10)	Intelligent . . . *Stupid*
(–).643	6)	*Changeable* . . . Stable
(–).638	4)	*Unpredictable* . . . Predictable
.637	21)	Verbal . . . *Uncommunicative*
(–).635	24)	*Delusional* . . . Reality oriented
(–).599	2)	*Excitable* . . . Calm
.567	7)	Outgoing . . . *Self-centered*
.553	22)	Highly insightful . . . *Without insight*
.366	1)	Thoughtful . . . *Carefree*
		Factor II
.373	25)	*Aggressive* . . . Submissive
(–).331	17)	Low education . . . *High education*
(–).329	12)	Old . . . *Young*
.302	26)	*Independent* . . . Dependent
.278	8)	*Emotional* . . . Unemotional
.245	13)	*City* . . . Farm
(–).211	20)	Customary . . . *Modern*

* The high scoring word in each pair is italicized.

dependent, rural, and perhaps custodial patient to the young, highly educated, modern, aggressive, urban patient. Diagnostically speaking the alternatives seem to be roughly the senile, custodial patient and the young patient with, e.g, schizoid or manic symptoms.

One may hypothesize that on this sort of a dimension, the aides, who are charged with maintaining peace and order on a ward, may prefer the old, and the psychiatrists, who may be more concerned with interesting cases and success of treatment, may prefer the young. Of the other occupations, nurses may prefer old, dependent, etc. patients, as nurses are also responsible for order on the ward, and as 'tender loving care' and a somewhat protective and maternal role vis-à-vis those who need help seem to go with their profession's approach to patients. On the other hand, social workers and counselors may be expected to be relatively more interested in getting people back to their homes, in changing and remodeling unsatisfactory conditions and habits, and thus to prefer younger, more educated patients who stand a better chance of cure and improvement.

When one compares factor II for the most liked and the least liked patients, one will notice that, while the same items make up both factors, the factor loadings are ranked somewhat differently. In contrast to the factor loadings for the preferred patient, the following items become more salient for the least liked patient: aggressiveness, independence, and emotionalism. The following issues become somewhat less central for the least liked patient: education, urban residence, and modernity.

While factor II seems to provide a choice between old and young, if one may use a simplifying abbreviation, Table 30 suggests that the items which constitute factor I stress more the standard citizen or middle class virtues.

The contrasts here tend to be between certain qualities and their absence. Among the qualities listed are cooperation, responsibility, reliability, steadiness, sociability, gentleness (as opposed to violence), politeness, stability, trust, calmness, and incidentally, next to each other, flexibility and morality. The scale as a whole might indicate the support of traditional values, of accepted norms or standards of behavior. In other words, we tend to deal here with conventional morality, with conformity to approved middle class ideals of behavior.

The discussion of the semantic differentials in the pilot study in Chapter 3 reviewed their application to the concepts of 'typical middle class person' and 'typical lower class person'. Of the qualities listed in the present factor I, ten scales tended to be associated with the 'typical middle class person'; namely those involving responsibility, reliability, steadiness, gentleness, politeness, stability, morality, intelligence, calmness, and thoughtfulness. A high score on factor I, then, might indicate a preference for patients with conventional 'middle class' values.

A low score on factor I could be interpreted as meaning less emphasis on the above values because of a less traditional or 'bourgeois' outlook. A low score may indicate one (or possibly both) of two opposites of a 'bourgeois' point of view; either a lower class outlook or a more sophisticated tolerance of unconventionality or variety of behavior. A patient who possessed all the qualities rated highly on this factor would be not only a model patient but would set an example for the healthy as well. One might wonder what brought him to a mental hospital in the first place.

It was not expected that any group in the sample would indicate a preference for the uncooperative, irresponsible, unreliable, etc. patients. However, it was anticipated that different groups would vary in the strength of their preferences. One might expect in the results for this factor an interplay of several variables. Occupational membership and functional role in the hospital might be related to stress on certain qualities. For example, ward personnel in constant contact with patients might stress responsibility, reliability, steadiness, etc., while psychiatrists, who see a patient only a few minutes a day, might be more interested in the diagnostically helpful expression of even unconventional symptomatic behavior. On the other hand, members of the professions may well have come under a stronger influence of a middle class education than aides with a working class background. In addition, hospital policies may set up different expectations and norms for an ideal patient. Cultural background may play a part through the different weights placed on conventions of preferred behavior both in a sample setting and generally within specific socio-economic groupings.

As with the rehabilitation scale one way analyses of variance were performed for occupations across hospitals and for hospitals across occupations. The analyses were conducted for the two factors and for the most liked and the least liked patients.

Tables 32 and 33 break down the samples for each semantic differential. There were some small differences in N, due largely to the impression some respondents got that the two semantic differentials were identical pages stapled together by mistake. Strictly speaking, the two distributions are largely but not entirely composed of the same respondents.

Table 32. *Number of respondents who completed the semantic differential – most liked patient*

	X	B	H	Y	Total
Attendants	46	63	84	24	217
Nurses	189	60	88	74	411
O. and R. therapists	13	15	12	6	46
Social workers and counselors	21	37	93	9	160
Psychiatrists	15	12	20	13	60
Psychologists	–	8	14	–	22
Total	284	195	311	126	916

Table 33. *Number of respondents who completed the semantic differential – least liked patient*

	X	B	H	Y	Total
Attendants	46	53	78	25	202
Nurses	199	59	89	74	421
O. and R. therapists	14	15	12	6	47
Social workers and counselors	20	36	88	9	153
Psychiatrists	15	11	20	16	62
Psychologists	–	8	14	–	22
Total	294	182	301	130	907

FACTOR I – 'MENTAL PATIENT I MOST ENJOY WORKING WITH'

Table 34 presents the findings of Factor I concerning the best liked patient. It may be remembered that a high mean score indicates high acceptance of the values underlined in Table 30. The potential range of scores is from 0 to 116 with a theoretical mean of 58. Limitations of space prevent the discussion and tracking down of all reasons for each measure, but the major trends will be reviewed.

It may be helpful to start with an account of the East coast American hospital B. This hospital's staff, or at any rate its psychiatrists and social workers, are most similar to Hollingshead and Redlich's New Haven psychiatrists and also to the pilot study's New York social workers. Both studies were discussed in Chapter 3, and

Table 34. *Semantic differential – most liked patient: Factor I: Means*

	X	B	H	Y	F ratios	Sign.	Range of means
Attendants	89.2	79.4	91.0	87.0	4.05	1%	11.6
Nurses	83.3	79.5	88.6	82.6	2.26	N.S.	9.1
O. and R. therapists	89.5	81.5	83.8	72.3	1.29	N.S.	17.2
Soc. workers and counselors	89.3	84.6	88.1	69.7	2.77	5%	19.6
Psychiatrists	76.9	89.4	85.2	76.6	2.60	N.S.	12.8
Psychologists	–	88.5	75.0	–			
F ratios	1.39	.86	2.20	2.38			
Significance	N.S.	N.S.	N.S.	N.S.			
Range of means	12.6	10.0	7.2	17.8			
	(excluding psychologists)						

Strongest possible response to 'Uncooperative' etc. patient — Neutral Midpoint — Strongest possible response to 'Cooperative' etc. patient

0 — 58 — 116

Theoretical range of Factor I scores

the arguments may be recalled that their subjects tended to prefer patients with 'middle class' characteristics. If in Table 34 one reviews the mean scores for the different occupations, one may notice a trend showing an increase of score size with professional status. Psychiatrists obtained the highest mean score, followed by psychologists and social workers and so on down to the attendants. These findings from the Eastern American hospital would tend to support Hollingshead and Redlich's notion of the preference of psychiatrists for patients from middle class backgrounds. The findings are not surprising considering that the semantic differentials in their original form were largely derived from Hollingshead and Redlich's account of their psychiatrists' preferences. It is interesting to see that the middle class bias of patient preferences in the Eastern hospital gets weaker as one descends the occupational ladder. A look at the standard deviations for the same data in Table 35 shows a rough

Table 35. *Semantic differential – most liked patient: Factor I: Standard deviations*

	X	B	H	Y	F ratios	Sign.	Range of S.D.'s
Attendants	20.0	24.3	18.9	14.5	4.05	1%	9.8
Nurses	24.7	22.3	18.0	17.4	2.26	N.S.	7.3
O. and R. therapists	18.6	16.6	17.8	15.2	1.29	N.S.	3.4
Soc. workers and counselors	19.6	18.3	18.7	24.3	2.77	5%	6.0
Psychiatrists	16.0	16.0	10.6	13.8	2.60	N.S.	5.4
Psychologists	–	11.3	9.1	–			
F ratios	1.39	.86	2.20	2.38			
Significance	N.S.	N.S.	N.S.	N.S.			
Range of S.D.'s (excluding psychologists)	8.7	8.3	8.3	10.5			

trend for variance to decrease inversely with professional status. This might reflect a tendency of aides to rate on the extreme points of the scales. With more education may go a tendency to be more careful and qualified in one's expression of preferences.

HAWAIIAN VIEWS ON THE MOST LIKED PATIENT – FACTOR I

So far, the results have tended to support and to extend the known findings on patient preferences of American mental health professionals. What happens if we leave familiar ground and the continental United States? Before going to England, let us first look at the Hawaiian hospital which shares a number of characteristics with the other American institution. At first sight, the results seem to run just about in the opposite direction with Hawaiian psychologists and psychiatrists presenting the lowest, and aides the highest scores. (See Table 34.) Why should this be? Occupational training in both hospitals was described as comparable (see Chapter 4). Hospital policy in Hawaii was referred to as more 'progressive', which might account for the lower scores of psychiatrists and psychologists but not for the higher scores of the other occupations compared with their mainland colleagues.

The hypothesis was proposed that cultural traditions would account for the difference from scores of the hospital B sample. The cultural argument was that white Hawaiians would score much like their mainland counterparts while Hawaiians of oriental descent would account for the difference, due to different traditional attitudes toward patients and preferences among them. The Hawaiian sample was broken down by ethnicity (see Table 36. As all psychologists were white, they were not included in this analysis).

The results tend to confirm the hypothesis. The white respondents are closer to the hospital B mean scores than their oriental colleagues (see Table 37). Oriental aides and nurses in particular obtain high mean scores. This would seem to support the earlier argument that cultural effects on attitudes toward mental patients are particularly strong among persons who have been least exposed to psychiatric theories. It may be noticed that among all the mean scores in Tables 34 and 37 it is only some oriental groups who reach scores above 90. The high mean score of the oriental psychiatrists may be also due to cultural traditions, but as the psychiatrists' N is only 4, no attempts will be made to derive conclusions from their performance. The white psychiatrists, as was noted, obtained a lower mean score than their colleagues in hospital B, presumably because they supported the more 'progressive' Hawaiian hospital policy. The scores of the auxiliary therapists run counter to the trends, but their respective N's are seven and five, and this occupational group was described as being composed of persons from somewhat heterogeneous backgrounds and training.

The standard deviations, presented in Table 37, follow for the white respondents a trend similar to hospital B. The four oriental psychiatrists show an unusually low variance. It may be observed, however, that while white Hawaiians' attitudes tend to follow trends of the mainland hospital, their mean scores and sigmas lie actually between hospital B and oriental Hawaiian measures. One may speculate that these white Hawaiian workers have been somewhat influenced by their oriental colleagues and by the many contributions of oriental cultures to life in Hawaii.

The fourteen Hawaiian psychologists, all whites, obtained the lowest mean score of the twelve American cells. (See Table 34.) The writer, who talked with each of the fourteen psychologists, is inclined to venture a guess regarding this result. These professionals are a strongly self-selected group, most or all of them came voluntarily

Table 36. *Semantic differential – most liked patient: Hawaiian sample – oriental (O) and white (W) respondents (Numbers)*

	O	W	Total
Attendants	55	19	74
Nurses	54	29	83
O. and R. therapists	7	5	12
Social workers and counselors	70	21	91
Psychiatrists	4	16	20
Total	190	90	280

Table 37. *Semantic differential – most liked patient: Hawaiian sample – oriental (O) and white (W) respondents*

	Means			
	Factor I		Factor II	
	O	W	O	W
Attendants	95.2	82.3	19.5	21.4
Nurses	90.3	83.1	18.0	16.9
O. and R. therapists	79.3	90.0	17.7	16.0
Social workers and counselors	88.6	85.8	16.7	15.3
Psychiatrists	91.3	83.6	14.5	13.1

	Standard deviations							
	Factor I				Factor II			
	O	W	F ratio	Sign.	O	W	F ratio	Sign.
Attendants	16.0	20.2	7.82	1%	6.6	5.0	1.29	N.S.
Nurses	17.3	18.3	3.06	5%	6.9	5.5	.54	N.S.
O. and R. therapists	15.9	18.4	.97	N.S.	3.7	3.5	.54	N.S.
Social workers and counselors	19.4	16.5	.37	N.S.	3.9	4.1	2.08	N.S.
Psychiatrists	4.7	11.1	1.62	N.S.	2.9	4.6	.29	N.S.

from the continental United States, and one might expect that curiosity and openmindedness for other cultures and varieties of behavior were strong in this group. This group, which was described in Chapter 4, consisted predominantly of clinical psychologists with strong interests in research and experimentation. For the American hospitals, the difference of means between psychologists is the largest for any occupation. This may suggest that factor I indeed measures the degree of acceptance of non-standard characteristics of patients.

A word may be due here on the difference between oriental and white preferences in Hawaii. In what way do 'oriental' traditions differ from white or mainland American ones in respect to mental patients? Only a few points will be mentioned here. During the field work in Hawaii, the author heard from a variety of persons working with mental patients that in the more traditional oriental families the mentally ill were rejected. Some mental health workers – including orientals – told the writer that among their patients those of oriental background tended to be ostracized and ignored by their families. Oriental patients in the hospital or in convalescent homes were reported to be more neglected by their families than white patients. These accounts struck the writer at first as implausible in view of the widely accepted view of the closely knit oriental family structure. However, further reports confirmed the claims of oriental stigmatization of mentally ill family members.

It may be that the close oriental* family order has exactly this negative effect for mentally ill members. They may embarrass or disgrace the family's name, and among people who have traditions of ancestor worship, mental illness may be seen as a kind of punishment that had better be hidden. At any rate, such traditional standards of behavior as filial piety can hardly be expected to be carefully observed by mental patients. It is commonly held that in some Japanese and Chinese traditions, e.g., the Confucian ethic, norms and standards of behavior vis-à-vis various persons are regulated in great detail. The high oriental mean scores on factor I may reflect belief in the importance of such behavior.**

* In Hawaii 'oriental' connotes primarily persons of Japanese and Chinese descent (see Chapter 4).

** The interrelationship of historical-cultural factors and psychotic symptomatology in Hawaii is a topic of great interest. Dr. Tim Wong of the Hawaiian state mental health service has over a period of years collected data for all mental patients being served by the state out-patient clinics. The data have not yet been analyzed, but certain consistencies have been noted. For instance, there is a 'Japanese first son's wife syndrome'. In traditional Japanese families, the eldest

One factor which affects the oriental responses may be the existence of some traditional ethical, e.g. Confucian norms. The ideal Confucian man is seen as a balanced, harmonious man, expressing politeness and using gracious and formal manners. This was discussed, e.g., by Max Weber (1951). The ideal Japanese is also reported to be polite and to exhibit formal behavior. One may expect that persons who have been brought up with this kind of an ideal may be particularly shocked by the formless, rude and anarchic behavior often associated with mental illness.

The replies of the English respondents will now be discussed and the interplay of cultural and occupational factors and of hospital policies should be noted.

ENGLISH VIEWS ON THE MOST LIKED PATIENT – FACTOR I

In Table 34 (which showed mean scores of all groups on Factor I) the English respondents (hospitals X and Y) appear at first to follow no clear pattern or at least to counter the trend found for the American hospital B. In the two British hospitals, curvilinear relationships are found which may be best discussed in three occupational groupings. Attendants, and to a lesser extent nurses, have high mean scores (i.e., they strongly prefer patients with conventional

son is held responsible to support his parents as long as they live. This means that his wife will be the all-around servant and second woman, after the mother, in the house. Reportedly, the unusual pressure on these wives has led to relatively frequent breakdowns which are characterized by symptoms of anxiety attacks and psychosomatic reactions.

One more symptom may be mentioned. Alcoholism is said to be virtually non-existent among Hawaiians of Polynesian descent, while Caucasians in the state show the highest incidence of this disorder.

It would be interesting to do research on the frequency and development of these symptoms in Hawaii. See, for example, Enright and Jaeckle (1963) who compared psychiatric symptoms and diagnoses for patients from two subcultures at the Hawaii state hospital. The hospital has published a series of *Psychology Research Reports* since 1960 which have presented statistics on mental illness in Hawaii. Unfortunately, a pursuit of this interesting topic is beyond the scope of the present study. The purpose in mentioning this topic has been to give support from another angle to the argument regarding the cultural effects on behavior of Hawaiians who were brought up in more or less different traditions.

characteristics). Psychiatrists obtain low mean scores (i.e., show less of this preference). Auxiliary therapists, social workers and counselors fall at opposite extremes in the two hospitals. A detailed discussion follows.

An attempt will be made here to account for these findings. The attempt is admittedly somewhat speculative, and it would be desirable to do additional research in order to determine the appropriateness of these interpretations. The psychiatrists in both English hospitals obtain lower mean scores than the American psychiatrists of all ethnic groups. This may be due to the reputed tradition of the educated English to be tolerant and even to find a certain appeal in eccentric behavior or in 'spleens'. This attractiveness of idiosyncratic characteristics has not been especially noted among American professional men. It may be that at one level of the British educational structure nonconformism is valued, while in American medical schools some emphasis seems to be placed on conformism. (See Christie and Merton, 1958.)

If we move to the opposite educational pole of the English institutions, we find British aides obtaining higher mean scores (that is, stronger preference for patients with conventional attributes) than white American aides. Oriental aides in Hawaii, however, obtained a still higher mean score. One may wonder whether perhaps English attendants conceived of themselves relatively more as members of the middle class than of the working class as compared with American attendants. Question 35 asked respondents for their class-self-identification (see Table 38). It can be seen that about half of the English attendants thought of themselves as members of the middle classes in contrast to a third or a fourth of the American attendants. It is not the writer's intention to scrutinize here the comparability of British and American class labels.* While British attendants may possess a somewhat higher status than their American counterparts, this alone may not account for their scores which are notably higher than those of American aides. Table 34 also indicates that in England aides have higher scores than nurses, who might be judged to be higher up in socio-economic status. (On question 35, British attendants and nurses rate themselves about

* It may be mentioned, though, that the appropriate British class terminology was carefully discussed in England before the present terms were included in the English questionnaires.

Table 38. *Self-designated social class of sample* (in percentages)

	Hospital B					
	N	Lower	Working	Middle	Upper	N/A
Aides	67	1	61	30	1	7
Nurses	61		25	69	3	3
O. and R. therapists	16		32	56	6	6
Social workers and counselors	39		5	85	5	5
Psychiatrists	12			92	8	
Psychologists	8			100		

	Hospital H					
	N	Lower	Working	Middle	Upper	N/A
Aides	95	3	73	21	2	1
Nurses	92	2	33	62	3	
O. and R. therapists	12		8	92		
Social workers and counselors	97	1	24	73	2	
Psychiatrists	20			80	20	
Psychologists	15		7	73	13	7

	Hospital X					
	N	Working	Lower Middle	Upper Middle	Upper	N/A
Aides	82	50	23	20	2	5
Nurses	206	51	31	13	2	3
O. and R. therapists	14	36	28	36		
Social workers and counselors	25	16	48	36		
Psychiatrists	16		13	68	13	6

	Hospital Y					
	N	Working	Lower Middle	Upper Middle	Upper	N/A
Aides	43	40	23	30		7
Nurses	86	40	33	21	1	5
O. and R. therapists	8	13	13	61	13	
Social workers and counselors	9	22	33	45		
Psychiatrists	16	6	19	62	13	

equally in respect to class membership.) In this writer's opinion, the British attendants do not react simply as lower or middle class persons in Hollingshead and Redlich's sense.

Rather, several factors may have influenced their preferences among patients. For one thing, their occupational role may enter, and they may think of themselves as protectors of society and of its values. On the other hand, it may be that in England, which is said to be a society with especially high regard for tradition, certain preferences and behavior norms have been more generally accepted by the public in the course of generations than in the United States with its population from diverse cultural backgrounds. One may repeat the argument used earlier, particularly in connection with the oriental sample members from Hawaii, that as one descends the ladder of psychiatric and general education, the influence of cultural traditions on attitudes toward the mentally ill becomes stronger. English nurses who score lower, or more permissive than attendants, may also have been influenced by their training with its emphasis on helping the needy and on 'tender loving care' (or its British equivalent).

This interpretation need not be taken as a disproof of Hollingshead and Redlich's view that social class membership of professionals affects their preference among patients. Rather, one may conclude that in different social systems, class membership may have become associated through history with different values and preferences. Thus, on the present semantic differential, white American aides on the average score somewhat like British psychiatrists, and white American psychiatrists score somewhat like British aides. If a moral were to be drawn from these findings, it might be this, that while social class may influence attitudes, cultural factors should not be ignored either.

The last occupational grouping in the British hospitals is the occupational and recreational therapists, social workers and rehabilitation counselors. At the more 'conservative' hospital X they score higher than their American counterparts (disregarding ethnicity). At the more 'progressive' hospital Y, they obtain the lowest mean scores of any occupational groups in the sample (see Table 34). Unfortunately, the N's are small for these occupations, especially in hospital Y. It is therefore assumed that the wide divergences between the two British hospitals for these occupations may be due to the small size of the samples. The small number of these workers, particularly at hospital Y, may maximize the effects of any bias in the selections for employment. It may be mentioned here parenthetically that among social workers and counselors, one-third at hospital X and two-thirds at hospital Y are women.

Finally, it may be observed that in England, all occupations have higher mean scores at the 'conservative' X than at the 'progressive' Y.

FACTOR I – 'MENTAL PATIENT I LEAST ENJOY WORKING WITH'

The respondents are asked to rate here the concept *logically* opposite to that of the *most* liked patient. *Psychologically* speaking, however, the two concepts need not be exact opposites *a priori.* For some persons at least, it seems to be easier to express approval than disapproval, and for others the opposite may be true. In the case of the least liked patient, the rater is asked not to express a preference but to identify a relatively rejected person, almost to make a confession that he in fact disapproves of patients who possess certain characteristics.

Occasionally a respondent said that he had no least liked patient, that to him they were all alike, and he proceeded to check off the neutral category (the central dash) for all twenty-eight scales. It is also conceivable that some persons tend generally to express likes or dislikes in a more extreme manner, depending on their respective outlook toward patients, toward mental illness or toward more inclusive concepts. Relatively persistent personality characteristics may incline a subject to express either likes or dislikes for persons more strongly. A perusal of a number of individual questionnaires showed that some respondents indeed gave a mirror image for the two semantic differentials, but others considered the differentials more independently.

The items for the most and for the least liked patients do not follow each other in quite the same sequence of factor loadings, e.g., the scales on shiftlessness, apathy and suspiciousness are considered more relevant in the disliked patient than in the liked patient. Tables 30 and 31 present the word pairs which make up each factor. These tables indicate also the generally higher factor loadings for the least liked over the best liked patient on factor I.

Tables 39 and 40 show the mean scores and standard deviations for the least liked patient on factor I. It may be recalled that the mean scores theoretically range from 0 to 116 and that the theoretical midpoint is 58. None of the found means comes near the midpoint. Instead, all mean scores fall safely in the expected side of the semantic differential. However, there are considerable differences among occupations and among hospitals.

Table 39. *Semantic differential – least liked patient: Factor I: Means*

	X	B	H	Y	F ratios	Sign.	Range of means
Attendants	42.1	37.7	21.4	45.7	7.13	1%	24.3
Nurses	36.5	32.9	23.6	32.9	4.19	1%	12.9
O. and R. therapists	24.0	31.0	25.7	45.7	1.35	N.S.	21.7
Social workers and counselors	22.1	29.5	22.5	22.8	1.08	N.S.	7.4
Psychiatrists	31.0	21.5	17.7	31.6	3.52	5%	13.9
Psychologists	–	17.1	32.8	–			
F ratios	2.19	1.26	1.00	1.86			
Significance	N.S.	N.S.	N.S.	N.S.			
Range of means (excluding psychologists)	22.1	16.2	8.0	22.9			

Table 40. *Semantic differential – least liked patient: Factor I: Standard deviations*

	X	B	H	Y	F ratios	Sign.	Range of S.D.'s
Attendants	33.6	34.6	21.2	34.3	7.13	1%	13.4
Nurses	31.1	27.9	23.8	26.7	4.19	1%	7.3
O. and R. therapists	24.7	20.0	20.4	25.4	1.35	N.S.	5.4
Social workers and counselors	19.9	24.0	19.0	16.4	1.08	N.S.	7.6
Psychiatrists	13.1	15.4	17.0	12.3	3.52	5%	4.7
Psychologists	–	10.6	16.4	–			
F ratios	2.19	1.26	1.00	1.86			
Significance	N.S.	N.S.	N.S.	N.S.			
Range of S.D.'s (excluding psychologists)	20.5	19.2	6.8	22.0			

At the outset it should be stated that a *low* score stands for a relatively strong identification of the disliked patient as being 'uncooperative', 'shiftless', and so forth. A *high* score indicates that the least liked patient is relatively more frequently described as 'cooperative', 'steady', etc., and/or relatively less strongly identified in terms like 'uncooperative', 'shiftless', etc. Looking at Table 31, one can say that a subject who strongly endorsed all underlined items to describe the least liked patient would receive a factor score of zero on factor I. A respondent who would have strongly agreed with all not-underlined alternatives would have obtained a factor score of 116. A relatively high score may thus be seen as indicating greater tolerance for patients lacking the standard citizen virtues or middle class values as they were described above.

In the sample geographically closest to the New Haven and New York studies, i.e. in the border state hospital B, the occupations run in a clear sequence, logically opposite to their descriptions of the best liked patient. Psychologists are strongest in their dislike for the 'unvirtuous' patient while attendants are most tolerant (see Table 39). Standard deviations tend to increase with the size of the mean scores.

In Hawaii, psychologists obtained the highest, i.e., most tolerant, mean score of any occupational group in that subsample. The other occupations were again divided by ethnic background (see Table 41) and show considerable differences in their mean scores (see Table 42). As for the most liked patient, the oriental attendants and psychiatrists reached again the most extreme (here lowest) scores. In the case of the attendants, this was ascribed to their relatively small psychiatric knowledge and to the opportunity for traditional cultural views to fill the perceptual vacuum in regard to the mentally ill.

Table 41. *Semantic differential – least liked patient: Hawaiian sample – oriental (O) and white (W) respondents (numbers)*

	O	W	Total
Attendants	51	18	69
Nurses	55	29	84
O & R therapists	7	5	12
Social workers & counselors	66	20	86
Psychiatrists	4	16	20
Total	183	88	271

Table 42. *Semantic differential – least liked patient: Hawaiian sample – oriental (O) and white (W) respondents*

	Means			
	Factor I		Factor II	
	O	W	O	W
Attendants	16.8	26.6	22.0	20.2
Nurses	25.2	21.6	23.2	24.0
O. and R. therapists	33.7	14.4	25.0	26.4
Social workers and counselors	23.6	18.9	23.7	27.7
Psychiatrists	8.2	20.0	28.0	27.3

	Standard deviations							
	Factor I				Factor II			
	O	W	F ratio	Sign.	O	W	F ratio	Sign.
Attendants	16.7	19.7	4.08	5%	5.7	4.8	1.37	N.S.
Nurses	27.0	16.7	.41	N.S.	6.5	5.2	.32	N.S.
O. and R. therapists	19.2	16.2	2.79	N.S.	3.7	5.3	.24	N.S.
Social workers and counselors	20.0	15.2	.91	N.S.	4.9	4.6	10.29	1%
Psychiatrists	4.1	18.2	1.48	N.S.	4.6	8.3	.02	N.S.

White attendants fall between their oriental fellow workers and hospital B aides.

White Hawaiian psychiatrists are somewhat closer to psychiatrists at hospital B than to their oriental colleagues, the four oriental psychiatrists reach the lowest mean score in any cell in either Table 42 or Table 39. Among the remaining occupational groups, nurses tend to be relatively tolerant, and the small group of auxiliary therapists is most strongly divided by ethnic background as it was on the most liked patient. As in hospital B, so in Hawaii, the sigmas tend to increase in size as one descends the occupational ladder. Both ethnic groups in Hawaii get lower mean scores than the hospital B personnel.

In the two British institutions X and Y, we find again psychiatrists exceeding their American fellows in tolerance for the unconventional. In respect to the least liked patient, they are, however, exceeded in openmindedness by the nurses and attendants. To interpret this finding, some English expert views might be profitably secured. One might venture a guess that while in England the populations from which attendants and nurses are recruited have their traditional preferences for persons with a certain behavior, they also have a strong sense of fair play and of tolerance for persons they dislike. Table 40 shows very high variances for aides and nurses which may suggest a split within the dislikes of these groups. In both English hospitals, social workers show the least tolerant scores. The small groups of auxiliary therapists are again sharply split with those of hospital Y clearly more openminded. The more 'progressive' hospital Y tends to get more permissive scores than hospital X across occupations.

Table 43. *Semantic differential – most liked patient means: Differences from midpoint*

	Factor I			
	X	B	H	Y
Aides	31.2	21.4	33.0	29.0
Nurses	25.3	21.5	30.6	24.6
O. and R. therapists	31.5	23.5	25.8	14.3
Social workers and counselors	31.3	26.6	30.1	11.7
Psychiatrists	18.9	31.4	27.2	18.6
Psychologists	–	30.5	17.0	–
	Factor II			
	X	**B**	**H**	**Y**
Aides	+1.1	.0	–1.0	+4.6
Nurses	– .7	–1.5	–3.6	– .2
O. and R. therapists	–2.8	–3.6	–4.0	–3.5
Social workers and counselors	+2.3	–5.3	–4.6	+ .7
Psychiatrists	–1.2	–7.7	–7.6	–4.7
Psychologists	–	–6.5	–5.7	–

When we compare the least liked patients of the various groups with their preferred patients, we see some reciprocity which is, however, by no means complete. In hospital B, the higher occupational groups are most distant and the attendants least distant from the theoretical midpoint (58) for factor I on both semantic differentials (see Tables 43 through 45). In England, however, differences between the two types of patients are less symmetric. The British psychiatrists' least favored patient is about 27 points below the theoretical midpoint. Their favorite patient is about 19 points above the midpoint. Thus they seem to be more openminded and less limited in their likes than in their dislikes. The English attendants see their preferred patient about 30 points above and their least liked patient about 14 points below midpoint. The attendants, then, seem to have more restricted preferences for a patient and to be more lenient or less specific in the qualities they dislike in a patient.

Table 44. *Semantic differential – least liked patient means: Differences from midpoint*

	Factor I			
	X	B	H	Y
Aides	15.9	20.3	36.6	12.3
Nurses	21.5	25.1	34.4	25.1
O. and R. therapists	34.0	27.0	32.3	12.3
Social workers and counselors	35.9	28.5	35.5	35.2
Psychiatrists	27.0	36.5	40.3	26.4
Psychologists	–	40.9	25.2	–
	Factor II			
	X	B	H	Y
Aides	– .4	–2.4	+ .3	–3.0
Nurses	– .2	+ .7	+2.6	– .7
O. and R. therapists	+3.1	+1.5	+4.6	+3.5
Social workers and counselors	–3.1	+3.1	+3.5	– .8
Psychiatrists	– .1	+6.2	+6.5	+3.2
Psychologists	–	+8.1	+6.3	–

Perhaps the point should be raised here whether, semantically, the word pairs in the scales have the same meanings to English respondents of different educational and occupational backgrounds. A direct answer to this point may be difficult to give. An indirect answer can be given, however. It may be recalled that the internal consistency measures for factor I were unusually high; in the case of the most liked patient, r_{xx} was .921, and for the least liked patient r_{xx} was .947. An item analysis was performed for both semantic differentials and for both factors in hospital X. A review of the 2 x 28 items for most and for least liked patients confirmed the impression that the different occupational groups tended to score very consistently in their relative answers on each item. This suggests that different meanings which certain words may have for English respondents from different social and occupational backgrounds do not account for much of the different responses of these groups.

Table 45. *Semantic differentials: Differences between means of most liked and least liked patients*

	Factor I			
	X	B	H	Y
Aides	47.1	41.7	69.6	41.3
Nurses	46.8	46.6	65.0	49.7
O. and R. therapists	65.5	50.5	58.1	26.6
Social workers and counselors	67.2	55.1	65.6	46.9
Psychiatrists	45.9	67.9	67.5	45.0
Psychologists	–	71.4	42.2	–
	Factor II			
	X	B	H	Y
Aides	1.5	2.4	1.3	7.6
Nurses	.5	2.2	6.2	.5
O. and R. therapists	5.9	5.1	8.6	7.0
Social workers and counselors	5.4	8.4	8.1	1.5
Psychiatrists	1.1	13.9	14.1	16.3
Psychologists	–	14.6	12.0	–

A last overall view of Tables 39 and 40 indicates that the British mean scores tend to be more tolerant than the American ones. As occupational status goes up standard deviations generally go down. The sizes of variances for the least liked patients indicate generally less consensus than the variance sizes for the most liked patients. (See Tables 35 and 40.)

FACTOR II – 'MENTAL PATIENT I MOST ENJOY WORKING WITH'

The factor's definition was given above. Tables 30 and 31 list the seven items of which it is composed in order of strength of factor loadings. It may be recalled that factor II contrasted old, submissive, rural, little-educated patients (presumably often corresponding to senile persons in custodial care) with young, aggressive, urban, highly educated patients.

The hypothesis was stated that on this dimension, attendants, being responsible for ward order and peace, might prefer the 'old', and psychiatrists, being presumably more interested in successful treatment, might prefer the 'young' patients. Nurses, being also mostly on wards and having undergone nursing training with its emphasis on the maternal and protective roles, were expected to show a tendency to prefer the more helpless and dependent mental patients. Social workers and counselors were thought to be more interested in bettering their patients and to find chances for social improvements greater among their younger and more educated patients.

Tables 46 and 47 present the mean scores and standard deviations for the most liked patient on factor II. The theoretical range of scores in this factor is from 0 to 42, and the theoretical midpoint lies at 21. A score above 21 indicates endorsement of the less educated, old, submissive, etc. patient. A score below 21 reflects relatively greater preference for the most educated, young, aggressive, etc. patient. In the following discussion, the two poles of factor II will be referred to, for brevity's sake, as 'old' and 'young', although it is fully realized that the respective clusters are more complex.

The first impression of Table 46 is that different respondent groups prefer on the average either 'old' or 'young' patients, i.e., the mean scores for the best liked patient fall on both sides of the midpoint, unlike the one-sided mean scores of factor I. A second impression, also unlike factor I, is the uniform trend in all four hospitals for 'young' patients to become increasingly more popular with the higher occupational groups. It may be recalled that the strongest factor loading was achieved by the educational scale. This characteristic may be accounted for by the preference of highly educated persons for patients from a similar educational background. Hollingshead and Redlich reported their psychiatrists' dislike of lower class patients whom they tended to see as 'dull' and 'stupid'. On the other hand, attendants may well prefer to work with less educated patients whose language they can understand, whom they can better empathize with. Lower class patients may be less resentful of this reversal of the usual status order than middle class patients who find themselves placed in the care of an aide with little formal education.

Table 46. *Semantic differential – most liked patient: Factor II means*

	X	B	H	Y	F ratios	Sign.	Range of means
Attendants	22.1	21.0	20.0	25.6	2.33	N.S.	5.6
Nurses	20.3	19.5	17.4	20.8	3.82	5%	3.4
O. and R. therapists	18.2	17.4	17.0	17.5	.12	N.S.	1.2
Social workers and counselors	23.3	15.7	16.4	21.7	16.29	1%	7.6
Psychiatrists	19.8	13.3	13.4	16.3	8.35	1%	6.5
Psychologists	–	14.5	15.3	–			
F ratios	1.91	3.89	6.71	4.16			
Significance	N.S.	1%	1%	1%			
Range of means	5.1	7.7	6.6	9.3			
	(excluding psychologists)						

Strongest possible response to 'young' etc. patient — Neutral midpoint — Strongest possible response to 'old' etc. patient

0 — 21 — 42

Theoretical range of Factor II scores

In general, then, the findings of Table 46 support the hypothesis which related job function to factor II scores. In hospital B, the trend noted is clear. Aides are exactly on the theoretical midpoint, closest within their hospital to preferring 'old' patients. The other occupations get increasingly stronger in their liking for the 'young' patients, following the occupation's status, with psychiatrists on top.

In Hawaii, the same overall trend is found. The Hawaiian sample was again divided into oriental and white respondents. (See Table 37.)

Table 47. *Semantic differential – most liked patient: Factor II standard deviations*

	X	B	H	Y	F ratios	Sign.	Range of S.D.'s
Attendants	7.4	6.3	6.3	5.3	2.33	N.S.	2.1
Nurses	6.6	11.5	6.6	5.7	3.82	5%	5.8
O. and R. therapists	6.5	4.4	3.7	5.9	.12	N.S.	2.8
Social workers and counselors	7.0	4.2	4.0	5.9	16.29	1%	3.0
Psychiatrists	4.1	3.8	4.4	3.5	8.35	1%	0.9
Psychologists	–	3.5	4.5	–			
F ratios	1.91	3.89	6.71	4.16			
Significance	N.S.	1%	1%	1%			
Range of S.D.'s	3.3 (excluding psychologists)	7.7	2.9	2.4			

No differences approaching significance were found between the two ethnic groups, although the oriental respondents tended to show slightly less preference for the 'young' patients.

In both English institutions, X and Y, the noted trends – of increasing preference for the 'young' with respondent's increasing education – are repeated with minor exceptions. The social workers and counselors for both hospitals, X and Y, state an average preference for less educated, old, submissive, etc. patients. This is in direct contrast to the American social workers of the pilot study (see Chapter 3) and of the present investigation. It is possible that the British social workers' training puts more emphasis on helping the 'old' etc. patients.

An item analysis was performed for the respondents of hospital X. Of all occupational groups at X, the social workers and counselors obtained the mean scores most in favor of patients who had little education and were old, submissive, dependent and customary. They also showed a slight preference for rural and for emotional patients.

The second exception to the educational trend in British hospitals is found among the psychiatrists of the 'conservative' hospital X who differ from the other psychiatrists by showing a slight relative tendency in the direction of the older patients. In contrast, at hospital Y, the psychiatrists were most strongly in favor of 'young' patients of all English occupational groups. The differences between the British psychiatrists at X and Y seems to reflect the two hospitals' difference in discharge rates and in policies.

For the preferred patients on factor II, thus, mean scores varied with cultural setting as well as with hospital and occupation. In England, only mean scores of attendants, social workers and counselors showed absolute preferences for 'old' patients. In the United States samples, only some aides reached even the midpoint dividing preferences for 'old' and 'young' patients. However, the British samples showed consistently less strong preferences for 'youth' than the American respondents. This may confirm the widespread view that in the United States an unusual emphasis is placed on youth in contrast to European societies like the United Kingdom.

In all four samples standard deviations tend to decrease in size inversely with occupational status. Thus, the respondents in the higher occupations tend to have more consistent views on factor II.

FACTOR II – 'MENTAL PATIENT I LEAST ENJOY WORKING WITH'

The results for this semantic differential factor are summarized in Tables 48 and 49. Scores range again potentially from 0 to 42 with the midpoint at 21. Scores above 21 indicate that the 'old' patient is least liked, below 21 that the 'young' patient is least liked. A comparison of Tables 30 and 31 shows that the sequence of the factor items is somewhat changed for the least liked patient. Aggressiveness, independence and emotionality are raised in relative importance while education and urbanism are lowered in importance.

The first impression of Table 48 is that again, as with the most liked patient on factor II, mean scores fall on both sides of the midpoint. This is in contrast to factor I in which mean scores for most and least liked patients each stayed on one side of the midpoint. The greater overlap for factor II seems to be due to the relative absence of 'civic virtues' in its constituent items in contrast to factor I and to greater relevance of a number of factor II items to the makeup of the custodial senile patient.

To return to Tables 48 and 49, hospital B shows the usual occupational trend with only aides disliking 'young' and more educated patients.

In Hawaii, generally the same trend is followed by both orientals

Table 48. *Semantic differential – least liked patient: Factor II means*

	X	B	H	Y	F ratios	Sign.	Range of means
Attendants	20.6	18.6	21.3	18.0	2.84	5%	3.3
Nurses	20.8	21.7	23.6	20.3	5.55	1%	3.3
O. and R. therapists	24.1	22.5	25.6	24.5	.81	N.S.	3.1
Social workers and counselors	17.9	24.1	24.5	20.2	8.05	1%	6.6
Psychiatrists	20.9	27.2	27.5	24.2	4.05	5%	6.6
Psychologists	–	29.1	27.3	–			
F ratios	2.09	7.01	5.99	3.96			
Significance	N.S.	1%	1%	1%			
Range of means (excluding psychologists)	6.2	8.6	6.2	6.5			

Table 49. *Semantic differential – least liked patient: Factor II standard deviations*

	X	B	H	Y	F ratios	Sign.	Range of S.D.'s
Attendants	7.0	7.5	5.5	4.7	2.84	5%	2.3
Nurses	6.1	5.7	6.0	6.0	5.55	1%	0.4
O. and R. therapists	6.6	4.6	4.5	2.1	.81	N.S.	4.5
Social workers and counselors	7.4	6.3	5.2	5.3	8.05	1%	2.2
Psychiatrists	3.7	6.6	7.7	3.6	4.05	5%	4.1
Psychologists	–	7.0	6.3	–			
F ratios	2.09	7.01	5.99	3.96			
Significance	N.S.	1%	1%	1%			
Range of S.D.'s (excluding psychologists)	3.7	2.9	3.2	3.9			

and whites (see Table 42). In that state, three out of five oriental groups show slightly less dislike for 'old' patients (i.e., lower scores), than their white colleagues do. Only among social workers and counselors does this trend reach significance. In Hawaii, white aides are the only group whose average shows an absolute dislike for 'young' patients.

In the British hospitals (see Table 48), a similar general trend is seen if one excludes the auxiliary therapists and social work groups. Social workers and counselors in both British hospitals show a relatively greater dislike for 'young' patients. The item analysis for the least liked patient on factor II showed the following results for social workers in hospital X. Among all occupational groups, these social workers and counselors least liked patients who are aggressive, independent and modern. Of all occupations, they showed relatively least dislike for patients with low education. They showed a relative distaste for young, emotional and urban patients.

At both British hospitals, the auxiliary therapists showed on the contrary least dislike for the 'young' patients. This may reflect their occupational training and outlook. See also Table 46 for their preferences on factor II. Young patients probably respond better to and show more improvement due to occupational and recreational therapy than senile patients do.

It is notable that seven out of ten British occupational means indicate greatest dislike for the 'young', aggressive, etc. patient. Among the twelve United States means, such a result is found only in one case, namely among aides, and specifically, only among non-oriental aides. As was noticed above, this difference appears to be

Table 50. *Semantic differential – most liked patient: Two-way analyses of variance*

	Factor I		Factor II	
	F ratio	Sign.	F ratio	Sign.
Hospital	.72	N.S.	9.38	1%
Occupation	4.22	1%	8.59	1%
Interaction	1.45	N.S.	1.20	N.S.

Table 51. *Semantic differential – least liked patient: Two-way analyses of variance*

	Factor I		Factor II	
	F ratio	Sign.	F ratio	Sign.
Hospital	2.91	5%	10.07	1%
Occupation	4.45	1%	7.14	1%
Interaction	1.00	N.S.	1.76	N.S.

accounted for primarily by cultural values which seem to differ somewhat between the two English-speaking nations.

Two-way analyses of variance were performed on factors I and II for both the most and the least liked patients. The results are shown on Tables 50 and 51. Three out of four F ratios are significant between hospitals. The highest significances are found on factor II which was said to refer to 'old' versus 'young' patients and thus may have some connection with the hospitals' policies in relation to a custodial approach which is more suited to senile patients and to a 'progressive' approach which has been advocated for younger patients. All four F ratios between occupations are significant at the 1% level. None of the interaction F ratios reach significance.

SUMMARY

Two semantic differentials were presented to the samples which were asked to rate on 28 scales the 'mental patient I most (or least) enjoy working with'. The responses were factor analyzed and two main factors emerged. Factor I involved qualities like cooperation, responsibility, politeness and morality. Factor II concerned attributes such as education, age, modernity, aggressiveness and independence. One-way and two-way analyses of variance were performed for the most and the least liked patients on both factors. Most respondents expressed clear preferences and dislikes among patients possessing various attributes. For example, ward personnel, whose function it is to maintain peace and order, tended to prefer older, less aggressive patients, while psychiatrists and psychologists tended to prefer more educated, younger patients who might have better chances of recovery. Differences among occupations and among hospitals were shown to be statistically significant. Other significant differences were found to go with certain cultural variations. In general, the British scores tended to show more 'tolerance' of 'non-conformist' patients than the American scores.

CHAPTER 7

Other distinctions made among mental patients

In the three following chapters, the discussion of the study's findings will deal with individual questions which are related to attitudes toward mental illness, mental patients, their treatment, and their rehabilitation, in particular their vocational rehabilitation. This discussion is organized around several topics which reflect answers to various items in the questionnaire. The first topic (Chapter 7) deals with distinctions made among mental patients and thus complements the views on the most and least liked mental patients reviewed in the preceding chapter. The second topic (Chapter 8) concerns opinions on the etiology of mental illness, on hospital policies and on the treatment of patients. The last topic (Chapter 9) deals with the rehabilitation of mental patients released from the hospital.

The present chapter reviews distinctions made among patients. In the semantic differentials, the subjects were asked to rate the mental patients they most (and least) enjoyed working with. The present discussion will deal with

(a) patients said to be easiest to work with,
(b) chances given patients to succeed in the respondent's own profession, and
(c) some predictions of vocational success of former mental patients.

EASIEST PATIENT TO WORK WITH – WHITE COLLAR VS. BLUE COLLAR WORKERS

The questionnaire contained certain items about the patient 'easiest to work with'. For instance, question 12 asked: 'Which of the following patients have you found it easiest to work with?

(a) white collar workers

(b) blue collar workers.

(In England, 'manual' was substituted for 'blue collar'.)

The question ostensibly asked for a somewhat more objective judgment than did the semantic differentials; still, it was felt that the expressed ease of working with different patients would reflect partly subjective experiences and preferences.

The purpose of the question was to determine whether respondents of different socio-economic and occupational backgrounds would find it easier to work with (a) or (b) and in what different proportions. It may be recalled that Hollingshead and Redlich's seventeen psychiatrists both preferred and found it easier to work with patients from the higher socio-economic strata. In the pilot study of social workers mentioned in Chapter 3, 16 out of 18 who answered a similar question preferred to work with white collar clients.

How would the present sample of occupations in the four hospitals respond to question 12? It was anticipated that psychiatrists, social workers and psychologists would support the earlier findings of a tendency to find work easier with white collar patients. Attendants, nurses, and auxiliary therapists were expected, because of their own socio-economic and educational background, to tend to find work less difficult with blue collar patients. These expectations were first formulated for hospital B, in the Eastern United States, as that setting is geographically and culturally closest to those of the New Haven and pilot studies. Expectations for the other hospitals were less confident, since cultural and historical factors might affect the issue in Hawaii and England.* Table 52 presents the results of question 12.

In hospital B, the expectations were fulfilled; in Hawaii the same held except for social workers and counselors. An – at least partial – explanation for the Hawaiian counselors may be found in the self-designated social class of the sample (see Table 38). In hospital B, of the respondent social workers and counselors, 85% described themselves as middle class, 5% as upper class and 5% as working class. In Hawaii, only 73% claimed middle class and 2% upper class membership, but 24% saw themselves as members of the working class and 1% of the lower class.

* See above the discussion of cross-cultural patient preferences on the semantic differentials.

Table 52. *Easiest patient to work with: White collar – blue collar* (in percentages)

	Hospital B				
	N	White collar	Blue collar	Both	N/A
Aides	67	33	58		9
Nurses	61	21	71	1	7
O. and R. therapists	16	19	81		
Social workers and counselors	39	56	31	8	5
Psychiatrists	12	50	25		25
Psychologists	8	63	12		25

	Hospital H				
	N	White collar	Blue collar	Both	N/A
Aides	95	14	77	2	7
Nurses	92	26	71	1	2
O. and R. therapists	12	8	84	8	
Social workers and counselors	97	37	52	7	4
Psychiatrists	20	80	5		15
Psychologists	15	73	20		7

	Hospital X				
	N	White collar	Manual	Both	N/A
Aides	82	18	55	4	23
Nurses	206	22	71	7	
O. and R. therapists	14	21	79		
Social workers and counselors	25	24	56		20
Psychiatrists	16	31	50	13	6

	Hospital Y				
	N	White collar	Manual	Both	N/A
Aides	43	12	65	2	21
Nurses	86	28	52	9	10
O. and R. therapists	8	38	63		
Social workers and counselors	9	44	22		33
Psychiatrists	16	31	31	6	31

In England, the main trend (of finding work easier with patients relatively close to one's own social class) was confirmed in hospital Y, although psychiatrists were split evenly and relatively large proportions of them and of social workers and counselors did not reply. In hospital X, 56% of the social workers and counselors and 50% of the psychiatrists found work easier with manual workers. Why did such a relatively large proportion of these professionals find it easier to work with manual workers?

Table 53. *Respondents' class self-identification and choice of easiest patient to work with, white collar or manual: Hospital X* (in percentages)

Professional		N	Patient: White collar	Manual	Both	N/A
Aides	Upper	2		50	50	
	Upper-middle	16	38	38		24
	Lower-middle	19	16	42	10	32
	Working	41	12	68	5	15
Nurses	Upper	5	20	60		20
	Upper-middle	33	30	61		9
	Lower-middle	69	26	70		4
	Working	106	14	68	11	7
O. and R. therapists	Upper	0				
	Upper-middle	5	40	60		
	Lower-middle	4	25	75		
	Working	5		100		
Social workers and counselors	Upper	0				
	Upper-middle	9	11	56		33
	Lower-middle	12	25	67		8
	Working	4	50	25		25
Psychiatrists	Upper	2		100		
	Upper-middle	11	36	36	19	9
	Lower-middle	2		100		
	Working	0				

The British responses (on patients easier to work with) were cross tabulated against the subjects' class self-assignments (see Tables 53 and 54). These tables show the general tendency within a given occupational group for those who claim higher social status to find it relatively easier to work with white collar patients. It is only among social workers and counselors at hospital X that the results show a reversal of the usual trend. The possibility cannot be excluded that a majority of this occupational group at X for some particular reason worked with more cooperative manual workers among their caseload.

Table 54. *Respondents' class self-identification and choice of easiest patient to work with, white collar or manual: Hospital Y* (in percentages)

Professional		N	Patient: White collar	Manual	Both	N/A
Aides	Upper	0				
	Upper-middle	13	23	46		31
	Lower-middle	10	10	70	10	10
	Working	17	12	71		17
Nurses	Upper	1		100		
	Upper-middle	20	40	45	5	10
	Lower-middle	28	25	43	18	14
	Working	35	23	57	6	14
O. and R. therapists	Upper	1	100			
	Upper-middle	5	40	60		
	Lower-middle	1		100		
	Working	1		100		
Social workers and counselors	Upper	0				
	Upper-middle	4	75		25	
	Lower-middle	3		67		33
	Working	2	50			50
Psychiatrists	Upper	2	50	50		
	Upper-middle	10	50	20	10	20
	Lower-middle	3		33		67
	Working	1		100		

For example, some local idiosyncrasies or memorable recent instances of patient assignment to the different social workers might have affected their responses. It is even conceivable that at this particular hospital some social workers and counselors in fact chose their occupation because of a preference for and ease in working with persons of the lower socio-economic groups. However, the N is too small to permit firm conclusions and to exclude the operation of chance factors. In previous discussions of results, differences in responses between the two British hospitals were pointed out in this occupational category.

For all four hospitals, it can be said that only small minorities stated that it was equally easy (or difficult) to work with both groups. This result is partly due to the deliberate provision of only two alternate answers.

Question 12 tried to get at the ease experienced in working with patients from different socio-economic backgrounds by providing alternate answers in quasi-occupational terms.

EASIEST PATIENT TO WORK WITH – FEE VS. NON-FEE PATIENTS

Question 13 approached the issue by presenting alternate answers in terms of hospital payment, as follows:

'Which of the following patients have you found it easiest to work with?
(a) fee patients
(b) non-fee patients.
In England, the alternatives were changed to:
(a) paying patients
(b) NHS patients
as all British residents are entitled to free hospital care under the National Health Service act. Thus, the question is not quite equivalent in the two countries. It was expected that in hospital B, and perhaps to a lesser extent in Hawaii, the results would again show respondents in the lower occupational groups to find it easier to work with non-fee patients (i.e., with those of lower socio-economic status) and those higher up in the hierarchy to find work with fee patients easier. Results of the question are presented in Table 55.

In hospitals B and Hawaii, the expectations were generally fulfilled. In the two British hospitals, patients easier to work with were almost unanimously said to be those supported by the National Health Service. Presumably most patients are now covered by the NHS, and they may tend to make fewer demands than private patients. As for the very small numbers of attendants and nurses at both hospitals who preferred paying patients, they might conceivably have received special benefits from the relatives of such patients.

Table 55. *Easiest patient to work with, fee or non-fee patient* (in percentages)

	Hospital B				
	N	Fee patient	Non-fee patient	Both	N/A
Aides	67	22	67	4	7
Nurses	61	11	75	5	9
O. and R. therapists	16	19	75		6
Social workers and counselors	39	41	33		26
Psychiatrists	12	50	25		25
Psychologists	8	50	12		38
	Hospital H				
	N	Fee patient	Non-fee patient	Both	N/A
Aides	95	12	77	2	9
Nurses	92	21	66	2	11
O. and R. therapists	12	25	67		8
Social workers and counselors	97	37	37	2	24
Psychiatrists	20	40	40		20
Psychologists	15	46	27		27
	Hospital X				
	N	Paying	NHS	Both	N/A
Aides	82	10	73	7	10
Nurses	206	3	86	2	9
O. and R. therapists	14		100		
Social workers and counselors	25		72	4	24
Psychiatrists	16		69	6	25
	Hospital Y				
	N	Paying	NHS	Both	N/A
Aides	43	7	79		14
Nurses	86	1	87	3	9
O. and R. therapists	8		88		13
Social workers and counselors	9		67		33
Psychiatrists	16		75		25

ANTICIPATED VOCATIONAL SUCCESS OF EX-MENTAL PATIENTS: WHITE COLLAR VS. BLUE COLLAR JOBS

The semantic differentials asked for a rather direct expression of preferences among patients. Questions 12 and 13, which were just discussed, inquired less directly about patients easiest to work with. Question 21 calls for a still more detached answer. It states: 'Check the kind of former mental patient you believe *most* likely to be successful in his job . . .

Ex-patient's new job is
(a) "white collar"
(b) "blue collar".
(In England, again 'manual' was substituted for 'blue collar'.)

This question would presumably evoke a relatively objective or informational answer. One would expect social workers and counselors to give the answers based on the most solid experience with ex-patients, and ward personnel's answers to reflect least knowledge and relatively most projection, if projection entered into the replies. If, indeed, respondents should tend to project their feelings for patients in the less direct questions, one might expect results of this question somewhat to parallel those of questions 12 and 13 which asked for identification of the patient easiest to work with.

The results, shown in Table 56, indicate that all sample groups alike, regardless of hospital or occupation, predict better chances for the success of blue collar (or manual) workers. This includes the presumably most knowledgeable group of social workers and counselors and the presumably least well informed group of ward personnel. In hospital B, all groups, including social workers and counselors, tend to assign somewhat better chances to white collar workers than the Hawaiian sample does. This finding suggests that the employment situation and possibly the patients' occupational backgrounds differ somewhat between the two American hospitals. Of the two British institutions, perhaps for similar reasons, manual workers get a slightly higher vote in hospital Y.

One may conclude from the consistency of social workers, counselors and others that this answer corresponds fairly well to the facts and that any projection of attitudes, though conceivably it may be present in some individuals, does not noticeably influence the results of any one group. A reversed question which asked for the 'former mental patient you believe *least* likely to be successful in his job' got

Table 56. *Ex-patient most likely to be successful in job, white collar or blue collar* (in percentages)

Hospital B

	N	White collar	Blue collar	Both	N/A
Aides	67	40	49	5	6
Nurses	61	26	69	2	3
O. and R. therapists	16	6	75		19
Social workers and counselors	39	33	49		18
Psychiatrists	12	33	59		8
Psychologists	8	25	63		12

Hospital H

	N	White collar	Blue collar	Both	N/A
Aides	95	18	66	2	14
Nurses	92	18	76	2	4
O. and R. therapists	12		92	8	
Social workers and counselors	97	13	79	2	6
Psychiatrists	20	25	70		5
Psychologists	15	27	60		13

Hospital X

	N	White collar	Manual	Both	N/A
Aides	82	12	49		39
Nurses	206	18	65	3	14
O. and R. therapists	14	21	50	8	21
Social workers and counselors	25	8	76		16
Psychiatrists	16	25	63		12

Hospital Y

	N	White collar	Manual	Both	N/A
Aides	43	12	65		23
Nurses	86	10	70		20
O. and R. therapists	8	37	63		
Social workers and counselors	9	11	78		11
Psychiatrists	16	6	81		13

virtually the reverse answers. Respondents of all occupations in all hospitals checked 'white collar' patients as least likely to be successful. The probable implications of these consistent replies are (1) that in fact former patients find it more difficult to obtain and to hold jobs which involve more responsibility than manual jobs do, and (2) that many respondents do not expect ex-patients to succeed in white collar jobs, because the former patients are not given a chance to work in such jobs and possibly because some respondents themselves think ex-patients less able to handle the more responsible positions.

Another reason is brought out by Olshansky, Grob, and Ekdahl (1960) who state, 'Again, since 60 percent of the ex-patients work on semi-skilled, unskilled, or service jobs, they are in jobs which are not likely to provoke much scrutiny of their past, especially during periods of high employment'.

EASIEST PATIENT TO WORK WITH – MALE VS. FEMALE PATIENTS

In question 11, respondents were asked to indicate whether they found male or female patients easier to work with. The results, presented in Table 57, show that in both American samples, majorities of all but one occupational groups find work with men easiest. (The only exception are physicians at hospital B.)

In England, the majority of all respondents (235 versus 171) also find work with men easier, but in some occupational groups women are predominantly chosen.

COULD FORMER MENTAL PATIENTS SUCCEED IN YOUR PROFESSION?

Question 21 sought for relatively impersonal information about ex-patients' chances for vocational success in blue collar vs. white collar jobs. Question 15, on the other hand, asked:

'Do you think that persons who once have been mental patients could successfully work in *your* profession?

(a) always
(b) probably
(c) probably not
(d) never.'

Table 57. *Easiest patient to work with, male or female* (in percentages)

	Border State				Hawaii				England			
	N	*Male*	*Female*	*N/A*	*N*	*Male*	*Female*	*N/A*	*N*	*Male*	*Female*	*N/A*
Aides	67	66	28	6	95	79	17	4	125	23	61	16
Nurses	61	66	28	6	92	72	23	5	292	60	23	17
O. and R. therapists	16	81	19	–	12	92	–	8	22	36	46	18
Social workers	26	54	27	19	79	56	34	10	19	26	48	26
R & E counselors	13	54	23	23	18	55	39	6	–	–	–	–
Physicians	13	38	46	16	26	54	42	4	32	53	22	25
Psychologists	8	50	25	25	15	33	47	20	–	–	–	–

In other words, the question asked for an association of the patient with the respondent's own position. To a larger extent than question 21 – which asked about chances for vocational success in a fairly abstract manner – the question presently under consideration involves the respondent himself and the feelings he has for his own position. If one excluded personal involvement of the respondents, one might expect a replication of the answers to question 21, so that 'blue collar' subjects would predict success in their profession for patients, and respondents higher up in the occupational scale would tend not to do so.

In American hospitals, former mental patients not infrequently find employment as aides, due partly to the shortage of persons applying for these positions. In England, on the other hand, there is reportedly an adequate supply of nursing personnel for mental hospitals. One might also expect some cultural differentiations, to the effect that in the United States change of occupations, at least horizontally – being 'Jack of all trades' – occurs more frequently than in England, where one might anticipate a more highly developed consciousness of one's occupational status and position in a hierarchical order. To a somewhat lesser extent, such a consciousness might be found in the Hawaiian sample due to traditions of some ethnic groups involved. The answers to question 15 are tabulated in Table 58.

In hospital B, majorities of all professions believe ex-patients could probably succeed in their own occupations; the ratio of those who believe in success to those who do not is about 3 : 1. Aides are the group which gives ex-patients the greatest chances for success (82% v. 14% non-success). Psychiatrists are relatively least hopeful for patients to succeed in their profession (58% v. 42% non-success). Among the aides, experience with ex-patient fellow workers may have combined with the expected success of blue collar ex-patients (see question 21). The psychiatrists' results may be due to the hospital's 'conservative' policy and to the generally poor prognosis for ex-patients' success in higher positions (see Table 56).

In the Hawaiian hospital, aides again give ex-patients the best chances for success in their occupation. Psychiatrists in this relatively more 'progressive' hospital are somewhat more hopeful than their mainland colleagues. The least optimistic group are the social workers and counselors. It may be recalled that in Hawaii these workers are distributed over different islands. Some of them may feel that

Table 58. *Could former patient succeed in your profession?* (in percentages)

	Hospital B					
	N	Always	Probably	Probably not	Never	N/A
Aides	67	9	73	10	4	4
Nurses	61	5	70	25		
O. and R. therapists	16		75	25		
Soc. workers & counselors	39	2	75	18	5	
Psychiatrists	12	8	50	34	8	
Psychologists	8	12	63	25		

	Hospital H					
	N	Always	Probably	Probably not	Never	N/A
Aides	95	1	82	15	1	1
Nurses	92		63	34	3	
O. and R. therapists	12		75	25		
Soc. workers & counselors	97	2	50	43	4	1
Psychiatrists	20		65	35		
Psychologists	15		60	33	7	

	Hospital X					
	N	Always	Probably	Probably not	Never	N/A
Aides	82	1	59	17	21	2
Nurses	206	1	49	28	20	2
O. and R. therapists	14		64	22	14	
Soc. workers & counselors	25		36	24	24	16
Psychiatrists	16		56	44		

	Hospital Y					
	N	Always	Probably	Probably not	Never	N/A
Aides	43		53	19	26	2
Nurses	86		40	38	21	1
O. and R. therapists	8		74	13	13	
Soc. workers & counselors	9		33	45		22
Psychiatrists	16	6	38	44	13	

in their small insular communities many local residents would distrust ex-mental patients in their profession which involves dealing with people in many walks of life rather than with patients in a hospital. Overall, respondents in Hawaii tend to be slightly less optimistic about ex-patients' success than subjects in hospital B. The Hawaiian ratio of expected success v. non-success is about 2 : 1.

In England, generally less success is predicted for patients in the respondents' position. Aides are still relatively high in granting a chance for success, though their optimism is lower than that of American aides. Also in contrast to American subjects, relatively high percentages (up to 26%) believe that ex-patients could 'never' succeed in the subjects' occupations. These results may be affected by the consciousness of one's own status and by the greater supply of labor for nursing positions in England. As in Hawaii, the social workers and counselors in both English institutions are especially pessimistic. Again, their job functions may be responsible as they require these workers to have very frequent contacts with many community members (some of whom probably distrust ex-patients) in contrast to other sample occupations which involve work in the relative shelter of a mental hospital.

EASIEST PATIENT TO WORK WITH – BY ETHNICITY

The questions to be discussed next deal with the ethnic background of patients. Question 14 inquired:

'Which of the following patients have you found it easiest to work with?

(a) Negro patients
(b) Oriental patients
(c) White patients.'

The original expectation was that respondents would state that it is easiest for them to work with members of their own ethnic group. Table 59 presents the initial results before division into respondents' ethnic groups.

In hospital B, the majorities of all occupations found it easiest to work with white patients. Orientals were hardly mentioned, and there were hardly any orientals among the respondents. Minorities, especially of nurses and aides, found Negroes easiest to work with, and minorities of these staff groups were Negroes.

Table 59. *Easiest patient to work with, negro – oriental – white* (in percentages)

	Hospital B					
	N	Negro	Oriental	White	All three	N/A
Aides	67	20	12	54	7	7
Nurses	61	25		64	2	9
O. and R. therapists	16	13	6	75		6
Soc. workers & counselors	39	13		74		13
Psychiatrists	12			91		9
Psychologists	8	13		50		37

	Hospital H					
	N	Negro	Oriental	White	All three	N/A
Aides	95	1	83	6	4	6
Nurses	92	1	67	24	2	6
O. and R. therapists	12		83	17		
Soc. workers & counselors	97	1	55	34		10
Psychiatrists	20	5	15	75		5
Psychologists	15		13	74		13

	Hospital X					
	N	Negro	Oriental	White	All three	N/A
Aides	82		2	73	9	16
Nurses	206	1	2	73	8	16
O. and R. therapists	14		14	79		7
Soc. workers & counselors	25			80		20
Psychiatrists	16	6		56	6	32

	Hospital Y					
	N	Negro	Oriental	White	All three	N/A
Aides	43		2	70	5	23
Nurses	86	3		79	3	15
O. and R. therapists	8			88	12	
Soc. workers & counselors	9			78		22
Psychiatrists	16		6	63		31

It may be recalled from the discussion of the samples in Chapter 4 that a minority of Negroes worked at hospital B, mostly as nurses and aides. To test their views on easiest patients to work with, a subanalysis was conducted by cross-tabulating the respondents' own ethnicity with the ethnicity of the patient said to be the easiest to work with. Results are shown in Table 60. Negro aides have only a slight preference for Negro patients. Of the Negro nurses who answer the question, most find it easiest to work with white patients. In the case of hospital B, work with white or Negro patients means work on different wards. This may be one reason why a relatively large proportion of Negro ward personnel find work with white patients easier. However, one should keep in mind the small N's involved.

Table 60. *Easiest patient to work with, negro – oriental – white, Hospital B: By respondents' ethnicity* (in percentages)

		N	Patient			
			Negro	Oriental	White	N/A
Aides	Negro	24	33	9	29	29
	White	41	12	15	68	5
Nurses	Negro	6	17		50	33
	White	52	27		65	8

In England, not surprisingly, most respondents chose white patients as easiest to work with. In Hawaii, majorities of all occupations except psychiatrists and psychologists found it easier to work with orientals than with white patients. As Table 8 indicates, the majority of respondents at the Hawaiian hospital were themselves of oriental background. However, a comparison of Tables 8 and 59 shows that not only respondents of oriental origin tended to find it easiest to work with oriental patients.

Two alternate hypotheses were proposed to account for the findings. Hypothesis I states that ward personnel who are concerned with peace and order on the wards find oriental patients – due to their upbringing and traditions – more aware of their relative position and less aggressive than white patients. On the other hand, psychiatrists, psychologists, social workers and counselors would find it easier to work with white patients who might be more outgoing and less submissive in bipersonal relationships involving authority figures. Hypothesis I predicted that the occupational preferences would cut across lines of respondents' ethnicity, so that a relatively large proportion of *white* nursing personnel would find work with oriental patients easier and a comparatively large proportion of *oriental* social workers, counselors, and psychiatrists would find work with white patients easier. To test hypothesis I, it was decided to cross-tabulate respondents' ethnicity with their choice of easiest patient to work with. Table 61 shows this cross-tabulation.

Table 61. *Easiest patient to work with, negro – oriental – white, Hospital H: By respondents' ethnicity* (in percentages)

Professional		N	Patient			
			Negro	Oriental	White	N/A
Aides	Negro	0				
	Oriental	59		96	4	
	White	24	4	62	13	21
Nurses	Negro	2			50	50
	Oriental	55	2	76	18	4
	White	32		56	31	13
O. and R. therapists	Negro	0				
	Oriental	7		86	14	
	White	5		80	20	
Social workers and counselors	Negro	0				
	Oriental	74		65	27	8
	White	21	5	19	62	14
Psychiatrists	Negro	0				
	Oriental	4		50	50	
	White	16	6	6	82	6
Psychologists	Negro	0				
	Oriental	0				
	White	15		13	74	13

This table indicates that majorities both of oriental and of *white* aides, nurses, and therapists found it easiest to work with oriental patients. Among white personnel, only social workers, counselors, psychiatrists and psychologists tended to report work easiest with white patients. In fact, between the two occupational clusters, there was a clear-cut reversal of responses for the white personnel. Among oriental respondents, 96% of aides, 76% of nurses, 86% of auxiliary therapists, 65% of social workers and counselors, and only 50% of psychiatrists preferred to work with oriental patients. The findings are in harmony with hypothesis I.

A second hypothesis suggested that the white professional workers who found it easiest to work with oriental patients actually might be persons who dislike accepting orientals as equals but who are willing to accept orientals in an inferior position, e.g., as mental patients. This hypothesis was tested in a subanalysis which cross-tabulated choice of patient easier to work with and relevant items from the social distance scales (question 31), namely, willingness to accept orientals as fellow workers or as relatives by marriage. No relationships were found to exist between ease of working with oriental patients and the social distance responses.

The conclusion was drawn that the first hypothesis seems to account best for the findings. The argument of this hypothesis is in accordance with existing general views on traditional orientals in Hawaii. In the general picture of Hawaiian mental patients, those of oriental extraction are seen as being more compliant than white patients and as continuing in the hospital to some extent the respectful relationship vis-à-vis recognized authority figures they are expected by cultural traditions to show in normal life. The relatively ready acceptance of ward and hospital discipline makes these patients easy to work with from the viewpoint of ward personnel who are charged with maintaining order and discipline.

As Parsons (1957, p. 128) said, 'At the same time, the auxiliary personnel (such as nurses, and aides) to whom responsibility is delegated may have tendencies in the direction of a custodial emphasis. This is, first, because they are often formally forbidden to assume therapeutic responsibilities. But because they stand in close operative relations with the daily lives of patients, they have a strong vested interest in the smooth functioning of the hospital or at least their ward'. On the other hand, psychiatrists, psychologists, and to some extent social workers and counselors whose function it is to help patients by having them more actively participate in the therapeutic relationships and processes may find the more aggressive white patients easier to work with in their particular functions. The white patients may tend to show more spontaneity and abreaction. They are said in Hawaii to give less formal responses and to be more outgoing and flexible than oriental patients. The most adequate explanation for the Hawaiian responses to question 14 then seems to be one which employs an interaction of occupational function, of traditional cultural roles, and partly of preference for one's own ethnic group.

ANTICIPATED VOCATIONAL SUCCESS OF EX-MENTAL PATIENTS: BY ETHNICITY

Question 26 asks:
'Check the kind of former mental patient you believe *most* likely to be successful in his job . . .
(a) Negro
(b) Oriental
(c) White.'
Again, as in the white collar – blue collar questions, a shift is made here from an inquiry into personal ease in working with given groups of patients to a more detached and impersonal issue. One might expect results which would show in England and in the border state hospital greatest success predicted for whites while in Hawaii this finding might be modified due to the greater number of orientals than of whites in the Islands. Results are reported in Table 62.

In the border state hospital, as expected, white ex-patients were given the best chances for occupational success. One should keep in mind that in this sample, a fairsized minority of aides and nurses are Negroes. Some of them apparently felt that white ex-patients had a better chance, which probably is a realistic viewpoint. Of the social workers and counselors, who are presumably especially knowledgeable in respect to this question, only 15% give Negroes the best chances to succeed. The parallel question for the patient *least* likely to succeed lists consistently Negroes although in smaller percentages than whites were thought to succeed (see Table 63).

In Hawaii, more aides, nurses and auxiliary therapists, social workers and counselors found it easiest to work with orientals (see Table 59) than expected orientals to succeed (see Table 62). This may reflect the feeling, based on facts, in Hawaii that while there is no official ethnic discrimination with regard to jobs, orientals, in reality, still find it somewhat more difficult than whites to obtain certain desirable positions. Majorities of the social workers, counselors and psychologists give a better prognosis for success to white ex-patients than to oriental ones. It has been said before that social workers and counselors are the professionals whose work should

Table 62. *Ex-patient most likely to be successful in job, negro – oriental – white* (in percentages)

	N	Negro	Oriental	White	All	N/A
Hospital B						
Aides	67	19	10	61	3	7
Nurses	61	7	8	85		
O. and R. therapists	16	31	13	50		6
Soc. workers & counselors	39	15	5	65	2	13
Psychiatrists	12	8		75		17
Psychologists	8	12		76		12
Hospital H						
Aides	95	5	53	31	2	9
Nurses	92	2	51	42	4	1
O. and R. therapists	12	8	42	42	8	
Soc. workers & counselors	97	3	35	49	2	11
Psychiatrists	20	5	45	40		10
Psychologists	15		33	54		13
Hospital X						
Aides	82	1	4	45	2	48
Nurses	206	7	6	64	3	20
O. and R. therapists	14	7	15	57		21
Soc. workers & counselors	25	8	8	60		24
Psychiatrists	16	6	13	13		68
Hospital Y						
Aides	43	7		47	5	41
Nurses	86	3	3	66	1	27
O. and R. therapists	8			100		
Soc. workers & counselors	9			89	11	
Psychiatrists	16			63	37	

make them best informed about the real chances for vocational success of different groups. Their prediction, if correct, may reflect (a) the reluctance of white employers to hire orientals for certain

Table 63. *Ex-patient least likely to be successful in job, negro – oriental – white* (in percentages)

	Hospital B					
	N	Negro	Oriental	White	All	N/A
Aides	67	39	20	22	3	16
Nurses	61	59	26	11		4
O. and R. therapists	16	54	26	20		
Soc. workers & counselors	39	54	10	15		21
Psychiatrists	12	50	25	25		
Psychologists	8	50	13	13		24
	Hospital H					
	N	Negro	Oriental	White	All	N/A
Aides	95	42	18	17	2	21
Nurses	92	62	8	14	2	14
O. and R. therapists	12	58	17	17		8
Soc. workers & counselors	97	64	10	10	1	15
Psychiatrists	20	60	15	15		10
Psychologists	15	53	13	21		13
	Hospital X					
	N	Negro	Oriental	White	All	N/A
Aides	82	21	9	20		50
Nurses	206	35	15	22	1	27
O. and R. therapists	14	7	21	29		43
Soc. workers & counselors	25	32	28	24		16
Psychiatrists	16	6		6		88
	Hospital Y					
	N	Negro	Oriental	White	All	N/A
Aides	43	12	9	21	2	56
Nurses	86	32	15	19		33
O. and R. therapists	8	63		37		
Soc. workers & counselors	9	33		11		56
Psychiatrists	16	50	12			38

desirable positions and perhaps also (b) a disinclination of oriental employers – who may be expected to employ a large proportion of orientals – to hire ex-patients, due to cultural traditions noted before. In the parallel question for the least successful patient, majorities of all occupational groups in Hawaii are most pessimistic about Negroes' success in employment. While there are only very few Negroes in Hawaii, not to mention Negro ex-mental patients, the prediction is probably realistic. Information from the social distance scales in the questionnaire showed that many Hawaiians who are ready to accept orientals and whites on a basis of equality, seem to have taken over mainland attitudes of greater social distance toward Negroes.

In the British hospitals, not surprisingly, majorities of respondents predicted greatest vocational success for white ex-patients. Least success was most often anticipated for Negro ex-patients, but many respondents abstained from answering the question. As the present question is asking primarily for knowledge, many English respondents may have been unable to answer in an informed manner a question which to them may have seemed academic.

SUMMARY

The present chapter reviewed (a) views on which patients were easiest to work with, (b) chances given ex-patients to succeed in the respondents' own profession, and (c) some predictions of vocational success of former mental patients.

A group of questions asked which patients the respondents found it easiest to work with. Respondents tended to select mental patients who were either closest to their own socio-economic background or to the social class to which the respondents assigned themselves.

Another question asked who was easier to work with, (a) fee patients or (b) non-fee patients. In England, the alternatives became (a) paying patients and (b) NHS (National Health Service) patients. (All British residents are entitled to free hospital care under the NHS.) In the American hospitals, occupations were divided again much as on the previous question. In the British institutions there was an almost unanimous designation of NHS patients as easier to work with.

Most respondents of all occupations and in all samples alike expected greatest vocational success for ex-patients in manual jobs and least vocational success in white collar jobs.

Majorities of the respondents in the English and especially in the

American samples found it easier to work with male than with female patients.

One question associated the patient with the respondent's own occupation: 'Do you think that persons who once have been mental patients could successfully work in your profession?' In American mental hospitals, ex-patients not infrequently are employed as aides, and aides were the group of which the largest percentage believed that ex-patients could make a success of working in their occupation. Majorities of all American groups believed that ex-patients could at least 'probably' make a career in their professions. In England, the optimism was generally somewhat reduced, and some hospital-occupational groups did not predict success for ex-patients in their fields.

Finally, some questions inquired into distinctions made among patients by ethnicity. One item asked, 'Which of the following patients have you found it easiest to work with? (a) Negro patients – (b) oriental patients – (c) white patients –.' In hospital B, majorities of all occupations found work easiest with white patients. Only Negro aides showed a slight preference for Negro patients. In the English institutions (which had practically no Negro patients), most respondents found white patients easiest to work with.

In Hawaii, majorities of all occupations except psychologists and psychiatrists found work easier with oriental than with white patients. The answers were cross-tabulated with respondents' ethnic background. The resulting table showed that majorities of both oriental and white aides, nurses, and auxiliary therapists found it easiest to work with oriental patients. Among oriental respondents, ease of work with orientals decreased as the subjects' occupational level increased. The finding was interpreted to mean probably that ward personnel, one of whose functions it is to maintain order and discipline on the wards, find oriental patients – due to their upbringing and traditions – to be less aggressive and more respectful vis-à-vis recognized authority figures like themselves. White patients – in view of their cultural background – might be more spontaneous and ready to participate actively in therapeutic relationships and processes novel to them, which would ease the job functions of psychiatrists, psychologists, and social workers. The most adequate explanation for the Hawaiian responses thus seemed to call for an interaction of occupational functions, of traditional cultural roles, and only partly of preference for one's own ethnic group.

A related question required respondents to 'Check the kind of former mental patient you believe *most* likely to be successful in his job . . . (a) Negro – (b) oriental – (c) white –.' In the border state and in the English hospitals, white ex-patients were given the best chances. In Hawaii, more respondents found oriental patients *easy* to work with than expected them to be *successful* in their jobs. The majority of social workers and counselors, i.e. the most experienced group, predicted greatest vocational success for white ex-patients. These findings may reflect the feeling that in Hawaii, even in the absence of official job discrimination by color, orientals still have somewhat more difficulty than Caucasians in obtaining certain desirable jobs. A parallel question for the ex-patient expected to be least successful resulted in greatest pessimism about the chances for success of Negro ex-patients.

CHAPTER 8

Views on mental illness and on its treatment

In the present chapter, the following topics will be discussed:

(a) Views on the causation of mental illness;
(b) Opinions on the most pressing need in the treatment of mental patients;
(c) What should be the primary goal of the mental hospital staff?
(d) What is the chief function of a mental hospital?
(e) Some views on open wards;
(f) Why do ex-mental patients get rehospitalized?

VIEWS ON THE CAUSATION OF MENTAL ILLNESS

Question 6 asked: 'Rank the following three statements. Put the number *1* behind the statement you think most important. Put the number *2* behind the statement you think next most important. Put the number *3* behind the statement you think least important.
(a) Mental illness is due to a patient's heredity
(b) Mental illness is due to a patient's social environment
(c) Mental illness is due to a patient's physical disease.'
Table 64 presents the first choices of the respondents. In all four hospitals the most frequent choice was 'social environment'. However, in the two British institutions, the selection of environment was consistently smaller than in the American hospitals. Conversely, larger proportions of subjects listed heredity as the first factor in importance at the English hospitals than in the American samples. The only exception to these results were the psychiatrists at the American 'conservative' hospital B, who together with this hospital's psychologists were the American group with the highest percentages who believed in the primacy of heredity in causing mental illness.

Table 64. *Mental illness is due to – first choices* (in percentages)

	Heredity				Social environment				Physical disease				No answer			
	X	B	H	Y	X	B	H	Y	X	B	H	Y	X	B	H	Y
Aides	22	9	4	26	39	57	67	40	24	31	19	23	15	3	10	11
Nurses	27	5	2	15	58	85	95	74	13	10	3	6	2			5
O. and R. therapists	15				43	75	92	87	21	25		13	21		8	
Soc. workers & counselors	24	5	5		52	90	87	56	12	5	5	11	12		3	33
Psychiatrists	19	25		13	56	58	95	50	19	17		31	6		5	6
Psychologists	–	13	7	–	–	87	93	–	–			–	–			–

The Hawaiian respondents generally produced the highest percentages of believers in the primacy of social environment and the lowest percentages of those who gave first choice to hereditary factors. Hawaii is followed by the border state and lastly by the English samples, both in increasing choice of heredity and in decreasing choice of environmental factors. The differences between the two American hospitals are pronounced, but they are present not only at the policy-setting level of psychiatrists which might be explainable in terms of hospital policies. Rather, the differences on the primacy of heredity and of social environment extend all the way down to the nurses and aides, who were earlier said to be relatively less affected by hospital policies. It then seems to be necessary to look for another explanation of the difference between the two American samples.

It is interesting to note the Hawaiian results in particular. The term 'heredity' (in contrast to 'social environment') was interpreted by the investigator in the general medical sense of whether mental disorders are or are not inherited. Notwithstanding the author's interpretation, it seems likely that some Hawaiian respondents thought of the heredity-environment choice as less a matter of individual heredity than of ethnically inherent characteristics. One of the outstanding characteristics of Hawaii is the heterogeneous origin of its population. It is interesting to observe that in Hawaii, i.e. in the subsample with the widest variety of ethnic groups, the greatest percentage of subjects discount heredity and select social environment as the prime factor in mental illness.

Compared with both American samples, the British respondents were found generally to assign more priority to heredity and less to social environment. There were no clearcut distinctions between the two British hospitals. The conclusion was reached that historical and traditional factors account for the different results in the two countries. Compared to the United States, England is a country where traditions are relatively more emphasized. The presence of a hereditary nobility and of a royal house is but one example of this. In English rural districts and in the smaller towns, families may have lived for many generations, and much about a person's family background – including medical history and occurrence of mental abnormality – is known to his neighbors. In contrast to this, in the United States less of a sense of historical continuity and of esteem for traditions is generally reported. Even in small towns, old families usually have lived for fewer generations than have families in English towns, and persons tend to feel less rooted to their place of birth.

Among the respondents in all four hospitals, aides provide the smallest proportions of environmentalist first choices. This may be due to (1) their having been least exposed to modern theories of psychiatry which stress the environmental influence on personality development and on the etiology of mental disorders* and to (2) the concomitant persistence of old popular explanations of mental illness. Aides are the most frequent supporters of the physical disease alternative in three hospitals. In the fourth institution, the British hospital Y, they are exceeded in frequency of this view by psychiatrists. It was a surprise to the writer that among psychiatrists, in spite of their medical training, only relatively few assigned primacy to causation by physical disease in the four hospitals studied, regardless of the hospital policy. Of the four hospitals, the Hawaiian respondents show least support for the primacy of causation by physical disease, and, as was noted, most support for the effectiveness of the social environment.

* One may consider the possibility that of the three alternate choices provided for answering the questions, 'social environment' might be least familiar to people of relatively low educational level, like aides. This possibility may also be related to this group's lack of exposure to environmental theories of personality.

OPINION ON THE MOST PRESSING NEED IN THE TREATMENT OF MENTAL PATIENTS

The first item in the instrument asked for a brief comment on the question 'In your opinion, what is the most pressing need in the treatment of mental patients?'

The question was meant to allow the respondents to express their own relatively uninfluenced concerns before the subsequent pages of the questionnaire might have directed their attention to particular issues. The item also was intended to introduce the questionnaire in an open way which might suggest that the respondents should feel free to express their views.

To sum up more than one thousand unstructured answers, it was necessary to condense the information by a coding system. All answers were copied from the questionnaires and reviewed. Inspection by two judges showed that they could be coded in eight pertinent categories. (A ninth category was provided for 'other or unclear' replies.) Then the answers were coded by two judges. Reliability of ratings was determined by having both judges code the same one hundred replies. Reliability was found to be higher than .90. Both judges were social psychologists and senior members of the project staff.

The results are presented in Tables 65 and 66. The most frequently felt need concerned mental health personnel, either their attitudes or else the requirement for more personnel. The next most frequent need dealt with activities outside of the mental hospital. Other but less commonly felt needs were medical treatment, physical or financial resources, research, and education and understanding by the public. Vocational rehabilitation was mentioned only occasionally, but it will be remembered that the question asked for the most pressing need in the *treatment* of patients.

In sum, the respondents found the most pressing needs in the treatment of patients to lie predominantly in staff attitudes, lack of personnel and matters outside of the mental hospital.

Table 65. *What is the most pressing need in the treatment of patients? Border state* (in percentages)

	N	Physical or financial resources	More personnel	Medical treatment	Outside of hospital	Voca-tional rehabili-tation	Research	Education & under-standing of public	Staff attitudes	Other or unclear	N/A
Aides	(67)	1	12	6			1	4	40	10	26
Nurses	(61)	5	25	3	5		2	10	41	1	8
O. and R. therapists	(16)	6	19						63		12
Social workers	(26)	8	34	12	23			4	15		4
R & E counselors	(13)	15	8	8		8		8	23		30
Physicians	(13)		23		8		8		8	22	31
Psychologists	(8)		50		37						13

Table 66. *What is the most pressing need in the treatment of patients? Hawaii and England* (in percentages)

	N	Physical or financial resources	More personnel	Medical treatment	Outside of hospital	Vocational rehabilitation	Research	Education & understanding of public	Staff attitudes	Other or unclear	N/A
Hawaii											
Aides	(95)	4	22	6	3	2	2	4	19	4	34
Nurses	(92)	20	33	10	7	1		12	15		2
O. and R. therapists	(12)	8	17		25	8			42		
Social workers	(79)	15	35	4	22	1	4	10		3	6
R & E counselors	(18)	6	17		22	6	16	6		11	16
Physicians	(26)	4	27	12	31		4	4	8		10
Psychologists	(15)	7	27		20		27	7		7	7
England											
Aides	(125)	2	10	5	1		1		36	3	42
Nurses	(292)	3	21	7	8	1	7	5	25	2	21
O. and R. therapists	(22)		18	18	5	5		9	27		18
Social workers	(19)	11	21	21		5	11		21		10
Physicians	(32)	3	9	12	12		16	6	22	3	16

WHAT SHOULD BE THE PRIMARY GOAL OF THE MENTAL HOSPITAL STAFF?

Respondents were asked to make a choice between the following alternatives:
'The primary goal of the hospital staff should be
(a) to cure the patients of their illness
(b) to rehabilitate patients into society.'
The purpose of this question was to find out how many mental health workers would realize the importance of the patient's general rehabilitation beyond the mere medical cure.

Table 67. *The primary goal of the hospital staff should be . . .* (in percentages)

	N	To cure the patients of their illness	To rehabilitate the patients into society	N/A	Both
Border State					
Aides	(67)	33	61	3	3
Nurses	(61)	18	82		
O. and R. therapists	(16)	19	81		
Social workers	(26)	23	77		
R & E counselors	(13)	38	54	8	
Physicians	(13)	8	92		
Psychologists	(8)	37	63		
Hawaii					
Aides	(95)	15	82	3	
Nurses	(92)	9	91		
O. and R. therapists	(12)	8	92		
Social workers	(79)	18	82		
R & E counselors	(18)	17	83		
Physicians	(26)	12	88		
Psychologists	(15)	7	93		
England					
Aides	(125)	50	44	4	2
Nurses	(292)	38	58	1	3
O. and R. therapists	(22)	27	73		
Social workers	(19)	26	69		5
Physicians	(32)	34	59	7	

The results, presented in Table 67, show a striking preponderance of respondents who choose rehabilitation as the staff's main goal. Of all occupational groups in all hospitals only the English aides show a slightly more frequent choice of the curative alternative.

Of the different samples, it is in the Hawaiian sample, that the largest proportions choose rehabilitation (between 82% and 93% for different occupations). In the East coast sample, the proportions range from 54% to 92%. Among the British occupational groups, the percentages range from 44% (for nursing assistants) to 73%.

WHAT IS THE CHIEF FUNCTION OF A MENTAL HOSPITAL?

In question 7, the sample was asked: 'The chief function of a mental hospital is:
(a) to safeguard society
(b) to return the patients to society
(c) to protect the patients.'
The alternatives can be seen as representing (b) a progressive and (c) a custodial point of view. To use Cohen and Struening's terminology, one might speak of (a) as 'social restrictiveness' and of (b) as approximating 'mental hygiene ideology'. It is also possible to consider both (a) and (c) as representing the custodial point of view with (a) being a more negative and (c) a more positive or paternalistic formulation.

The present question deals fairly directly with issues of hospital policy. One may ask then, do the respondents reflect the policies of the four hospitals as they have been described earlier? If there is a reflection, does it apply to all occupations? The expectations for the results in this question were that hospital policy would indeed affect the responses and that psychiatrists would express policy most and aides least. Results are shown in Table 68.

It is first noticeable that all groups give strongest support to the view that patients should be returned to society. The strength of this viewpoint varies among hospitals and among occupations. In all four institutions, aides give least support to this view and most support to the combined two custodial alternatives.

Among hospitals, too, differences emerge. Of the four institutions, the 'conservative' American hospital B tends to support least the 'progressive' alternative. In England, the 'conservative' hospital X gives less support to this alternative than the 'progressive' hospital Y.

Table 68. *Chief function of a mental hospital – first choices* (in percentages)

	To safe-guard society				To return patients to society				To protect patients				No answer			
Hospital	X	B	H	Y	X	B	H	Y	X	B	H	Y	X	B	H	Y
Aides	9	5	11		52	49	65	67	23	41	16	23	16	5	8	10
Nurses	6	3	5	6	78	57	75	72	14	38	20	17	2	2		5
O. and R. therapists	7	6			79	75	75	100	7	19	25		7			
Social workers & counselors	8	3	4		64	82	71	78	16	15	21		12		4	22
Psychiatrists	19	8	5		69	59	75	74	6	33	15	13	6		5	13
Psychologists	–	13	7	–	–	74	86	–	–	13	7	–	–			–

In the 'conservative' American hospital B, relatively greatest agreement is found with the alternative to protect the patients. Among the four hospitals, the English ones give comparatively least support to this protective alternative. On the other hand, the 'conservative' English hospital X gives strongest support to the 'socially restrictive' view (a); in particular, its psychiatrists are the one group in all hospitals which most actively supports the view of the hospital's function as safeguarding society. Of all occupational groups at the 'progressive' English hospital Y, only some of the nurses agree with this interpretation of the mental hospital's role.

It has been stated before that psychiatrists as a group are most concerned with the policy of mental hospitals. Table 69 shows how the psychiatrists in the four institutions are distributed in their views on question 7. Among the psychiatrists, those in hospital X give relatively most support to the 'safeguard society' viewpoint. The American 'conservative' hospital B shows the strongest 'protective' sentiment. The 'progressive' hospitals' psychiatrists tend to give least agreement to the 'custodial' views and most to the 'progressive' view.

Table 69. *Psychiatrists' views of chief function of a mental hospital – first choices* (in percentages)

	Hospitals			
Views	X	B	H	Y
To safeguard society	19	8	5	
To protect the patient	6	33	15	13
To return patients to society	69	59	75	74
No answer	6		5	13

The results seem to confirm the earlier evaluation of the hospitals, which was based on background information and on personal impressions. Table 69 also suggests that hospital policy is not a unidimensional matter but that, e.g., within the 'custodial' outlook, relatively more emphasis may be placed on a 'socially restrictive' or on a 'paternalistic' aspect.

SOME VIEWS ON OPEN WARDS

It may be recalled from Chapter 4 that the hospitals sampled varied in the extent of wards that had been opened. In the Eastern United States hospital, about 20% of all aides and nurses stated that they worked on open wards on an average day; in Hawaii this percentage reached 40% and in England it climbed to over 90%.

How are the different hospital practices reflected in attitudes toward open wards? A series of seven statements about open and closed wards was presented in question 9 and respondents could indicate their agreement or disagreement.

The first statement claimed that 'patients escape more often from open wards than from closed wards.' Majorities of all occupational groups in all samples disagreed (see Table 70). However, in all occupations, the English respondents gave the relatively greatest proportion of agreement with the skeptical view. Presumably in the course of years of the English respondents' experience with open wards, more patients did 'escape' from open than from closed wards.

Table 70. *Opinions on open wards* (in percentages)

(a) *Patients escape from them more often than from closed wards*

Key – Disagree
+ Agree

	Border State				*Hawaii*				*England*			
	N	–	+	N/A	N	–	+	N/A	N	–	+	N/A
Aides	67	73	27	–	95	87	13	–	125	53	32	15
Nurses	61	80	20	–	92	82	18	–	292	64	25	11
Therapists	16	88	13	–	12	92	8	–	22	64	23	13
Social workers	26	81	19	–	79	89	11	–	19	47	21	32
Counselors	13	100	–	–	18	88	12	–	–	–	–	–
Physicians	13	62	38	–	26	77	23	–	32	47	9	44
Psychologists	8	75	25	–	15	93	7	–	–	–	–	–

The second statement held that 'open wards motivate patients in a hospital to improve' (see Table 71). Majorities of all occupations in all samples agreed, but again all English groups showed relatively least faith in this effect of open wards.

Table 71.

(b) *Open wards motivate patients to improve*

Key – Disagree
+ Agree

	Border State				*Hawaii*				*England*			
	N	–	+	N/A	N	–	+	N/A	N	–	+	N/A
Aides	67	10	90	–	95	16	84	–	125	29	56	15
Nurses	61	3	97	–	92	7	93	–	292	9	80	11
Therapists	16	6	94	–	12	–	100	–	22	9	77	14
Social workers	26	8	92	–	79	5	95	–	19	5	63	32
Counselors	13	38	62	–	18	28	72	–	–	–	–	–
Physicians	13	23	77	–	26	8	92	–	32	3	53	44
Psychologists	8	13	87	–	15	13	87	–	–	–	–	–

The next statement proposed that 'closed wards are more efficient' (see Table 72). Again, majorities in all groups opposed this view, and again the English groups were relatively least opposed.

Table 72.

(c) *Closed wards are more efficient*

Key – Disagree
+ Agree

	Border State				*Hawaii*				*England*			
	N	–	+	N/A	N	–	+	N/A	N	–	+	N/A
Aides	67	82	18	–	95	85	14	1	125	70	20	10
Nurses	61	93	7	–	92	89	11	–	292	–	–	–
Therapists	16	100	–	–	12	92	8	–	22	77	14	9
Social workers	26	88	12	–	79	85	15	–	19	68	–	32
Counselors	13	92	8	–	18	77	23	–	–	–	–	–
Physicians	13	92	8	–	26	92	8	–	32	53	6	41
Psychologists	8	100	–	–	15	93	7	–	–	–	–	–

The following assertion held, 'it is hard to maintain order and discipline in an open ward' (see Table 73). Once again, most respondents in all groups disagreed with the assertion, and in England there was least disagreement.

Table 73.

(d) *It is hard to maintain order and discipline in an open ward*

Key – Disagree
+ Agree

	Border State				Hawaii				England			
	N	–	+	N/A	N	–	+	N/A	N	–	+	N/A
Aides	67	78	22	–	95	85	14	1	125	61	23	17
Nurses	61	95	5	–	92	84	16	–	292	75	14	11
Therapists	16	94	6	–	12	92	8	–	22	77	9	14
Social workers	26	85	15	–	79	80	19	1	19	53	16	32
Counselors	13	77	23	–	18	83	17	–	–	–	–	–
Physicians	13	100	–	–	26	92	8	–	32	53	3	44
Psychologists	8	75	25	–	15	100	–	–	–	–	–	–

The next sentence declared, 'patients in open wards get cured faster' (see Table 74). The English occupational groups give majorities in support of this view. In the American samples, majorities of only the counselors and the nurses (and of auxiliary therapists in Hawaii) disagree with the optimistic view.

Table 74.

(e) *Patients in open wards get cured faster*

Key – Disagree
+ Agree

	Border State				Hawaii				England			
	N	–	+	N/A	N	–	+	N/A	N	–	+	N/A
Aides	67	39	60	1	95	49	49	2	125	26	54	20
Nurses	61	52	48	–	92	59	41	–	292	19	69	12
Therapists	16	13	87	–	12	75	25	–	22	36	50	14
Social workers	26	27	73	–	79	37	62	–	19	5	58	37
Counselors	13	62	38	–	18	67	33	–	–	–	–	–
Physicians	13	38	62	–	26	38	62	–	32	12	41	47
Psychologists	8	13	87	–	15	33	67	–	–	–	–	–

Another sentence maintained, 'closed wards are easier on the staff' (see Table 75). The preponderance of answers in most groups opposed this view. (Only physicians in hospital B and English social workers tended to support the statement.)

Table 75.

(f) *Closed wards are easier on the staff*

Key – Disagree
+ Agree

	Border State				*Hawaii*				*England*			
	N	–	+	N/A	N	–	+	N/A	N	–	+	N/A
Aides	67	72	27	1	95	68	31	1	125	60	23	17
Nurses	61	61	39	–	92	54	46	–	292	70	19	11
Therapists	16	81	19	–	12	58	42	–	22	59	27	14
Social workers	26	65	35	–	79	51	49	–	19	26	42	32
Counselors	13	85	15	–	18	55	44	–	–	–	–	–
Physicians	13	38	62	–	26	73	27	–	32	44	12	44
Psychologists	8	75	25	–	15	73	27	–	–	–	–	–

The last statement in the series alleged that 'open wards often lead to trouble with the community' (see Table 76). Majorities of all groups disagreed with the statement, but in England once again there was least disagreement.

Table 76.

(g) *Open wards often lead to trouble with the community*

Key – Disagree
+ Agree

	Border State				*Hawaii*				*England*			
	N	–	+	N/A	N	–	+	N/A	N	–	+	N/A
Aides	67	85	13	2	95	85	14	1	125	54	29	17
Nurses	61	93	7	–	92	91	9	–	292	68	21	11
Therapists	16	87	13	–	12	100	–	–	22	59	27	14
Social workers	26	88	12	–	79	91	8	1	19	63	5	32
Counselors	13	100	–	–	18	94	6	–	–	–	–	–
Physicians	13	77	23	–	26	92	8	–	32	47	9	44
Psychologists	8	63	25	12	15	87	13	–	–	–	–	–

To sum up this series, one might say that generally most groups favor open wards and think them superior to closed wards. In

England, where open wards are much more widely used, the support for them was relatively smallest. The comparatively less one-sided English expressions on this topic may reflect a more sober and realistic view on open wards.

WHY DO EX-MENTAL PATIENTS GET REHOSPITALIZED?

In question 8, respondents were asked to choose the three most important among seven reasons for rehospitalization. Their first choices are shown in Table 77. The relatively most frequent choice was the argument that the 'patient was not well enough to be released'. Among American respondents, the argument checked off next most frequently was that the patient's 'family didn't try hard enough'. In England, the second most common statement was that the 'patient was too used to being hospitalized'. Less frequent reasons were seen in lacking efforts by members of the general community, by the patients themselves, by employers or fellow workers and by public agencies.

SUMMARY

Notions about the causation of mental illness were tapped. Generally, 'social environment' was the most frequent first choice over 'heredity' and 'physical disease', but considerable variations were found. In all four hospitals, aides assigned least importance to environmental factors, presumably because of their relative unfamiliarity with modern psychiatric thinking and because of the concomitant persistence of old popular explanations of mental illness. Compared with both American samples, the British respondents in general assigned more priority to heredity and less to social environment. As no clearcut distinctions between the English hospitals were found, the conclusion was reached that historical-cultural factors were responsible for the greater English belief in the importance of heredity. The Hawaiian sample, on the other hand, produced the largest percentage of support for the primary importance of social environment and least agreement with the inheritance view. It is interesting to find that the one sample which possesses the widest ethnic

Table 77. *Reasons for rehospitalization of former mental patients – first choice* (in percentages)

	N	Patient didn't try	Family	Employer or fellow workers	Communi-ty members	Public agencies	Too used to hospi-talization	Patient released too soon	N/A
Border State									
Aides	(67)	13	28	3	9	1	9	25	12
Nurses	(61)	15	18	5	13		5	38	6
O. and R. therapists	(16)	12	32	6	6			44	
Social workers	(26)	4	15		12	4		62	3
R & E counselors	(13)			15	15		23	38	9
Physicians	(13)	8	23	8		8	15	31	7
Psychologists	(8)	12			25			63	
Hawaii									
Aides	(95)	19	23	4	3	1	5	37	8
Nurses	(92)	9	36		4	2	3	45	1
O. and R. therapists	(12)	8	17		8	8	8	42	9
Social workers	(79)	10	20	1	13	3	4	49	
R & E counselors	(18)	6	17		6		6	55	10
Physicians	(26)	4	54		4	4	11	23	
Psychologists	(15)		13		27	20	7	27	6
England									
Aides	(125)	11	16	5	4	1	26	26	11
Nurses	(292)	8	13	8	10	3	26	30	2
O. and R. therapists	(22)	4	9	18	4		32	27	6
Social workers	(19)		10		10	5	32	32	11
Physicians	(32)	6	9		12	16	19	28	10

diversity and the most extensive experience in living with markedly different cultural groups believes least in the causation of mental illness by heredity and most in the relevance of social environment.

Respondents were asked to comment briefly on what they considered to be the most pressing need in the treatment of patients. The most frequent needs were said to concern staff attitudes, lack of personnel and matters outside the mental hospital.

When asked what the primary goal of the mental hospital staff should be, most respondents in all samples stated that it was 'to rehabilitate the patients into society' rather than merely 'to cure the patients of their illness'.

What is the chief function of a mental hospital? (a) to safeguard society, (b) to return the patients to society, or (c) to protect the patients? Respondents were asked to indicate their preference for a 'custodial' (a) and (c) or a 'progressive' (b) outlook in mental hospitals. All groups of respondents expressed strongest support for the 'progressive' alternative, but there were variations among occupations and among hospitals. In all four samples, aides had the relatively strongest tendency to endorse a 'custodial' outlook. On the other hand, those hospitals which are still most custodial in their practices also have the largest proportions of staff members who support a 'custodial' outlook. This holds for both the English and the American hospitals. Psychiatrists' views, in particular, tended to vary with the overall ranking of hospitals in terms of 'progressivism' which was discussed above.

A series of seven questions on open and closed wards showed that majorities of all occupations in *all* samples tended to favor open wards. Surprisingly, English respondents (who are most familiar with open wards) were generally less strongly in favor of them. It was felt that they might be expressing a more sober and realistic view of the pros and cons involved.

Why do ex-mental patients get rehospitalized? The 'most important' reason most frequently given was that the 'patient was not well enough to be released'. The next most common argument in the American samples was that the patient's 'family didn't try hard enough' while in England it was said that the 'patient was too used to being hospitalized'.

CHAPTER 9

Views on the vocational rehabilitation of former mental patients

The present chapter reports specific views on issues concerning the vocational rehabilitation of former mental patients. The following issues are discussed:

(a) Views on the discrepancy between vocational rehabilitation needs and facilities;
(b) Opinions on the greatest difficulties in the vocational rehabilitation of former mental patients;
(c) When should job planning for a mental patient best be started?
(d) Views on how best to help an ex-mental patient in finding a job;
(e) Should an ex-patient tell the employer about his hospitalization?
(f) Former mental patients believed most likely to succeed in their jobs.

VIEWS ON THE DISCREPANCY BETWEEN VOCATIONAL REHABILITATION NEEDS AND FACILITIES

Question 16 asked, 'In your opinion, about how many per cent of mental patients in your state *need* help in vocational rehabilitation? (Check ONE)

(a) very few (2% or less)
(b) few (about 15%)
(c) about a quarter (25%)
(d) about half (50%)
(e) most (more than 50%)
(f) all.'

Item 17 asked the complementary question, 'In your opinion, about how many per cent of mental patients in your state have *received* help in vocational rehabilitation? (Check ONE)

(a) very few (2% or less)
(b) few (about 15%)
(c) about a quarter (25%)
(d) about half (50%)
(e) most (more than 50%)
(f) all.'

The replies of the presumably best informed groups, i.e. of counselors, social workers and physicians are shown in Tables 78 and 79.

Table 78. *What proportion of mental patients in your state need help in vocational rehabilitation?* (in percentages)

	N	Very few (2% or less)	Few (about 15%)	About a quarter (25%)	About half (50%)	Most (more than 50%)	All	N/A
Border State								
R & E counselors	(13)	0	15	0	23	24	15	23
Social workers	(26)	4	8	19	23	35	4	7
Physicians	(13)	0	23	38	15	8	8	8
Hawaii								
R & E counselors	(18)	6	6	39	11	33	0	5
Social workers	(79)	3	15	28	15	37	1	1
Physicians	(26)	0	4	19	42	35	0	0
England								
Social workers	(19)	5	0	26	26	26	0	17
Physicians	(32)	6	9	38	10	34	0	3

There appears to be a discrepancy between the need of ex-mental patients for vocational rehabilitation services and the availability of such services. For instance, in Hawaii, 96% of the sampled physicians answered that one-quarter or more of all ex-mental patients in their state need help in vocational rehabilitation. Only 23% of the same physicians thought that one-quarter or more of the state's ex-mental patients have received such help. In the Atlantic border state, 69% of the physicians felt that at least one-quarter of ex-patients in the state need assistance in vocational rehabilitation. Only 8% of the same physicians felt that one-quarter or more of ex-patients in their state have been given such assistance. In England, on the other hand, where 82% of physicians stated that a need existed on this scale, 54% of the physicians felt this need had been met.

Among the sampled rehabilitation and employment counselors in the two states the results were as follows: In Hawaii, 83% noticed the need for services on this scale, and only 12% felt that the services have been provided. In the Atlantic border state, 62% of the sampled counselors stated the need for such vocational rehabilitation, and 16% of the same counselors expressed their belief that rehabilitation on this scale has been practiced.

Table 79. *What proportion of mental patients in your state have received help in vocational rehabilitation?* (in percentages)

	N	Very few (2% or less)	Few (about 15%)	About a quarter (25%)	About half (50%)	Most (more than 50%)	All	N/A
Border State								
R & E counselors	(13)	15	38	8	0	8	0	31
Social workers	(26)	23	50	12	4	0	0	11
Physicians	(13)	38	31	8	0	0	0	23
Hawaii								
R & E counselors	(18)	55	22	6	6	0	0	11
Social workers	(79)	35	42	13	4	1	1	4
Physicians	(26)	31	35	15	4	4	0	11
England								
Social workers	(19)	26	21	16	10	10	0	17
Physicians	(32)	6	34	25	10	16	3	6

Similar results were obtained for the other occupational groups. Among social workers, the comparative results were as shown in Table 80.

Table 80. *Social workers who felt at least one quarter of ex-mental patients need and have received help in vocational rehabilitation* (in percentages)

	Border state	Hawaii	England
(a) *Need help*	81	81	78
(b) Have *received* help	16	19	36
N	(26)	(79)	(19)

One may conclude that the specialists in the field find a serious discrepancy between the need of ex-mental patients for vocational rehabilitation and the services that have been provided.

WHAT ARE THE GREATEST DIFFICULTIES IN THE VOCATIONAL REHABILITATION OF FORMER MENTAL PATIENTS?

Question 30 inquired, 'In your opinion, what are the three *greatest* difficulties in the vocational rehabilitation of former mental patients? . . .
(a) weakness of the ex-patients
(b) reluctance of employers to hire ex-mental patients
(c) the patient's family doesn't understand him
(d) lack of program in the hospital
(e) lack of program among community mental health agencies
(f) most people in the community don't understand the problems of former mental patients.'

The first choices of the presumably most knowledgeable groups of counselors, social workers and physicians are presented in Table 81.

Table 81. *Sources of greatest difficulties in the vocational rehabilitation of former mental patients – first choices* (in percentages)

	N	Ex-patients	Employers	Family	Hospital	Mental health agencies	Community	N/A
Border State								
R & E counselors	(13)	23	38		8		31	
Social workers	(26)	4	58	4	15	8	11	
Physicians	(13)	16	39		15	15	15	
Hawaii								
R & E counselors	(18)	33	28	11	17		11	
Social workers	(79)	10	51	5	9	4	21	
Physicians	(26)	15	19		38	8	15	5
England								
Social workers	(19)	16	16	5	5	16	37	5
Physicians	(32)	25	12	6	3	6	28	20

In the American samples the primary difficulty was seen in the reluctance of employers to hire ex-mental patients. In England, on the other hand, the most frequent first selection was (f), lack of understanding by members of the general community. Other sources of difficulties that were chosen relatively frequently were (a) weakness of the ex-patients and (d) lack of program in the hospital.

WHEN SHOULD JOB PLANNING FOR A MENTAL PATIENT BEST BE STARTED?

This question was posed in item 28, and the following choices of answers were provided:
(a) with his admission to the hospital
(b) early in his treatment
(c) late in his treatment
(d) after his treatment has been completed.
Results are given in Table 82. They show that most of the counselors, social workers and physicians choose (b) and (c), i.e., early or late during the patient's treatment. Counselors in particular prefer job planning to start late in the treatment.

Table 82. *When should job planning for a mental patient best be started?* (in percentages)

	N	With his admission to the hospital	Early in his treatment	Late in his treatment	After his treatment has been completed	N/A
Border State						
R & E counselors	(13)	8	31	54		7
Social workers	(26)	8	58	23	11	
Physicians	(13)		46	38	17	
Hawaii						
R & E counselors	(18)	6	33	44	17	
Social workers	(79)	24	53	18	5	
Physicians	(26)	15	50	35		
England						
Social workers	(19)		32	47	21	
Physicians	(32)		28	60	9	3

VIEWS ON HOW BEST TO HELP AN EX-MENTAL PATIENT IN FINDING A JOB

Question 29 stated, 'When a released mental patient asks for help in finding a job, it would be best: (check ONE)
(a) to return him to his old job
(b) to find him first an easy job to get him used to regular work

(c) to delay his getting a job until it is fairly certain he can keep it
(d) to find him a new job as soon as possible
(e) to find him a new permanent job.'

Results for counselors, social workers and physicians may be seen on Table 83. In general, Americans tended to choose most frequently the 'springboard' view (b) of getting the ex-patient started on an easy job. The next most common choice was (a) to return him to his old job. (In England the popularity of these two choices was reversed.) Other relatively frequent choices were (c) to delay work until the ex-patient has a better chance of succeeding and (d) to find a new job as soon as possible. The least frequent choice was (e), 'to find him a new permanent job'.

Table 83. *When a released mental patient asks for help in finding a job, it would be best . . .* (in percentages)

	N	To return him to his old job	To find him first an easy job to get him used to regular work	To delay his getting a job until it is fairly certain he can keep it	To find him a new job as soon as possible	To find him a new permanent job	N/A
Border State							
R & E counselors	(13)	23	15	8	31	8	15
Social workers	(26)	19	19	35	23		4
Physicians	(13)	38	54			8	
Hawaii							
R & E counselors	(18)	28	33	22	6	11	
Social workers	(79)	25	32	28	6	9	
Physicians	(26)	27	31	15	19	8	
England							
Social workers	(19)	26	21	11	26	11	5
Physicians	(32)	35	31	19	3	6	6

SHOULD AN EX-PATIENT TELL THE EMPLOYER ABOUT HIS HOSPITALIZATION?

Question 27 in the instrument inquires: 'When a former mental patient is applying for a job, should he tell the employer about his hospitalization?

(a) Yes
(b) No.'

Grob and Olshansky (1958) in their study of employers in Massachusetts found that about three-quarters of their respondents stated a willingness to employ former mental patients, but only one-quarter reported having knowingly hired mental patients. Their finding does not necessarily mean that the one-half of their respondents (who said they would hire ex-patients but hadn't hired any) were hypocrites. It may well be that some of these employers had hired ex-patients who did not tell them about their hospitalization and that some of these employers were never approached by a self-admitted ex-patient. At any rate, there seems to be a widespread view that ex-mental patients' chances for employment are considerably reduced if they tell a potential employer about their former illness (see Ferguson, 1965 and Dightman and Marks, 1968). Considering this background, it would appear that the more sophisticated or better informed persons would give relatively most support to the 'realistic' negative answer and that the less informed or less educated respondents would tend to give relatively strongest support to the affirmative answer with its moralistic implications of honesty and straightforwardness. Table 84 presents the responses to the item.

With the exception of psychiatrists and psychologists in Hawaii, all respondent groups predominantly favor telling the employer of the hospitalization. Across hospitals, generally psychologists, psychiatrists, social workers and counselors provide the largest proportions of negative answers, which imply a realistic, or if one prefers, a cynical view of the employers' reactions to being told of former hospitalization. In all fairness, it should not be forgotten that the employers' concern is primarily with their company's efficiency and only secondarily with the humanitarian goal of helping ex-mental patients. The value conflicts involved were confirmed for the same question in the parallel study on the attitudes of community samples toward mental patients and toward their vocational rehabilitation, to be discussed in Part II. Social workers and counselors, of course, may be expected to be best informed about the realities of the situation facing a job-seeking ex-patient. Interestingly, though, the social workers and counselors at hospital Y, who were previously shown to differ widely from those at the other English hospital, here come out 100% for telling the employer.

The responses of aides, nurses and auxiliary therapists favored most strongly the 'moralistic' alternative of telling the employer about one's former hospitalization. As the traditional job function of these groups does not involve them to a large extent in the vocational rehabilitation of ex-mental patients, it might be more useful to attempt an explanation of their responses in terms of their general education and social background. For example, one may speculate that phenomena like the 'lower class authoritarianism' described by Lipset (1960) are involved in their preference for the relatively intolerant answer.

Table 84. *When a former mental patient is applying for a job, should he tell the employer about his hospitalization?* (in percentages)

	Hospital B				Hospital H			
	N	Yes	No	N/A	N	Yes	No	N/A
Aides	67	94	6		95	90	6	4
Nurses	61	90	8	2	92	91	7	2
O. and R. therapists	16	75	19	6	12	92	8	
Soc. workers and counselors	39	62	28	10	97	82	15	3
Psychiatrists	12	75	25		20	45	55	
Psychologists	8	63	37		15	47	53	
	Hospital X				**Hospital Y**			
	N	Yes	No	N/A	N	Yes	No	N/A
Aides	82	84	11	5	43	67	33	
Nurses	206	87	12	1	86	87	12	1
O. and R. therapists	14	93	7		8	100		
Soc. workers and counselors	25	60	36	4	9	100		
Psychiatrists	16	56	38	6	16	56	44	

Psychiatrists are relatively most responsible for the cure of patients. If concern for cure of patients and for getting them back on their feet is important for psychiatrists, and if this concern varies between 'conservative' and 'progressive' hospitals, it should be reflected in different degrees of emphasis shown in psychiatrists' responses to the question. This tends to be the case, as a comparison of the hospitals shows. In the 'conservative' institutions B and X, respectively 25% and 38% of psychiatrists state an ex-patient should not tell his employer. In the 'progressive' hospitals H and Y, respectively 55% and 44% of psychiatrists feel the same way.

FORMER MENTAL PATIENTS BELIEVED MOST LIKELY TO SUCCEED IN THEIR JOBS

A series of questions asked to 'check the kind of former mental patient you believe most likely to be successful in his job'.

In Chapter 7, responses in terms of 'white collar jobs' versus manual jobs and in terms of ethnicity were discussed. Question 20 provided these alternatives:
'Ex-patient's new job mostly:
(a) requires dealing with things
(b) requires dealing with people.'
Results are listed in Table 85. It appears that majorities of all occupational groups (except some aides) in the border state, in Hawaii and in England predict greater success for ex-patients who deal with *things.* The proportions of respondents who choose (b)

Table 85. *Ex-patient believed most likely to be successful in his job – if the new job mostly requires dealing with things or with people* (in percentages)

	(Number of respondents for tables 85 to 91)			If the new job mostly requires dealing with things		
	B	*Hawaii*	*England*	*B*	*Hawaii*	*England*
Aides	(67)	(95)	(125)	46	53	41
Nurses	(61)	(92)	(292)	62	84	63
O. and R. therapists	(16)	(12)	(22)	75	83	50
Social workers	(26)	(79)	(19)	81	95	63
R & E counselors	(13)	(18)	–	62	88	–
Physicians	(13)	(26)	(32)	85	88	84
Psychologists	(8)	(15)	–	100	93	–

	If the new job mostly requires dealing with people			Both or N/A		
	B	*Hawaii*	*England*	*B*	*Hawaii*	*England*
Aides	49	36	26	4	11	32
Nurses	36	13	21	2	3	16
O. and R. therapists	19	17	32	6	0	18
Social workers	12	4	16	8	1	21
R & E counselors	0	6	–	38	6	–
Physicians	8	8	3	8	4	12
Psychologists	0	0	–	0	7	–

dealing with people, tends to decrease as one goes up the educational ladder.

Question 18 related vocational success to sex of the ex-patient (see Table 86). Majorities in all occupational groups predicted more success to male ex-patients. This finding may be related to general attitudes toward the roles of the sexes in the community and especially in working life. There may be an underlying expectation that in Western societies men do not have the alternative of a household to fall back on and that male ex-patients may thus experience a stronger need and motivation to succeed in a job.

In Question 19, vocational success was to be judged according to the ex-patient's age as follows:

(a) below 20
(b) 20 - 29
(c) 30 - 39
(d) 40 - 49
(e) 50 - 59
(f) above 59

Replies of counselors, social workers and physicians are shown in Table 87. Greatest likelihood of success was predicted for ex-patients between 20 and 39 years of age, especially for those in their thirties. The next most favored groups are ex-patients below twenty and in their forties. The outlook is least optimistic for ex-patients fifty years old or older.

Question 22 contrasted the ex-patient who (a) has to compete with his fellow workers, with the one who (b) works independently.

The results on Table 88 indicate that by far most respondents are more optimistic about the success of ex-patients who work independently. Not a single rehabilitation or employment counselor believed the ex-patient who competes with his fellow workers would be more likely to succeed.

In Question 23, chances for success were to be assigned to ex-patients who in their new jobs:

(a) supervise others,
(b) take orders from others, and
(c) neither supervise nor take orders.

Findings are tabulated in Table 89. Hardly any respondents chose (a); none of the rehabilitation and employment counselors did so. Most respondents felt that the most successful ex-patients would either hold jobs where they neither supervise nor take orders, or

Table 86. *Ex-patient believed most likely to be successful in his job – by sex* (in percentages)

	Female			*Male*			*N/A*			*Both*		
	B	Hawaii	England	B	Hawaii	England	B	Hawaii	England	B	Hawaii	England
Aides	27	18	31	66	72	33	4	7	32	3	3	4
Nurses	21	30	13	79	59	62	0	4	22	0	7	3
O. and R. therapists	38	17	9	62	75	73	0	8	14	0	0	4
Social workers	15	22	16	69	71	63	12	5	21	4	2	0
R & E counselors	0	22	–	69	61	–	31	17	–	0	0	–
Physicians	8	19	22	69	81	53	8	0	19	15	0	6
Psychologists	0	7	–	88	87	–	12	6	–	0	0	–

Table 87. *Ex-patient believed most likely to be successful in job – by age* (in percentages)

	N	Age: -20	20-29	30-39	40-49	50-59	59+	N/A or mixed
Border State								
R & E counselors	(13)		15	54	8			23
Social workers	(26)	15	38	19	15			13
Physicians	(13)	23	8	31	23		7	8
Hawaii								
R & E counselors	(18)	22	39	22				17
Social workers	(79)	17	34	41		1		7
Physicians	(26)		27	46	19	4		4
England								
Social workers	(19)	5	16	32	10	5		32
Physicians	(32)		25	28	28	3	3	13

Table 88. *Ex-patient believed most likely to be successful in his job if he has to compete or works independently* (in percentages)

	Ex-patient has to compete with his fellow workers			Ex-patient works independently		
	B	*Hawaii*	*England*	*B*	*Hawaii*	*England*
Aides	36	28	20	53	63	48
Nurses	28	5	24	69	93	61
O. and R. therapists	25	8	27	75	92	59
Social workers	12	6	10	85	90	79
R & E counselors	0	0	–	69	94	–
Physicians	31	8	6	69	92	88
Psychologists	0	20	–	100	80	–

	N/A			Both		
	B	*Hawaii*	*England*	*B*	*Hawaii*	*England*
Aides	4	9	30	7	0	2
Nurses	2	2	14	1	0	1
O. and R. therapists	0	0	14	0	0	0
Social workers	3	3	11	0	1	0
R & E counselors	31	6	–	0	0	–
Physicians	0	0	6	0	0	0
Psychologists	0	0	–	0	0	–

Table 89. *Ex-patient believed most likely to be successful in his job if he supervises, takes orders or does neither* (in percentages)

	Supervises others			Takes orders from others		
	B	*Hawaii*	*England*	*B*	*Hawaii*	*England*
Aides	6	6	4	66	57	38
Nurses	5	2	6	39	39	40
O. and R. therapists	0	8	0	44	42	46
Social workers	4	1	5	15	27	21
R & E counselors	0	0	–	23	11	–
Physicians	0	8	3	54	23	47
Psychologists	0	0	–	37	33	–

	Neither supervises nor takes orders			Both or N/A		
	B	*Hawaii*	*England*	*B*	*Hawaii*	*England*
Aides	24	21	28	4	16	30
Nurses	46	51	34	10	8	20
O. and R. therapists	38	33	41	18	17	13
Social workers	69	68	47	12	4	27
R & E counselors	46	83	–	31	6	–
Physicians	46	65	41	0	4	9
Psychologists	63	67	–	0	0	–

where they only take orders from others. Majorities of the counselors were most optimistic about former patients who neither supervise nor take orders.

Finally, questions 24 and 25 related job success to income before and after illness. Table 90 shows that among four income groups vocational success was in general considered most likely for the group which had the lowest income before the onset of illness. Table 91 indicates that similarly, success in their jobs is relatively most often believed to come to those who are in the lowest of four income groups after their illness.

As will be pointed out in Part II, employers and employees in the Eastern state, in Hawaii and in England are most willing to accept ex-patients in jobs which require least responsibility and which presumably are associated with the lowest income group.

Table 90. *Ex-patient believed most likely to be successful in job – by yearly income before illness* (in percentages)

	N	$ -4,000	4,000 -6,000	6,000 -8,000	8,000+	N/A
Border State						
R & E counselors	(13)	23	8	31	8	30
Social workers	(26)	23	15	15	31	16
Physicians	(13)	62	15		15	8
Hawaii						
R & E counselors	(18)	39	22	11		28
Social workers	(79)	30	23	19	19	9
Physicians	(26)	31	10	15	27	17
	N	£ -800	801 -1,200	1,201 -1,600	1,600+	N/A
England						
Social workers	(19)	58	11		5	26
Physicians	(32)	47	16		19	18

Table 91. *Ex-patient believed most likely to be successful in job – by yearly income after illness* (in percentages)

	N	$ -4,000	4,000 -6,000	6,000 -8,000	8,000+	N/A
Border State						
R & E counselors	(13)	38		15	15	32
Social workers	(26)	19	19	4	42	16
Physicians	(13)	62	23		8	7
Hawaii						
R & E counselors	(18)	50	22	6	6	16
Social workers	(79)	28	34	10	18	10
Physicians	(26)	23	19	19	27	12
	N	£ -800	801 -1,200	1,201 -1,600	1,600+	N/A
England						
Social workers	(19)	53	10		5	32
Physicians	(32)	41	12	3	22	22

SUMMARY

What proportion of former mental patients *need* help in vocational rehabilitation? What proportion have *received* such help? Replies to these two questions showed a striking discrepancy between the need which was felt to exist and the limited help that has been provided in the American areas sampled.

What are the greatest difficulties in the vocational rehabilitation of ex-mental patients? American counselors, social workers and physicians tended to point most frequently at the reluctance of employers to hire ex-mental patients. English social workers and physicians tended to place most emphasis on the lack of understanding by the general community.

When should job planning for a mental patient best be started? Early or late during his treatment in the hospital, according to most counselors, social workers and physicians. Counselors tended to prefer a start late in the treatment process.

How could one best help an ex-patient who looks for a job? The most frequent answers were, 'to find him first an easy job to get him used to regular work' and 'to return him to his old job'. Only few respondents felt that one should 'find him a new permanent job'.

When a former mental patient applies for a job, should he tell the employer about his hospitalization? 'Yes', is the answer predominantly chosen. However, relatively large proportions of psychiatrists and psychologists doubt the advisability of passing on this information.

A series of questions asked for identification of the kind of former mental patient believed most likely to succeed in his job. Majorities felt:

(1) that successful ex-patients would hold jobs which require them to deal with things rather than with people,
(2) that male ex-patients would be more likely to succeed than female ex-patients,
(3) that the ages most favorable for vocational success of ex-patients were the twenties and especially the thirties,
(4) that success was more likely for ex-patients who work independently than for ex-patients who have to compete with their fellow workers,
(5) that little success was to be expected for ex-patients who supervise others, and that the outlook was better for ex-patients who

neither supervise nor take orders or who only take orders, and

(6) that vocational success was thought to be most likely for ex-patients who belonged to the lowest income group before their illness and

(7) for those who belong to the lowest income group after their illness.

CHAPTER 10

Variables influencing attitudes of mental health workers

Chapters 5 through 9 summarized major findings of the study which were obtained by the different scales and questions. The following discussion will attempt to show the relative effects of different variables on the attitudes under consideration.

In the first chapter, the argument was advanced that the attitudes of mental health personnel toward mental illness, mental patients and their rehabilitation are influenced by an interplay of factors. The discussion of the findings has shown that different results can be best explained by different factors in varying degrees or by different combinations of factors. There might be a certain appeal of simplicity if the results could be accounted for uniformly by one explanatory principle or if one single factor were seen as triumphant over other factors. It is unfortunate for a parsimonious view that the data do not lend themselves to this concise or simple explanation.* Rather, they seem to require an explanation which takes into consideration the complexity of the samples, their range of occupations, of hospitals, and of cultural settings. The primary concern should be to do justice to the facts found.

The selection of the samples from different settings invited complex results. In one sense, the investigation may be seen as self-corrective, like a sequence of several studies. Thus, Hollingshead and Redlich's (1958) or Cohen and Struening's (1959; 1960; 1962) conclusions might explain the findings in the East coast sample. As one proceeds to the Hawaiian sample, however, the data are often seen as requiring additional explanation which calls new factors into

* In Chapter 2, Gilbert and Levinson's unidimensional interpretation of attitudes of mental health personnel was rejected in favor of a multifactorial approach.

play. The British data frequently go beyond the now present assembly of factors and open a still wider perspective.

The study ranged not only over these sampling regions, but it also employed different techniques. One may suppose that if one had taken only one single scale, the resulting data might have been interpreted in a comparatively clearcut fashion. The use of different scales and of items on various topics provoked more complex results. To some extent the situation is similar to that which would have been obtained if another instrument with new questions had been given to the same samples under the same conditions.

In this study, the respondent who professionally works with mental patients is perceived as belonging to a specific occupation with its special training and functions vis-à-vis the patient, to a specific hospital setting and to a cultural setting. These factors will next be viewed separately. Some attention will be given to the conditions under which a given variable plays a dominant role.

VARIATION BY OCCUPATION

The first characteristic which distinguishes the samples of this study from the general population is the subjects' work with mental patients and presumably their self-selection for this kind of work. Earlier research, notably that of Cohen and Struening (1959; 1960; 1962), has shown that attitudes toward mental illness vary with the respondents' occupation. It may be worthwhile to consider what underlying factors are implied in the 'occupation' of mental health workers. Cohen and Struening noted that attitudinal responses are influenced not only by occupation, but by amount of education as well, and that the two factors run largely parallel. One may go further and note that status in the occupational hierarchy implies socio-economic class background. Hollingshead and Redlich's (1958) work has shown the class-relatedness of psychiatric preferences among patients. Education involves not only the general amount of schooling received but also exposure to professional and pre-professional training, as e.g. in a pre-medical course. Membership in an occupation implies not only certain general and professional training and socio-economic status but also specific responsibilities and job functions vis-à-vis the mental patient.

Three major occupational groups could be distinguished in terms of job functions. First, the nursing personnel – aides and nurses – and the auxiliary therapists, who are generally in daily and relatively routinized contact with patients on the wards or in occupational and recreational therapy. Second, the social workers and vocational counselors whose role consists in mediating between and in helping the patient in the transition from the hospital to the community. Finally, the group of psychiatrists and psychologists play a predominant role in the active treatment and diagnosis of the patients. Their concern is not with maintaining peace and order on a ward but with leading patients into new forms of behavior. In some instances it was possible to explain attitudinal differences by reference to these three occupational clusters, and sometimes a unidimensional progression of scores was found with increasing occupational-educational status.

Frequently, however, it was necessary to look at the six occupational groups separately. For example, one might contrast nurses and aides, whose educational and class background is dissimilar even if their hospital functions overlap to some extent. Among the various occupations, aides were said to have been least exposed to psychiatric theories and in some respects to have been least indoctrinated by specific hospital ideologies. Correspondingly, the attitudes of aides were expected to have retained and to reflect most strongly traditional popular views on the subject of mental illness. At the same time, it should be remembered that aides are a self-selected group in a somewhat unusual job and that their attitudes cannot be taken automatically to stand for popular attitudes in general. Aides or attendants, across samples, tended to show a relatively strong support for 'custodial' views as compared to the responses of other occupational groups. Aides generally assigned little importance to the effect of environmental factors in the causation of mental illness. Psychiatrists, at the other extreme, have the greatest say in setting the hospital's policies and were found to reflect these policies most strongly. Psychiatrists were usually at or near the top of their hospitals in the rehabilitation scale scores (see Chapter 5).

Hollingshead and Redlich (1958) suggested that psychiatrists tend to prefer work with middle class patients. The question was asked whether members of other occupations prefer to work with patients from class backgrounds similar to their own. This question was answered generally in the affirmative. Ease in working with patients from various socio-economic backgrounds was found to be somewhat related to respondents' perception of their own class membership.

Within limitations imposed by culture and traditions, Hollingshead and Redlich's views on psychiatric attitudes can thus be extended beyond their New Haven setting. They were well supported in the East coast hospital B, somewhat less in Hawaii and still less in England.

Quite generally, the findings made it possible to say that workers in the mental health occupations have preferences and dislikes among mental patients. Two-way analyses of variance for the semantic differentials were highly significant for occupations across hospitals. The semantic differentials dealt with the most and least liked patients. The rehabilitation scale was concerned with attitudes toward mental illness, mental patients in general and their rehabilitation. For this less personal scale, the two-way analysis of variance showed variation among hospitals to account for greater attitudinal differences than variation among occupations. The conclusion was reached that occupation – with its social, educational and other implications – plays an important role in affecting the attitudes studied, but that its effect is modified by the hospital and cultural settings.

VARIATION BETWEEN HOSPITALS

Gilbert and Levinson (1957a) investigated the effects of hospital policy on staff attitudes and concluded that policies and attitudes are correlated. In the present study, hospitals varied not only by their policies but also in their cultural and national settings. Although in the United States and in England both there was one relatively 'conservative' and one more 'progressive' hospital and some attitudinal variations were found between these hospitals, the variations were found primarily at the level of psychiatrists, i.e. of the occupational group which has greatest influence on setting the hospitals' policies. Other occupations were much less affected by the institutional policies. Gilbert and Levinson's (1957a) conclusion putting different hospital and occupational groups in one unidimensional sequence correlated with attitudes was not supported.

Overall comparisons were made of the effects of occupations and of hospitals on attitudes. On the rehabilitation scale and its subscales, variance due to 'hospital' exceeded variance connected with occupation. On the semantic differentials, which deal less with policies and general views and more with individual preferences among patients, occupation was found to be more important than hospital in the analyses of variance. In these computations, however, hospitals varied not only in their policies but in other respects as well. Cultural differences due to the hospital's geographical locations were also involved and will be discussed below. The possibility may be considered whether an analysis of variance should be performed which would contrast hospital policy with country (England v. United States). It was felt, however, that while for each country one relatively 'progressive' and one comparatively 'conservative' institution was included in the sample, the hospitals varied not only by policy and by nationality. For one thing, although the two British institutions were serving adjoining areas which included parts of the same county, the American hospitals were separated by a continent and several thousand miles of ocean. The Hawaiian and the Eastern American samples differed strongly in cultural traditions and in historical background but no comparable differences could be found within England. Furthermore, the hospitals varied also in other ways, e.g., in their discharge rates, in the proportion of open wards, and in the employment of ex-patients. If one were dealing here with two relatively 'pure' dimensions, as in an experiment, a 2 by 2 table or analysis of variance (for hospital 'progressiveness' v. country) might have been very enlightening. As the 'cultural' and 'hospital policy' parameters were thus seen as fairly complex, it was feared that analysis of variance might be somewhat misleading. It was therefore decided not to perform an analysis of variance on hospital policy v. geographic setting. However, throughout the evaluation of the results, all tables were reviewed with the consideration in mind of which findings could be explained in terms of hospital characteristics and which in terms of cultural background.

One particular instance of how hospital policies affect attitudes could be tested in the British hospital X. This institution had a long-established reputation for being 'conservative', but within the year before the field study, a new superintendent with a 'progressive' outlook had tried to bring about rapid reforms. The transitional status of this hospital was reflected in unusually large standard deviations.

Hospital policy was found to have a certain limited connection with staff attitudes. The relation seemed to be strongest for psychiatrists, that is for the occupational group which has the largest say in determining policies. Among the different questionnaire scales and items, hospital 'progressivism' or lack of it was most reflected in questions concerning general issues, e.g., the item on the chief function of a mental hospital, or the rehabilitation scale. In the hospitals studied and presumably in most institutions in the two countries, the less trained an occupation is in psychiatric thinking, the more its members tend to reflect popular preconceptions concerning mental illness. This does not mean that policies need necessarily be ineffective below the higher occupational levels. In a model hospital and in the future, it may well be possible, for instance, to educate hospital aides to see mental patients in a more psychiatric perspective and to get personally more involved in their treatment. In the present study, not only hospital policies and practices were shown to have some effect on staff attitudes, but also the sociocultural setting and the respondents' occupational background.

VARIATION BY CULTURAL SETTING

At the outset of this study, it was argued that the attitudes of professionals in the mental health field would vary not only with their occupational and institutional background, but that the professionals must also be considered as members of the society in which they grew up, went to school and of which they continue to be members. Sociocultural factors were said in Chapter 1 to be related to the symptomatology of mental illness and were hypothesized to be also related to attitudes toward mental illness.

In the samples used, cultural variation existed both between hospitals (England versus United States) and to some extent within a hospital (the Hawaiian institution). Sociocultural factors might be related to ethnic variation – as in Hawaii –, historical continuity, as in the internationally contrasted hospitals, or fairly recent events – such as the social changes in England reflected in, e.g., National Health Service legislation.

When the English and the American hospitals were compared, some specific differences were found between the attitudes of the two national samples. In part, these differences were attributed to historical and traditional factors, in part to recent developments. Overall, the findings showed the samples in both countries to overlap considerably in their views. In some questions, culture clearly outweighed hospital policy, in others it did not. An example of English consistency across hospitals and occupations – in contrast to the American subjects – was the relatively greater priority attached to heredity and the smaller emphasis put on environment in causing mental disorders. On the semantic differentials, the British respondents tended to show more tolerance of 'non-conformist' patients than their American colleagues did. Other instances of international attitude variations were found.

Another major effect of cultural variation on attitudes was noted within the Hawaiian sample. In this sample, a number of statistically significant differences were found between the workers of oriental and of Caucasian descent. These differences were typically strongest in the two occupations least exposed to higher professional training, that is, among aides and nurses. As acculturation takes its course in Hawaii, these differences may be expected to diminish. Interestingly, the responses of white Hawaiians tended to fall between those of oriental Hawaiians and of the other American sample. It was speculated that there might be some mutual cultural assimilation between whites and orientals. Very little antagonism toward either orientals or Caucasians was shown by respondents of the other ethnic group.

In summary it appeared that the less formal training a respondent had received, the stronger were the effects of cultural traditions on his attitudes. By proposing this general relationship, it is not meant to say that professional training by necessity will wipe out the effects of a professional's cultural and social background on his attitudes, but rather that this background would play a less influential role. As Klineberg (1950) has pointed out, national characteristics need not be unimodally distributed but can form a bimodal distribution, particularly in a culture in transition. Inkeles and Levinson (1954) similarly argued that within a national group characteristics might be dispersed in multimodal fashion. Even in the relatively mild cultural variations between England, the American mainland, and Hawaii, it was found that cultural and historical factors have some bearing on attitudes toward mental illness. It is expected that culture would play an even greater role if attitudes were compared in more diverse cultural settings.

INTERPLAY OF FACTORS AFFECTING ATTITUDES OF MENTAL HEALTH WORKERS

Just one example will be recalled here to demonstrate interaction of variables. When Hawaiian respondents were asked whether they found work easier with oriental or white patients, their responses appeared to be most adequately explained by an interaction of occupational functions, of traditional cultural roles, and only partly by a preference for their own ethnic group. Throughout the study, the multiplicity of influences on attitudes was stressed. Some seeming inconsistencies in the responses of a group should be seen in the light of the different techniques used and of the different topics that were presented. Diverse issues and items might have called forth in a respondent to a greater or lesser extent his professional training or experience, his personal predilections, or his wider socio-cultural background. For example, little relation was found between the subjects' choices of the kind of patient they found it easiest to work with and the patients they expected to be most successful in future employment.

This study set out to discover whether any one of the factors proposed in the literature is of overriding importance in determining attitudes toward mental patients or whether an interplay of factors would best account for the findings. In the writer's opinion, the results presented above did not encourage a simple overall explanation; the data appeared not to be reducible to a unidimensional continuum. Instead, it was attempted to do justice to the findings through a multifactorial explanation. Some of the interpretations were tentative; to test their adequacy, further data from additional samples should be collected.

The findings of this investigation showed mental health workers to respond in terms of their occupational background which becomes effective within an institutional setting that in turn exists within a socio-cultural matrix. The intent of this study was to find out how attitudes are affected by different dimensions in this wider perspective.

SUMMARY

Relative effects of different variables on attitudes toward mental illness and mental patients were discussed. Occupation – with its social, educational and other implications – was found to play an important role in affecting the attitudes studied. This effect was modified by policies and by other hospital characteristics. Cultural factors also were shown to influence attitudes significantly when English and American hospitals were contrasted. It was concluded that to do justice to the found attitudes of mental health personnel, one has to think of an interplay of factors.

CHAPTER 11

Recommendations for research and rehabilitation

RECOMMENDATIONS FOR FURTHER RESEARCH

The problems involved in the vocational rehabilitation of former mental patients are not unique to the United States and England. How have other societies been dealing with these common problems? What can be learned from their experiences? Which of their practices are applicable to American or British conditions? Here is an important field for future research.

The present study has shown the feasibility of a cross-cultural study of attitudes toward mental patients and their rehabilitation. As cultural factors were found to affect attitudes even within comparatively similar English-speaking samples, it might be fruitful to extend future sampling to non-English-speaking areas so as to see how members of more diverse cultures view mental illness and mental patients. To collect data for such research, care should be taken to develop instruments which are biased as little as possible by the investigators' cultural background.

Of considerable practical interest would be an inquiry into the experiences and views of former mental patients themselves. A number of ex-patients were interviewed in England as a part of the background for the present project. In what ways do the views of ex-patients differ from those of the community and from those of the mental health workers whose function it is to restore them to society? Which attitudes are seen as helpful and realistic by the former patients? One might mention that Giovannoni and Ullmann (1963) compared hospitalized mental patients with a matched sample of non-patients and found no differences in their attitudes toward the mentally ill.

What effects have attitudes of experts and of members of the general community on mental patients and on their rehabilitation? Some objective criteria might be set up, and various attitudes could be correlated with the criteria.

In the present study it was found that mental health personnel tend to assign the best chances for vocational success to ex-patients who are manual rather than white collar workers, to men rather than to women, to persons in non-competitive jobs, to ex-patients who deal with things rather than with people, and to individuals who do not supervise others. Some of these findings are corroborated in the study of attitudes of employers and employees reported in Part II of this volume. These respondents saw ex-patients as being more successful in jobs with little responsibility than in more responsible positions. Since the mental health personnel in our study were not asked to express their attitudes but rather their guesses on the success of ex-patients, we do not know to what extent their statements reflect the real situation or the respondents' own belief that mental patients may not be fit for more demanding jobs. Additional research might determine whether the mental health personnel's expectations for less vocational success reflect prejudice encountered by ex-patients or less ability of former patients to hold certain positions.

Intensive work should be done to determine ways in which members of the different mental health occupations can play optimal roles in the vocational rehabilitation of former mental patients.

How can attitudes toward mental patients be changed? An experiment might be run with four matched groups of one mental health occupation. Different groups could be (a) exposed to a specific educational program, (b) given no instruction, but experience with mental patients under specified conditions, (c) given both education and specified experience, and (d) a control group might be exposed to neither the experience nor specific education. Attitudes and behavior toward mental patients could be measured again after a given period of time. Variations of this suggested study could be readily developed. For example, the roles played by members of a given mental health profession might be systematically varied.

The point here is that to evaluate recent theories and practices in mental hospital operation and staff functions one need not rely on their proponents' claims nor on overall conclusions resulting from the simultaneous introduction of various new techniques. Contemporary social science research is capable of testing by experimental methods specific therapeutic or rehabilitative practices, and of providing objective data which allow comparisons of the effects of various techniques. This is one of the ways in which social research can contribute to the understanding and alleviation of the problems faced by mental patients in their search for rehabilitation.

RECOMMENDATIONS FOR THE VOCATIONAL REHABILITATION OF MENTAL PATIENTS

The relevance of attitudes for the perception of mental patients was discussed in Chapter 1. There is little doubt that many members of the general population have a picture of former mental patients which is at least partially characterized by distrust and apprehension. This might be expected of persons who have little or no experience or formal training in the area of mental illness. The question may be asked, however, whether mental health personnel are free from unprofessional biases when they perceive mental patients.

Before looking more closely at the attitudes of mental health personnel, it may be appropriate to consider the position of a former mental patient in society. In a rural static society, a mentally ill person, if he is not entirely excluded from the community, may be absorbed with comparative ease in the extended family's home and farm to engage in some kind of work which he is able to do. Some eccentricities of behavior might be considered irrelevant in, say, a shepherd. In modern industrialized societies with crowded urban living the mentally ill pose more of a problem. They are often hospitalized not so much because of their symptoms but because no one in a small family is both able and willing to take care of them. Once the patient is 'put away', he is placed in a position of being discriminated against. He finds himself without civil rights. In a conflict of views with, for example, a hospital attendant, the patient's word usually is not taken seriously. He is in short considered to be not fully human.

How can such a person make a come-back? Will he be seen as capable of rehabilitation or as a hopeless case? The answer involves not only members of the community and of the immediate family. The road back to normal life as a fully recognized citizen starts in the hospital. The social workers and vocational counselors are an important connecting link between hospital and community. Therefore, one may ask: What are the attitudes of the mental health personnel? Are they directed toward the recovery and subsequent rehabilitation of the patient?

If in an industrialized society's labor market supply exceeds demand ex-mental patients are apt to be especially hard hit. American vocational rehabilitation counselors report that the placement of these persons is exceptionally difficult. In England, where all companies above a certain size have to hire a given quota of handicapped persons, ex-mental patients are frequently left out as least desirable. It is understandable that many modern employers, unlike the owner of a family farm, may hesitate to offer work to someone who only recently was excluded from society and who may be feared to involve the employer in a risk of damage, danger or the firm's reputation.

If such reluctance is found among employers, it may be partly explained by their lack of knowledge. Are the attitudes of mental health personnel more positive toward mental patients and their rehabilitation? Are these attitudes realistic? Are they consistent? Should and could they be changed?

Our results indicate that mental health personnel both felt a need for more extensive vocational rehabilitation services and showed a certain readiness to acknowledge the importance of rehabilitation. For example, majorities of the samples felt that the primary goal of the hospital staff should be 'to rehabilitate the patients into society' rather than just 'to cure the patients of their illness'. Also, majorities of all occupations stated that the chief function of a mental hospital is 'to return the patients to society' rather than to 'protect' either patients or society.

On the rehabilitation scale and its subscales, the averages for all hospitals and occupational groups were in the direction considered favorable to mental patients, although there was much individual and inter-group variation. This scale involved mostly general issues. When, however, the questions dealt less with general issues and more with specific matters, the attitudes were not always so favorable. The average scores for all occupational groups in the four hospitals indicated preferences for the least eccentric patients. Many of the respondents, especially aides and nurses, stated that they most enjoyed working with poorly educated, old, submissive, and dependent patients. Workers who express such a preference may find it easy to work with senile or custodial patients. One may ask, however, whether such an attitude would facilitate the treatment and future rehabilitation of other patients who might be expected to leave the hospital. Attitudes which are very appropriate for one type of patient may be inappropriate for other kinds of patients.

Several practical questions arise. What are the traditional functions and goals of the mental health occupations as they have been defined historically in their cultural settings? Is the traditional occupational training experienced by different groups, notably aides and nurses, suitable for the demands currently made on these occupations? What, if any, are the attitudes toward rehabilitation which are instilled in trainees for these positions? Do they realistically match the changing job functions and the needs for vocational rehabilitation? The Cummings (1957) showed that a quick exposure to mental hygiene indoctrination did not change attitudes appreciably. The present study found that policies set at the hospitals' top administrative levels had but little effect at the level of ward personnel, that is, of the staff members who have by far the most frequent daily contact with the patients. It is not intended here to put the blame on the already overworked hospital administrators for not educating their nursing personnel more thoroughly in a rehabilitation outlook.

Rather, the point is that in order to maximize the future rehabilitation of patients, ways and means should be found so that a concerted effort in this direction could start at the ward level beginning from the day when the patient enters the hospital. Overcrowded hospitals and chronic staff shortages can *explain* why there is room for improvement, but they should not distract from the *need* for purposeful changes.

If a hospital administration feels that it would like to pave the way for a more successful adjustment of ex-patients, then it can not take for granted that the spirit of new policies will *eo ipso* filter down to all personnel. It will not be sufficient to establish new policies, but the attitudes and the assumptions on which policies are based must be shared by personnel on all levels. Active efforts are required to implement the new purpose. Continuous education, information, and examples might demonstrate what the hospital staff can and should do to facilitate the patients' rehabilitation. It is unlikely that the change from a custodial to a rehabilitation approach could be sustained without a change in attitudes. That attitude changes can be brought about by education was suggested by the differential responses of groups with different professional training. It may be recalled that in Hawaii the more highly trained subjects tended to lose increasingly the traditional perceptions of mental illness of their respective cultural groups.

It may also be remembered that many hospital workers, for instance, aides, do not have extensive psychiatric knowledge. To impress upon them the therapeutic potential of their position, it is insufficient to pass on to them some vague noble-sounding declarations. It would seem to be potentially more fruitful to combine statements of aims with specific recommendations that make sense in practical behavior. Attempts should be made to translate 'progressive' aims into terms of the respondents' own purposes and job satisfactions. Some explorations could be made in this direction.

Unlike psychiatrists and social workers who may receive some information about ex-patients, the nursing personnel usually do not learn what becomes of patients after they are released. Possibly these staff members might become personally more involved in the future of their patients if they deliberately were given some feedback on what happens to their ex-patients. Another possibility might be mentioned. This study found that regardless of their general expressions on the subject of mental illness and of rehabilitation, many mental health workers show preferences for certain types of patients. It might be a practicable improvement to assign some staff members, for instance, to chronic wards if such persons prefer work with passive and dependent patients (as shown, e.g., by the semantic differentials). This comment is not meant to contradict the argument for changes of attitudes but rather to supplement it by reassignment of some staff members to positions for which their views may make them more suited.

It is urged here to support progressive ideals of patient treatment with practical measures that follow from a realistic perception of what the hospital and its personnel can do within limitations of budget and of staff size. A striking contrast exists between highly reputed model institutions with generous endowments and good staff-patient ratios and on the other hand the big publicly financed mental hospitals. The view is getting more widely accepted that there will be no sudden abundance of psychiatrists and psychiatric nurses in public hospitals, but that their shortage will continue and that other workers like aides should correspondingly receive preparation for wider responsibilities and a larger role in treatment than they have officially been holding in the past. When our respondents were asked, 'what is the most pressing need in the treatment of mental patients?' the most frequent answers involved staff attitudes and lack of personnel.

The above discussion has mostly focussed on the nursing staff, particularly on aides, as their expressed views tended relatively least to reflect a rehabilitation approach. However, it is not meant that the attitudes and job roles of other occupations are perfect and that these occupations could not benefit by a redefinition of their job functions and by corresponding reeducation which might facilitate the rehabilitation of former patients.

One of the findings of this study was that in spite of their work with and presumed expertise on mental patients, the respondents' attitudes are still influenced by their socio-cultural background. Even in England, where hospital doors have been generally opened, the staff attitudes overlapped considerably with those of American hospitals which have started only more recently to open their doors. It is one of the hopeful outcomes of this investigation that purposeful training and experience can overcome some traditional popular views which are directed against an acceptance of mental patients.

The mental health personnel are only part of the rehabilitation picture. Even their most well-intentioned efforts are limited in their effectiveness by the community's attitudes. It is important that the general public acquires a more factual picture of what are the risks and the rewards involved in the employment of former mental patients.

As Pratt, Scott, *et al.* (1960) stated, not only are mental hospital workers influenced by the community they come from, but they in turn can participate in changing the attitudes of the wider community.

Part I of this study closes with a plea to find ways for mental health personnel to maximize their ability to prepare patients for rehabilitation.

PART II

Community attitudes toward mental illness and mental patients

By

MARISA ZAVALLONI

International Center for Intergroup Relations
École Pratique des Hautes Études at the Sorbonne
University of Geneva

and

ALEXANDER ASKENASY

CHAPTER 12

Introduction

WHAT ARE THE POPULAR VIEWS OF MENTAL ILLNESS?

Part I of this volume dealt with the attitudes of mental health workers toward mental patients. Part II will deal with the views held by members of the working public.

In the literature, there is far from general agreement on the nature of popular attitudes toward mental patients (Halpert, 1965, 1969; Rabkin, 1972). On the one hand, it has been repeatedly found that the general public regards mental patients with fear, distrust and dislike. This 'pessimistic' view of mental illness has been supported by a number of studies (Cumming and Cumming, 1957; Joint Commission, 1961; Philips, 1964, 1966; Rosen, 1970; Star, 1956; Tereshima, 1969; Tringo, 1970). On the other hand, there are researchers who feel that the public is well disposed toward the mentally ill, and they in turn present research evidence to support their view (Bentz and Edgerton, 1971; Crocetti, Spiro and Siassi, 1971; Lemkau and Crocetti, 1962; Meyer, 1964).

In addition to these two contradictory views, one author has suggested that not only is there a strong negative halo associated with the mentally ill, but also that attitudes toward mental illness tend to be highly inconsistent so that people frequently either agree with inconsistent opinion statements or fail to agree with apparently consistent statements (Nunnally, 1961).

AIMS OF THE STUDY

This study attempts to answer three general questions. First, whether a 'pessimistic' or an 'optimistic' view on mental patients can be confirmed, second, whether inconsistent attitudes exist, and third, if this should be the case, how the inconsistency can be accounted for.

In addition to this probing of general orientations toward mental patients, some specific issues related to their employment will be investigated. Special emphasis will be given to popular expectations of the occupational performance of released mental patients. Such expectations can explicitly or implicitly limit the opportunities for employment and the levels of attainment open to ex-mental patients.

An attempt will be made to distinguish the cognitive component of popular notions of mental illness from attitudes. Another question to be considered is: Does the public perceive mental illness as a general undifferentiated entity or does it recognize distinct types and degrees of mental disorder?

The study was conducted in three areas, 1) the state of Delaware, 2) Southeastern England and 3) the state of Hawaii. The three areas will be identified henceforth as border state, England and Hawaii. Since this study has been conducted across cultures, it will be possible to ask if the conclusions can be generalized cross-culturally. For instance, American mainland data show that educational and occupational variables are consistently linked to differences in attitudes. Will the same variables also affect the views of English respondents and of those of orientals in Hawaii?

THE INSTRUMENT

During the preliminary phase of instrument preparation, a series of intensive unstructured interviews were given. The final instrument reproduced in Appendix II was a questionnaire combining open ended and multiple choice questions. Most of the questions were specifically developed for this study. The instrument also included twelve items from Cohen and Struening's OMI (Opinions about Mental Illness) scale (Cohen and Struening, 1962). The questionnaires were administered by specially trained interviewers, after being pretested in the three areas sampled.

THE SAMPLE

All the respondents in Part II come from catchment areas served by the hospitals in Part I. The sample includes only persons who are actively engaged in the productive life of the community and who might therefore play a role in the employment of former mental patients, either as gatekeepers of the world of work (managers, supervisors and foremen) or as potential co-workers (professionals, white collar, skilled and unskilled workers). Both men and women were included. The total number of respondents in the three areas was about 1170. The occupational distribution is given in Table 92.

Table 92. *The community samples by occupational level*

	Border State	Hawaii	England
Managers of large and medium companies and professionals	116	112	41
Managers of small companies	35	24	51
Clerical and low supervisory personnel	213	135	89
Foremen	22	27	36
Skilled workers	46	39	29
Unskilled workers	47	67	39
Totals	479	404	285

The selection of respondents was based on the following procedure. In each area studied, a number of business firms were randomly selected from official census data, covering all the manufacturing, service and retail establishments of the community. Large, medium and small companies were included in the sample. The cooperation of each company was then secured. The selection of individual respondents was based on company personnel lists obtained from the management.

The principles underlying the selection of respondents from the different companies were as follows: It was attempted to include respondents from all occupational levels, starting with manual labor and reaching up to company management. In order to obtain a sufficient number of respondents in each category, the upper levels were overrepresented.

THE CONTEXTUAL HYPOTHESIS OF ATTITUDES TOWARD MENTAL PATIENTS

The concept of 'mental patient' may be thought of as conveying at least two connotations, one implying 'deviancy' and the other 'illness'. Correspondingly, this concept may arouse different types of reaction in a population. On the one hand, the 'mental patient' may be viewed as a deviant who fails to fulfill normative social expectations, and as a threatening figure who must be kept at a distance. On the other hand, as a 'sick person' he may be entitled to a certain amount of help and understanding. By overtly rejecting a 'sick person', a community member violates an implicit social norm of helping the needy and the underdog. One of the hypotheses governing this study was that the expressed attitudes toward the mentally ill will vary if the context within which they are formulated is altered. We would expect that a respondent who perceives a mental patient as a sick person requiring help will exhibit more positive attitudes toward him than he will if the patient is perceived as a deviant or an outcast.

It is our contention that the contradictory results obtained in assessing attitudes toward mental illness may just reflect differences in the dimensions tapped by different researchers. If we consider attitudes as a multidimensional phenomenon, then it is entirely possible, as we intend to show, for the same persons to express more or less negative sentiments in regard to different aspects of a complex attitudinal object.

For the purpose of testing the hypothesis, the two dimensions of 'deviancy' and of 'illness' were successively made salient to the respondents.

For the purpose of evoking the 'deviancy' aspect of the attitudinal object, a set of questions were asked which emphasized the requirements demanded by society in order to fulfill various occupational roles. For instance, the respondents were asked: 'Do you think that a patient released from a mental hospital, who had been properly trained, may be trusted in the following occupations? . . .' and 'if an employer knows that an applicant is a former mental patient, should he hire him for jobs in which he has to supervise other people, jobs in which there are important decisions to be made, etc.? ' The underlying characteristic of these questions has to do with the 'normative dimension' in the sense that the demands of occupational roles are set by universalistic social norms.

In order to evoke a more positive attitude toward mental patients the respondent as a private individual was confronted in the questionnaire with a hypothetical person who needs a job and help. This type of questions is exemplified by the following: 'In general, how would you feel about a person who has had a mental illness?' 'Would you be willing to take a job alongside such a person? . . . to hire such a person?' Now the emphasis is no longer on the normative requirements of the job but on the private good will of the respondent. We may summarize the character of the dimension tapped here by labeling it the 'affective-conative' dimension.

In line with the contextual hypothesis we would expect that a more favorable picture of the community view of mental illness will emerge by tapping the 'affective-conative' dimension of attitudes rather than the 'normative' one.

THE CONSISTENCY HYPOTHESIS OF ATTITUDES TOWARD MENTAL PATIENTS

While we expect that views toward mental illness will be conflicting, we do not intend to suggest that they need be inconsistent. So far we discussed the contextual aspect of attitudes toward mental patients by emphasizing the possibility of obtaining apparently 'inconsistent' views from a given individual, even though he may possess a stable underlying attitude. We may call this a 'pseudo-inconsistency'.

The second hypothesis which guides the present study is that persons who rank relatively high on the normative dimension also rank relatively high on the affective-conative dimension. If the data support this hypothesis, then we may speak of 'consistency' of attitudes in spite of the absolute differences of responses on the two dimensions. If, on the other hand, people who are relatively favorable on one dimension are unfavorable on the second dimension when compared to other people, then we would have to reject the hypothesis and to speak of an 'inconsistency' of attitudes.

The following chapters will deal with the results of this investigation.

SUMMARY

A number of studies were cited on popular attitudes toward mental patients. The studies reached pessimistic or optimistic conclusions about popular views. The aims of the present study were then identified: whether a pessimistic or an optimistic view on mental patients could be confirmed; whether inconsistent attitudes exist; and, if so, how the inconsistency could be accounted for. The contextual hypothesis of attitudes toward mental patients was stated: The expressed attitudes toward the mentally ill will vary if the context within which they are formulated is altered. The context may be one of deviancy or of illness. More favorable attitudes are expected for the latter. To test this hypothesis, questions were asked in a deviancy context to tap what was labeled the normative dimension, and in an illness context, to tap what was called the affective-conative dimension. The second hypothesis, dealing with the consistency of attitudes, was that persons who rank relatively high on the normative dimension also rank relatively high on the affective-conative dimension. The instrument and the sample were described.

CHAPTER 13

The normative dimension

The empirical counterpart of what we have called the 'normative' dimension may be found in the range of occupations which people consider suitable for a former mental patient. The respondents were asked: 'Do you think that a patient released from a mental hospital, who had been properly trained, may be trusted in the following occupations?: a medical doctor, an actor, a carpenter, etc. . .' In each of the three areas, 23 occupations were ranked according to the percentage of respondents who trusted mental patients to work in them. The occupational ranking obtained indicates the performance level at which the respondents in the three areas are ready to trust a former mental patient.

Based on these rankings, we may now answer some questions. Does a history of mental illness preclude eligibility for some occupations? If so, for which occupations? The answers to these questions have practical consequences for former mental patients who have been trained in various skills. Table 93 gives the distribution of the results. There is striking agreement in all three areas studied on the rank order of occupations in which a former mental patient may be trusted. These occupations are either characterized by little skill and little prestige such as that of a doorman, a grocery-man, a farmer, etc., or they represent more unconventional occupations like acting, painting, and journalism. There is general consensus that former mental patients cannot be trusted as doctors, judges, generals and foreign service officers.

The ranking of occupations found in Table 93 repeats in reversed form the one obtained by Hatt and North (Reiss, Duncan, Hatt and North, 1961) on the *prestige* rating of occupations by a cross-section of the general population. Hatt and North found that the occupations which were given the highest prestige ratings were those requiring highly specialized training and a considerable degree of responsibility for the general community. Therefore, what has been called the 'stigma' of mental illness may include the notion that no high responsibility and therefore no high prestige should be bestowed on those who happen to have been affected by it.

Table 93. *Rank order of occupations in which ex-patients are trusted*

Do you think that a patient released from a mental hospital, who had been properly trained, may be trusted in the following occupations?

	Percentage answering: Yes		
	Border State (N = 479)	Hawaii (N = 404)	England (N = 285)
Farmer	92	96	92
Doorman	92	92	94
Grocery man	92	94	92
Housekeeper	92	94	92
Painter (artist)	90	92	94
Salesclerk	90	86	95
Carpenter	90	90	84
Actor	85	84	84
Journalist	80	75	79
Clergyman	70	66	69
Foreman	66	58	55
Cashier	63	47	45
Scientist	60	44	48
Bus driver	60	52	35
Teacher	53	47	45
Dentist	50	34	38
Lawyer	48	34	27
Foreign Service Officer	38	25	36
Druggist	40	34	20
Policeman	36	22	23
Doctor	30	22	23
Judge	26	16	19
General	22	13	22

THE INDEX OF OCCUPATIONAL TRUST

Using as a point of departure the data presented in Table 93 an individual score of occupational trust or index of occupational trust was developed. Respondents were classified into four categories according to the number of occupations they were ready to entrust to a former mental patient. If a respondent agreed to trust a former mental patient in no more than 9 occupations out of the total of 23 presented to him, he was given a 'very low' score on the index of occupational trust. Respondents who trusted ex-patients in 10 to 12 occupations, were given a 'low' score; those who trusted ex-patients in 13 to 19 occupations received a 'medium' score. Finally, agreement to trust a former mental patient in 20 or more occupations earned a 'high' score on the index of occupational trust. The number of occupations in which an ex-patient was trusted was closely linked to the level of prestige and responsibility. To have a 'very low' score, as closer analysis showed, virtually always means to trust a former mental patient only in those occupations which are characterized by low prestige and low responsibility.

Table 94 shows the distribution of scores on the index of occupational trust in the three areas studied. The overall findings show that respondents in the border state sample appear to be willing to trust former mental patients in more occupations than either the English or the Hawaiian sample members. 22% of the total border state sample and only 13% in Hawaii and 15% in England fall in the 'high' category on the index of occupational trust. Correspondingly, only 12% of respondents in the border state sample fall in the 'very low' category as compared to 27% in England, and 23% in Hawaii.

Since the Hawaiian sample is ethnically highly diversified, the opportunity arose to break down the sample according to different cultural-ethnic subgroups. Table 95 shows the distribution on the index of occupational trust among different ethnic groups of Hawaii. The findings show that the white group resembles very much the respondents from the continental United States in Table 94 in their relatively high level of occupational trust.

The Chinese respondents tend to cluster in the middle categories and to avoid the extremes. Filipinos and Hawaiians* show a relative-

* The sample of Hawaii refers to all respondents from this state in contrast to the other samples. 'Hawaiian' as an ethnic group refers to respondents of

ly low trust. However, these results should be appraised with caution. In our study, Filipinos and Hawaiian respondents are mainly drawn from the 'blue collar' ranks and have had on the whole much less schooling than the other ethnic groups. Differences in education may be a crucial factor in determining expressed attitudes and may outweigh cultural differences.

Table 94. *Index of occupational trust by area* (in percentages)

	N	Very low	Low	Medium	High
Border State	479	12	19	46	22
Hawaii	404	23	24	40	13
England	285	27	21	37	15

Very low occupational trust = 9 or fewer occupations out of 23 for which ex-mental patients may be trusted.

Low occupational trust = 10-12 occupations out of 23 for which ex-mental patients may be trusted.

Medium occupational trust = 13-19 occupations out of 23 for which ex-mental patients may be trusted.

High occupational trust = 20 or more occupations out of 23 for which ex-mental patients may be trusted.

Table 95. *Occupational trust by ethnic affiliation: Hawaii* (in percentages)

	N	Very low	Low	Medium	High
White	134	16	21	40	22
Chinese	39	8	46	46	–
Filipino	27	41	22	33	4
Hawaiian	33	42	12	36	9
Japanese	155	26	23	41	10

OCCUPATIONAL TRUST AND JOB CHARACTERISTICS

We may ask ourselves, what is behind the willingness or refusal to trust a mental patient in a given occupation? Can we identify specific

Polynesian descent as contrasted to orientals, Filipinos and Caucasians who together comprise the Hawaiian sample.

job requirements for which former mental patients are deemed unsuitable by those who show little occupational trust? Three types of job activities were considered relevant here: (1) supervision, and (2) decision making, both of which are usually associated with positions of prestige, and (3) close contact with other people. This latter job characteristic is not necessarily linked to prestige, but reflects the expectation for a minimum of *savoir faire* and of emotional stability.

Respondents were asked whether an employer should hire an applicant who was a former mental patient for jobs possessing the above characteristics. The responses to these questions were then cross-tabulated with the scores on the index of occupational trust.

The findings reported in Table 96, as expected, help us to clarify the meaning of 'occupational trust'. There is a strikingly strong and clearcut trend as we progress from respondents with 'very low' to those with 'high' occupational trust for increasingly 'favorable' opinions of which types of jobs are appropriate for former mental patients. A direct relationship is found in all three sampling areas between degree of trust and the feeling that an employer should hire ex-patients for supervisory and decision making positions. Only 10% or less of the 'very low trust' respondents as against 70% or more of the 'high trust' ones agree that an employer should consider a former mental patient for 'jobs in which he has to supervise other people', or in which 'there are important decisions to be made'. 'Jobs with close personal contact' show the same trend between the respondents, but it is less pronounced.

Table 96. *Occupational trust and job characteristics* (in percentages)

	Ex-patient should be hired for jobs with these characteristics											
	Border State				Hawaii				England			
Occupational trust	N	A	B	C	N	A	B	C	N	A	B	C
Very low	58	9	10	45	94	8	7	40	75	7	7	61
Low	93	23	15	72	95	11	8	61	61	20	17	80
Medium	222	45	46	79	162	39	33	75	106	51	42	92
High	108	80	82	88	51	75	73	89	43	74	70	91

A. Jobs in which he has to supervise other people.

B. Jobs in which there are important decisions to be made.

C. Jobs with close personal contact with other people.

The pattern of tolerance (meaning willingness to have ex-patients in supervisory and decision making jobs) follows with perfect regularity and consistency the increase of trust. A look at Table 96 will clearly show this progression. These results support the notion that lack of occupational trust in mental patients reflects the belief that they are unable to make important decisions and to supervise others and, to a certain extent, also are unable to work in close contact with other people. In all three sampling areas people who are distrustful of mental patients are somewhat more tolerant when asked about this last category. Such tolerance for close personal contact in a job situation is most characteristic of our English respondents.

OCCUPATIONAL TRUST AND PREDICTION OF VOCATIONAL SUCCESS OF FORMER MENTAL PATIENTS

Is there a relationship between trust in general and expected success of former mental patients in one's own line of work? To test such a relationship, the respondents were asked to agree or to disagree with the following statement:

'Former mental patients could successfully work in my occupation.'

Table 97 indicates that occupational trust is strongly related to expectation of vocational performance of former mental patients. Expectation of probable success in the respondent's line of work increases directly with the score on the index of occupational trust.

Table 97. *Occupational trust and prediction of vocational success* (in percentages)

	Former mental patients could successfully work in my occupation (strongly agree or agree)		
Occupational trust	Border State	England	Hawaii
Very low	35	40	20
Low	40	46	34
Medium	69	59	56
High	90	84	84

In the border state high trust respondents agree nearly three times as often as very low trust ones that former mental patients could successfully work in their own occupations. In England the proportion is two to one and in Hawaii four to one. Since a large proportion of respondents do not hold positions of responsibility, we see that there is something else which accompanies an attitude of distrust besides skepticism in the supervisory and decision making capacities of former mental patients. This new factor may be seen as something akin to distrust of the ex-patient's general adequacy of performance.

OCCUPATIONAL TRUST AND CHARACTERISTICS OF WORK PERFORMANCE OF EX-MENTAL PATIENTS

Is it possible to identify further job attitudes which are related to occupational trust? If supervisory activity and decision making constitute a very high performance level, what can be expected of those aspects of work performance which are also required in less demanding types of jobs? Carefulness, independence, and the ability to get along well with one's fellow workers are important dimensions of most types of jobs. Table 98 shows that respondents who are trustful (high and medium trust) and those who are distrustful (low and very low trust) sharply differ in their evaluations of former mental patients' performances along these dimensions. The 'distrustful' respondents are more likely to consider former mental patients as being 'easily antagonized by fellow workers', 'dangerous to those who work around them', 'requiring close supervision in their work', and they are less likely to believe that ex-patients 'work as carefully as anybody else'.

Therefore, the willingness to trust former mental patients only in occupations of little responsibility which characterizes the view of the very low and low trust groups, is far from implying a confidence in ex-patients' ability to carry out satisfactorily the less demanding jobs. Lack of trust is not limited to high levels of performance, but seems to be a generalized view of the total capacity of former mental patients.

Table 98. *Occupational trust and views on work performance of former mental patients* (in percentages)

Occupational trust	Ex-pat. work as carefully as anybody else (always, mostly)			Ex-pat. require close work supervision (always, mostly)			Ex-pat. dangerous to co-workers (rarely, never)			Ex-pat. get along well with co-workers (always, mostly)			Ex-pat. easily antagonized by co-workers (always, mostly)		
	B.S.	Ha.	Eng.	B.S.	Ha.	Eng.	B.S.	Ha.	Eng.	B.S.	Ha.	Eng.	B.S.	Ha.	Eng.
Very low	50	53	45	55	59	69	59	45	63	48	45	65	33	41	20
Low	60	71	57	47	42	46	94	88	85	59	64	67	22	29	17
Medium	82	76	74	20	35	24	89	90	74	77	69	70	6	12	13
High	84	80	82	9	22	14	78	82	84	78	80	84	3	6	9

SUMMARY

An index of occupational trust was empirically derived from the respondents' expressed willingness to trust ex-mental patients in 23 specific occupations. A striking agreement was found in the rank orders assigned to occupations in which ex-mental patients were trusted by the members of the Hawaiian, English and border state samples. Respondents were allocated to four groups, very low, low, medium and high in occupational trust.

Occupational trust was correlated with various other responses. The respondents' willingness to see ex-mental patients hired for positions of supervision and decision making followed with perfect regularity and consistency their position on the index of occupational trust. Occupational trust was correlated with various other responses. The vocational success, the respondents' belief in ex-patients' carefulness, their independence and their ability to get along with their fellow workers.

CHAPTER 14

The affective-conative dimension

On the whole, tolerance and understanding do not seem to be widespread when we explore the occupational boundaries set for the previously mentally ill. However, in accordance with the initial hypothesis about the possibility of altering the expressed views on mental illness by altering the context within which they are formulated we would expect that the level of acceptance will be increased by approaching the respondents within the frame of what was called the affective-conative dimension. By this we mean that the respondents are confronted not with impersonal, normative themes such as '*should* ex-patients be trusted?' or '*should* en employer hire him?', but with questions involving a particularistic emphasis on their private good will, as in 'are *you willing* to?' and 'how do *you feel* about it?'

ACCEPTANCE IN WORKING SITUATIONS

The topic under scrutiny here will still have a bearing on tolerance toward former mental patients, only now this tolerance is seen in a different context. In addition to the previous questions, tolerance of social contacts with ex-patients will be tested.

As said before, the 'personal' good will of the respondents will be determined, as the following questions attest: 'In general, how would you feel about a person who has had a mental illness?' 'Would you be willing to take a job alongside such a person?' 'Would you be willing to have such a person as your boss?' 'Would you be willing to hire such a person?'

As Table 99 shows, the distributions of responses to two of these questions – on the willingness (1) to work alongside, and (2) to hire such a person – are overwhelmingly positive in all three areas studied. These results express more tolerance than our data reported so far (on the normative dimension) have suggested. Now it is the English and not the American respondents who exhibit the greatest tolerance. The third alternative, to have an ex-patient as a boss, generally is endorsed less readily, and slightly more often by the border state sample.

Table 99. *The affective-conative dimension* (in percentages)

In general, how would you feel about a person who has had a mental illness?

	Willing to take a job alongside such a person	Willing to have such a person as your boss	Willing to hire such a person
Border State	79	43	72
Hawaii	72	27	68
England	86	38	80

	Willing to invite such a person to your home as a guest at a party	Willing to have such a person live next door	Willing to have such a person in the same household
Border State	78	77	67
Hawaii	72	69	58
England	86	91	67

ACCEPTANCE IN SOCIAL SITUATIONS

The second topic included in the 'affective-conative' dimension has to do with the acceptance of former mental patients in social rather than in occupational contacts. The respondents were asked about their willingness (1) to invite ex-patients as party guests into their homes and (2) to accept them as neighbors. The more extreme alternative (3) asks for their readiness to live with an ex-patient in the same household.

The results are presented in Table 99. Again, English respondents, in the first two questions, exhibit the greatest willingness to have social contacts with former mental patients, and the Hawaiians show the least willingness. As for the third alternative, living in the same household, there is less readiness in accepting it than there is for more casual contacts.

ATTITUDES AS A FUNCTION OF CONTEXT

These results confirm the initial expectation that a more favorable view toward mental illness will emerge by shifting the context of evaluation. They have also a bearing on the interpretation of some findings in the research literature. Lemkau and Crocetti (1962), in their study conducted in Baltimore, found 80% of their respondents saying that they would not hesitate to work with someone who had been mentally ill. The authors inferred from this that the general public is well disposed toward the mentally ill. Their distribution of positive answers is exactly reproduced in the present study (see Table 99) where 79% of the border state respondents say they are willing to take a job alongside a person who has had a mental illness.

These writers' optimistic findings may be dependent on the form of the questions they asked. We would suggest an additional note of caution in regard to the optimistic interpretation of Lemkau and Crocetti. Not only do their questions emphasize personal good will, but they also leave completely unspecified the type of roles and positions open to former patients. One may express willingness to work with and to hire a former mental patient and yet hide no less important forms of rejection, such as limiting the permitted occupational range to menial positions. The same caution applies to the findings of Grob and Olshansky (1958) on the stated willingness of a sample of businessmen to hire discharged mental patients.

Since the context within which a question is raised affects the answers, one will hesitate to infer a general orientation, either favorable or unfavorable, from a single set of questions. Our data suggest a more plausible interpretation which may solve the apparent inconsistency between perceiving the mentally ill as a 'deviant' or 'transgressor' who threatens society and as a patient or a 'sick' person who needs help. The solution may be precisely the respondents' readiness to accord the ex-patient some help as a general form of good will but to limit vocational opportunities to a narrow range.

Variations in the focus of the question or the amount of specification may very well evoke more or less favorable responses even if the underlying attitude is stable.* Thus, an apparent inconsistency may merely reflect variation in the saliency of different aspects of mental illness as it is perceived by the general public.

SUMMARY

Items implying the affective-conative dimension were reviewed in the present chapter. As expected from the contextual hypothesis, results on the affective-conative dimension were more favorable than on the normative dimension. Both in working and in social situations respondents were more willing to accept ex-mental patients than they were in a normative context. The bearing of these results on findings in the literature was discussed.

* In a different context, Campbell (1963) arrived at a similar notion when he speaks of the existence of a 'differential attitudinal threshold'.

CHAPTER 15

Consistency and inconsistency of attitudes

The second hypothesis which guided the present study is that persons who rank relatively high on the normative dimension will also rank relatively high on the affective-conative dimension. If the data support this hypothesis, we may speak of 'consistency' of attitudes in spite of the absolute differences of responses on the two dimensions. In order to investigate the consistency of individual attitudes, the *relative position* of an individual on the various attitudinal dimensions should be compared. One may start such a comparison by inquiring whether people who are *relatively* low on the index of occupational trust tend also to be *relatively* low in the affective-conative dimension, regardless of the absolute degree of tolerance expressed.

Table 100 shows that there is a striking congruence between the two types of responses. In virtually all cases when the score on the index of occupational trust increases, there are parallel increases in expressed willingness to hire, to have as a boss, and to work with a former mental patient.

We have here, then, a neat demonstration of the high consistency in the individual's relative position on both normative and affective-conative dimensions. That is, those segments of the population which are more likely to agree that mental patients should be trusted in a large number of occupations are also more likely to express their personal willingness to work alongside ex-patients, to hire them, and even to have them as a boss.

We now switch from the work situation to one which involves social contacts by asking the respondents how they would feel about inviting a former mental patient to their home as a guest at a party, having such a person live next door or in the same household. A similar pattern emerges. As Table 101 shows, in the border state and

Hawaii only approximately half of the respondents representing the subgroup characterized by very low occupational trust are willing to invite a former mental patient to their home, to live next door to him, or to have such a person in the same household, while almost everyone in the highly trustful groups is willing to do so. In England there is relatively greater tolerance for casual social contacts even among those respondents who are least trustful.

Table 100. *Occupational trust and willingness to accept a former mental patient at work* (in percentages)

Occupational trust	Willing to take a job alongside a former mental patient			Willing to have a former mental patient as your boss			Willing to hire a a former mental patient		
	B.S.	Haw.	Eng.	B.S.	Haw.	Eng.	B.S.	Haw.	Eng.
Very low	57	44	76	5	8	11	57	41	65
Low	71	71	85	19	12	23	67	65	83
Medium	86	83	84	43	36	45	82	77	75
High	88	94	95	81	69	79	85	90	91

Number on which the percentages are based:

	B.S.	Hawaii	England
Very low	58	94	75
Low	93	95	61
Medium	222	162	106
High	108	51	43

Table 101. *Occupational trust and willingness to accept a former mental patient in a social context* (percentage who agree)

Occupational trust	Willing to invite a former mental patient to your home as a guest at a party			Willing to have a former mental patient live next door			Willing to have a former mental patient in the same household		
	B.S.	Haw.	Eng.	B.S.	Haw.	Eng.	B.S.	Haw.	Eng.
Very low	57	45	74	59	41	82	45	30	53
Low	80	73	83	77	67	93	57	50	58
Medium	85	85	81	87	84	84	76	75	65
High	88	96	93	88	90	95	84	86	86

Even though there are great similarities in the views toward mental illness in the three areas studied, some differences in trends and in tendencies may be detected. English respondents were the most tolerant ones on the affective-conative dimension, i.e., when asked about their personal good will. Border state respondents gave the most favorable responses on the normative dimension, i.e., when trust in the occupational performance of ex-mental patients was tapped. The border state respondents tended also to be more consistent in their views toward mental patients whether they were favorable or unfavorable. The English were more ready to *accept* an ex-patient personally even though they had more doubts about his performance than mainland Americans did. This suggests greater tolerance of deviancy by the English respondents as a whole, which may be related to a cultural variable.

IS THERE A CLUSTER OF ATTITUDES TOWARD MENTAL ILLNESS?

The results so far suggest the existence of a general orientation toward mental illness which may be expected to guide the various aspects of behavior and of cognition which are related to it.

Such cognitive aspects might include the following questions. How is mental illness perceived? What are the differences in optimism or pessimism about its outcome and curability? How should family members advise a former mental patient? If our results show the existence of an attitudinal cluster, we may also inquire into its origin and into its possible link to background factors such as education and special experience with the issue, e.g., first hand contact with the mentally ill. If such a cluster is found, a practical consequence will be that for any program of attitudinal change one will have to deal simultaneously with the various facets of it, rather than attempt to alter only a single facet. These questions will be treated in the following chapters.

SUMMARY

The second hypothesis which guides the present study is that persons who rank relatively high on the normative dimension also rank relatively high on the affective-conative dimension. Striking consistencies were found between respondents' occupational trust and their expressed willingness to hire a former mental patient, to work with him and to have him as a boss. Similar consistencies were obtained for occupational trust and acceptance of ex-patients in social situations.

CHAPTER 16

Clusters of acceptance and rejection

TRUST AND PERCEPTION OF MENTAL ILLNESS

The inquiry into the existence of an integrated attitudinal cluster may begin with the question of whether trustful and distrustful people differ in their perceptions of mental illness. The answer is presented in Table 102.

Respondents who are characterized by high occupational trust, in contrast to those who are not, are less likely to believe that 'it is easy to recognize someone who once had a serious mental illness,' and that 'there is something about mental patients that makes it easy to tell them from normal people'.

According to Table 102, the more people distrust mental patients at work, the more they tend to perceive them as qualitatively different from the general population, and, also, the more likely they are to think of mental patients as dangerous. Thus, while about one out of two respondents characterized by a very low score on the index of occupational trust agrees with the statement that:

> 'Although some mental patients seem all right, it is dangerous to forget for a moment that they are mentally ill',

only one out of four among those with a high score does so.

TRUST AND OPTIMISM ABOUT OUTCOME OF HOSPITALIZATION

If a general orientation of trust or distrust toward mental patients exists we should expect considerable differences in notions concern-

Table 102. *Occupational trust and perception of mental patients* (percentage who agree)

Occupational trust	It is easy to recognize someone who once had a serious mental illness			Although patients discharged from mental hospitals may seem all right they should not be allowed to marry			There is something about mental patients that makes it easy to tell them from normal people		
	B.S.	Haw.	Eng.	B.S.	Haw.	Eng.	B.S.	Haw.	Eng.
Very low	31	35	38	45	34	46	35	49	51
Low	23	32	27	29	40	35	18	35	37
Medium	17	14	15	14	24	17	18	26	19
High	7	16	12	5	16	12	3	14	16

Occupational trust	People who were once patients in mental hospitals are no more dangerous than the average citizen			Most women who were once patients in a mental hospital could be trusted as baby sitters			Although some mental patients seem all right it is dangerous to forget for a moment that they are mentally ill		
	B.S.	Haw.	Eng.	B.S.	Haw.	Eng.	B.S.	Haw.	Eng.
Very low	60	60	78	41	25	36	55	60	62
Low	62	76	85	41	56	48	57	55	47
Medium	70	83	86	62	62	63	36	41	37
High	85	90	91	84	84	88	25	22	28

ing the curability of mental illness. Data relevant to this aspect of the problem may be found in Tables 103 and 104 which show with great consistency that occupational trust and optimism in the curability of the illness increase together. In all three areas studied, respondents who are characterized by very low or low occupational trust are less likely to believe that,

'Most patients leaving a mental hospital are completely cured',

than are respondents with high occupational trust. As Table 103 shows, the percentages of 'yes' answers to the above question by very low trust respondents are the following: 14% in the border state sample,

25% in the Hawaiian sample, and 16% in the English sample. For the highly trustful respondents the percentages of 'yes' answers are respectively 29%, 42%, and 56%.

Table 103. *Occupational trust and belief that most patients leaving a mental hospital are completely cured* (in percentages)

Occupational trust	B.S.	Hawaii	England
Very low	14	25	16
Low	17	18	15
Medium	21	33	32
High	29	42	56

Table 104. *Occupational trust and belief that one can never be sure that a person released from a mental hospital is completely cured* (in percentages)

Occupational trust	N	B.S.	N	Hawaii	N	England
Very low	58	64	94	72	75	63
Low	93	57	95	56	61	61
Medium	222	54	162	51	106	51
High	108	49	51	49	43	37

Correspondingly it may be seen in Table 104 that 64% of respondents in the border state sample who are least trustful agree with the statement that:

'One can never be sure that a person released from a mental hospital is completely cured.'

Only 49% of very high trust respondents agree with it. Differences in optimism about the outcome of mental illness as related to trust and distrust are even greater for the Hawaiian sample, with 72% and 49% agreeing respectively among people with very low and high trust, and for the English sample with 63% and 37% respectively agreeing with the statement above. The intermediate categories of respondents follow perfectly these trends. Disbelief in the curability of mental illness and the notion of a constant possibility of relapse are, therefore, part of an overall cluster of attitudes toward mental illness.

TRUST AND DEGREE OF IMPAIRMENT IN WORK PERFORMANCE

That belief in impairment due to mental illness is a function of one's trust and distrust is further confirmed by the distribution obtained in all three areas to the following question:

'Do you think that when a patient is released from a mental hospital, his family should encourage him to take a job easier than the one he had before? '

As Table 105 shows, very few respondents in the very trustful group agree that the family should do that, while more than a third among the very low trust group think so in the border state and in England, and 59% in Hawaii do.

Table 105. *Occupational trust and belief that if a patient is released from a mental hospital his family should encourage him to take an easier job than before* (in percentages)

Occupational trust	B.S.	Hawaii	England
Very low	35	59	38
Low	29	43	33
Medium	16	43	31
High	14	13	16

TRUST AND DESIRE FOR ASSURANCES

Table 106 shows that regardless of degree of trust, in the Hawaiian and in the border state sample many respondents agree that if they had to work closely with a former mental patient, they would want to have some specific information and assurances about him, while fewer respondents in England express the same wish. However, there are also consistent differences according to the respondents' trust and distrust, with the trustful respondents less often wanting assurances than the distrustful ones.

Table 106. *If you had to work closely with a former mental patient, would you want to have some specific information and assurances about him?*

	Percentages answering: Yes		
Occupational trust	B.S.	Hawaii	England
Very low	79	85	49
Low	72	73	43
Medium	66	72	44
High	62	59	19

TRUST AND EVALUATION OF CHANCES OF EMPLOYMENT OF FORMER MENTAL PATIENTS

When the respondents are asked to express not their attitudes but their evaluation of the chances of employment of former mental patients, we do not see any differences that may be related to trust or distrust. The question was asked:

'What do you think an employer *generally does* when he knows that an applicant has been a patient in a mental hospital? '

As Table 107 shows, one out of three respondents in the border state sample and one out of five in the English sample believe that the employers prefer to hire someone else. In the Hawaiian sample the proportion who believe so is even greater. Only cultural differences emerge when we tap this belief about hiring policies concerning former mental patients. This means trustful and distrustful respondents do not differ in their evaluation of employers' readiness to hire a former mental patient. Differences emerge, however, when instead of inquiring about what an employer does, we ask instead:

'What do you think an employer *should do?*'

A few of the very distrustful say, 'he should hire someone else', but none among the trustful respondents say so.

Table 107. *What do you think an employer generally does when he knows that an applicant has been a patient in a mental hospital?*

	Percentage saying that the employer prefers to hire someone else		
Occupational trust	B.S.	Hawaii	England
Very low	31	44	20
Low	25	25	17
Medium	24	30	20
High	31	43	21

What do you think an employer should do?

	Percentage saying that the employer should hire someone else		
Occupational trust	B.S.	Hawaii	England
Very low	9	19	7
Low	3	8	3
Medium	2	4	–
High	–	–	–

TRUST AND IMPUTED MOTIVES FOR HIRING FORMER MENTAL PATIENTS

An interesting finding has to do with the kind of motives respondents attribute to an employer who hires a former mental patient. Table 108 shows that people who differ in their attitudes of trust and distrust also differ in guessing the reasons an employer may have had for hiring a former mental patient. They were asked to complete the following open ended item:

'When an employer knowingly hires a former mental patient, he does this because . . .'

The responses were classified into several categories. Two types of responses were most frequent. One category of responses gives as reason behind the employer's decision a desire to help; his action is imputed to be based purely on a humanitarian motive. The second most frequently used category may be summarized as follows: The ex-patient can do the job. The respondents' emphasis on the motive for hiring in the second instance involves the fitness of the ex-patient to perform a job well.

As Table 108 shows, there is a striking difference in proportion of the two reasons given for hiring when we look at the trustful versus the distrustful people. More of the trustful ones stress the patient's ability, while the distrustful respondents are most likely to attribute the hiring of ex-patients to the good will and humanitarianism of the employer. A view of former mental patients as either self-reliant or as dependent emerges thus spontaneously through a largely unstructured question, and it is closely linked to a general orientation of trust or distrust toward the mentally ill.

Table 108. *When an employer knowingly hires a former mental patient, he does this because . . .* (in percentages)

Occupational trust	Desire to help him			The ex-patient can do the job		
	B.S.	Hawaii	England	B.S.	Hawaii	England
Very low	57	39	76	7	24	9
Low	56	42	82	19	26	17
Medium	42	45	62	29	34	26
High	31	16	27	36	41	10

Numbers upon which the percentages are based:

Occupational trust	B.S.	Hawaii	England
Very low	58	94	75
Low	93	95	61
Medium	222	162	106
High	108	51	43

TRUST AND CONTACT WITH MENTAL PATIENTS

There is a regular increase in favorableness toward mental patients when we go from very low, to low, medium and high occupational trust. We may now test, at least in part, the widely held assumption of the effect of first hand knowledge and contact in dispelling distrust and prejudice and in increasing tolerance toward specific groups. Following this line of reasoning we would expect that the trustful subgroup should have had more first hand experience with mental patients than the distrustful subgroup.

The respondents were therefore asked whether they had any contact with people who were hospitalized because of mental illness. Interestingly enough, the trustful subgroup mentioned more often that they had known personally people who had been hospitalized because of mental illness. Table 109 shows that in the border state sample only 22% of the very trustful respondents, as against 40% of distrustful respondents, say they did not have such contacts. In Hawaii lack of contact is reported by 59% of the very low trust groups and by 42% of the high trust groups. In England 31% of the very low trust and 15% of the high trust groups had no contact with mental patients. In other words, familiarity with mental patients goes with increased tolerance of them.

Table 109. *How many people who are or have been in a mental hospital have you had contact with?*

	Percentage saying they have had no contact with people in a mental hospital		
Occupational trust	B.S.	Hawaii	England
Very low	40	59	31
Low	31	49	27
Medium	28	47	25
High	22	42	15

	Numbers upon which the percentages are based		
Occupational trust	B.S.	Hawaii	England
Very low	45	91	73
Low	70	93	59
Medium	178	158	105
High	80	48	39

TRUST AND PERSONAL CLOSENESS TO A MENTAL PATIENT

What happens when the mental patient is presented not as a generalized attitudinal object, but as a close friend or relative? To assess the problems encountered in the community by a discharged mental hospital patient it will be of paramount importance to know how his close friends and relatives will act toward him. The following question was asked:

'Let's suppose that a close relative of yours or a very close friend, after a stay in a mental hospital had been released and came to you for help in getting a job. What would you most likely do?'

The answers are found in Table 110. People who may be considered distrustful of mental patients, in general, do not differ from those who may be considered highly trustful, in their readiness actively to help a close friend or relative in securing a job. Only 4%, 7% and 3% of the least trustful in the border state, Hawaii and England respectively 'would prefer to have nothing to do with it'. None among the highly trustful respondents in all three areas subscribed to this view.

CLUSTERS OF ACCEPTANCE AND REJECTION

The findings so far clearly show a strong relationship between the various aspects of belief, attitudes and perception relating to the mentally ill. This holds true even though expression of tolerance is higher on the affective-conative than on the normative dimension. In confirmation of both of our initial hypotheses, such relationships have been found to exist among the respondents of each of the three areas sampled.

Thus, a coherent cluster emerges by which a humanitarian subgroup may be isolated, that is, a minority in the community who tend to perceive a mental patient as quite indistinguishable from the general population, as able to succeed, not dangerous, and trustworthy in positions of prestige and responsibility.

This highly tolerant group may be contrasted with a group of people exhibiting a cluster of intolerance. They also represent a minority of the total population sampled and tend to perceive a former mental patient as qualitatively different from people in general, as dangerous and untrustworthy, as unlikely to succeed in the respondent's line of work, as probably incurable, and as always liable to relapse.

Table 110. *Let's suppose that a close relative of yours, or a very close friend, after a stay in a mental hospital had been released and came to you for help in getting a job. What would you most likely do?* (in percentages)

Occupational trust	N	I would ask people I knew to hire him	If I knew of an opening, I would tell him to go and see for himself	I would prefer to have nothing to do with it
Border State				
Very low	58	43	50	4
Low	93	40	55	2
Medium	222	35	61	1
High	108	30	62	–
Hawaii				
Very low	94	45	46	7
Low	95	44	53	1
Medium	162	54	42	1
High	51	51	49	–
England				
Very low	75	41	56	3
Low	61	40	58	–
Medium	106	31	59	2
High	43	35	65	–

The concept of 'mental patient' or 'ex-mental patient' has been purposely left unspecified and vague all along in this study, so that it may be used as a kind of projective stimulus. Mental illness should be considered as a continuum covering different states, ranging from a benign disturbance to insanity. In spite of mental illness being such a heterogeneous entity our respondents reacted to it with a coherent cluster of perception and attitudes. This generalized orientation was found by their implicit choice of a point either on the positive or on the negative side of the continuum and by their corresponding reactions. Now the problem arises of whether attitude or perception had the genetic primacy in determining this generalized orientation. If one assumes a primacy of perception, then one may link distrust to the way in which an undefined mental patient is conceived, i.e., either as dangerous and qualitatively different from the general population or as indistinguishable from it. According to a primacy of attitude, we would consider the findings to be an illustration of the phenomenon that given a certain attitude, selective perception will result. This phenomenon has been repeatedly documented in studies of prejudice toward ethnic and religious minority groups. A study dealing with attitudes toward psychoanalysis in a cross-section of the French public also shows the existence of a structured coherent attitudinal cluster even though the representation of the issue may be cognitively diffuse (Moscovici, 1960).

SUMMARY

Further probings into a possible consistency or inconsistency of perception and attitudes toward mental patients were made, and clusters of acceptance and rejection were found.

Degree of occupational trust was parallel to the degree of favorableness of the perception of mental patients. Trust also increased with optimism about the outcome of hospitalization. The respondents who showed most occupational trust saw ex-patients as least impaired in their work performance. Such respondents also expressed least need for reassurances about ex-patients.

No relationship was found between occupational trust and the evaluation of employers' hiring practices for ex-mental patients. Neither was occupational trust seen to vary with respondents' readiness to help a formerly hospitalized close friend or relative in securing a job.

The respondents were asked to guess the motives of employers who hire ex-mental patients. The trustful respondents tended to give the ex-patients' ability as the main reason, while distrustful respondents were more likely to attribute employment of ex-patients to the humanitarianism of the employer. Respondents' occupational trust increases when they have had personal contact with ex-patients.

The findings so far make possible the identification of clusters of acceptance and rejection. Among respondents, two groups could be identified. A humanitarian cluster may be isolated, that is, the attitudes of a minority in the community who tend to perceive a mental patient as quite indistinguishable from the general population, as able to succeed, not dangerous, and trustworthy in positions of prestige and responsibility. A contrasting group exhibits a cluster of intolerance. Its members tend to perceive former mental patients as qualitatively different from the general population, as dangerous and untrustworthy, as unlikely to succeed in the respondent's line of work, as probably incurable, and as always liable to relapse.

CHAPTER 17

Education and attitudes

Until now we have attempted to determine the existence of consistent orientations, either favorable or unfavorable, toward ex-mental patients, in the population sampled. Our next step will be an attempt to relate these different results to some characteristics of the population sampled. Cumulative findings in social research strongly suggest a link between people's level of education, their type of occupation and their attitudes on a wide range of issues. We will, therefore, relate the views expressed so far on the issue of mental illness, first to the respondents' educational background, and in the next chapter, to their occupational level.

Table 111 shows that in all three areas the less educated respondents are, the more likely they are to be very distrustful. Aside from this similarity of the three areas, at every educational level border state respondents have a tendency to be more trustful than Hawaiian and English respondents. This corroborates our earlier findings (see Table 94) when occupational trust was related only to sample by areas. Therefore, the relatively greater tolerance exhibited by the border state sample in the normative dimension is not due to an artifact of sample composition.

The aforementioned relationship between attitudes and educational level of the respondents may be related to two district lines of social research. Along one line, the found relationship corroborates the view that intolerance may be an attribute of lower class personality. This view has been consistently supported by studies on ethnic prejudice (Allport, 1954), attitudes toward 'civil liberties' (Stouffer, 1955), and authoritarianism (Adorno *et al.*, 1950; Lipset, 1959). All these findings tend to agree that tolerance, whatever its object, increases with education which obviously may be considered to be a principal indicator of social class. As Stouffer writes in his study of

Table 111. *Educational level and occupational trust* (in percentages)

	B.S. Occupational trust					*Hawaii* Occupational trust				
	N	Very low	Low	Medium	High	N	Very low	Low	Medium	High
Some high school or less	103	21	20	48	11	93	40	27	28	5
Completed high school	145	10	23	41	27	153	22	27	40	11
Some college	126	11	16	50	23	84	14	19	46	20
Completed college	106	8	18	47	27	71	16	18	49	17

		England Occupational trust				
		N	Very low	Low	Medium	High
	Elementary	131	33	24	31	12
Secondary school	Ordinary level	57	23	18	44	16
Secondary school	Advanced level	57	26	25	30	19
	Some university or more	36	5	14	57	24

attitudes toward civil liberties: 'Intolerance may be a systemic factor in personality, whatever its object, and distrust of political deviants may be only one phase of a larger social and psychological problem – distrust of one's fellow man' (Stouffer, 1955).

Following this lead, one sees that the tendency of respondents with little education to be very distrustful of former mental patients fits into the general pattern of lower class authoritarianism, which has been defined as a lack of tolerance of human differences. Within this pattern, mental illness may very well be seen as one subcategory of human differences; ethnicity, cultural and ideological nonconformism may be others.

It has been argued in the literature that this lower class authoritarianism with the concomitant tendency to perceive the world as a dangerous place and the lack of optimism all complement a basic perceptive strategy, which has been linked to patterns of child rearing (see Frenkel-Brunswik, 1948).

The second line of research emphasizes not different personalities, but different life experience of the various social strata. If we integrate our findings with this second line of research it will lead us to a different interpretation. The results of this line of research have a bearing more specifically on mental illness and on different ways in which people from various social classes experience mental illness. The case for the hypothesis of 'differential experiences' as we may call it, may be made in the context of Hollingshead and Redlich's (1958) findings. They show that the symptoms of mental illness and modes of referral to mental hospitals differ by social class. Violence and anti-social behavior are common features of such illness among the lower class and are infrequent among the upper or middle strata. To support their claim, the authors show that in their community study, 72% of the psychotics in class V (which designates the slum dwellers and unskilled workers) were brought to treatment by police, courts and social agencies (52% were referred by the police). On the other hand, none of the psychotics of the upper and upper middle classes (classes I and II) were referred to the psychiatrist by the police. Violence and physical assault were thus described as the usual symptoms leading to referral in class V. (Hollingshead and Redlich, 1958.)

In an intensive analysis of a small number of patients from classes III (roughly the lower middle class) and V, who were included in the original Hollingshead and Redlich sample, Myers and Roberts note in the symptomatology of schizophrenics the following differences which can be linked to class affiliation: 'Class V patients were extremely suspicious and convinced that people were conspiring against them; patients were extremely violent and aggressive.' (Myers and Roberts, 1959.)

In contrast to class V patients, schizophrenics in class III displayed superiority feelings, grandiose ideas and ritualistic behavior. Among neurotics, suspiciousness and paranoid tendencies were found in class V, while neurotics in class III tended to consider themselves as failures in life. Such data tend to make us reconsider the reasons behind class differences in stated attitudes toward mental illness. Rather than expressing suspicion and distrust as a fact of the 'authoritarian' syndrome, the lower class respondents may be faithful to their actual experiences with the mentally ill around them. Suspiciousness and anomie seem to be widespread reactions of lower class people, and lower class mental patients may thus exhibit the usual characteristics of their milieu. Thus we may conclude that it is not so much different views of the *same* attitudinal object which are a function of respondents' education; rather, there may be a vicious circle between a tendency to be easily provoked to express suspicion fostered by a typical lower class milieu and the actual characteristics exhibited by the attitudinal object.

Finally, the tolerance exhibited by people of a high educational level, as contrasted to the relative intolerance of people with less education, may stem less from a difference in the underlying attitudes than from their notions of what may be a socially desirable answer. Education may inhibit the expression of intolerance and hostility in a verbal response to a questionnaire.

In our study, the relationships between education and the affective-conative dimension in the border state and the Hawaiian samples are similar to those found between education and the normative dimension (compare Tables 111 and 112).

Respondents who do not have a high school diploma are less likely to be willing to work with, to hire and to have as a boss, a former mental patient than are those who have had more schooling. There is also a tendency toward a consistent increase of favorable responses to these questions when other educational levels are considered, especially in the American sample. The same is true when favorable attitudes are conveyed by willingness to have an ex-patient as a party guest, as a neighbor, or living with him in the same household (see

Table 112. *Educational level and affective-conative dimension* (in percentages)
In general, how would you feel about a person who has had a mental illness?

	N	Willing to take a job alongside such a person	Willing to have such a person as your boss	Willing to hire such a person	Willing to invite such a person to your home as a guest at a party	Willing to have such a person live next door	Willing to have such a person in the same household
Border State							
Some high school or less	103	74	29	66	61	69	53
Completed high school	145	82	46	84	88	86	78
Some college	126	87	49	82	88	86	73
Completed college	106	85	55	79	91	90	79
England							
Elementary	131	84	33	76	82	88	59
Ordinary level	57	91	48	85	85	91	66
Advanced level	57	88	40	79	79	91	76
Some university or more	36	81	38	79	93	87	70
Hawaii							
(White)							
Some high school or less	18	72	33	55	61	67	61
Completed high school	39	77	33	82	82	79	74
Some college	38	92	59	92	95	90	79
Completed college	41	93	41	90	93	93	81
(Oriental)							
Some high school or less	46	49	9	45	55	55	36
Completed high school	89	75	25	62	71	67	55
Some college	35	78	31	67	86	75	61
Completed college	26	69	23	65	65	69	65

Table 112). The Hawaiian sample, on the whole, follows a similar pattern: people with less schooling express less favorable attitudes than people with more schooling. However, there is an over-all tendency for the oriental respondents to be less favorable than their Caucasian counterparts, regardless of educational level.

In England, when the affective-conative dimension is tapped, respondents with little schooling tend to display as much tolerance as those with more education. These results confirm our previous observation, that while English respondents are more likely than the American sample to express distrust concerning the occupational fitness of previously hospitalized patients, the English respondents are nevertheless more likely to *accept* ex-mental patients, if they are asked about their *private willingness* to do so. This paradoxical finding suggests that there seems to be in England a high tolerance of deviation on the level of personal contacts.

EDUCATION AND PERCEPTION OF MENTAL ILLNESS

When the data pertaining to the perception of the mentally ill are analyzed in terms of the respondents' educational level we see that while the same trend exists, there are also variations in the three areas sampled, which may be imputed to cultural characteristics. We will now consider the three samples one by one.

The border state sample

As Tables 113 and 114 show, the majority of respondents agree that, 'mental illness is an illness like any other', that 'many mental patients are capable of skilled labor, even though in some ways they are very disturbed mentally', and that 'people who were once patients in mental hospitals are no more dangerous than the average citizen'. However, even though a majority agree with the above statements, a trend may be seen in the usual direction, i.e., agreement increases when education increases, but the trend is slight.

Striking differences between highly educated and less educated respondents appear in a special set of questions which deal specifically with the notion that mental patients are visibly recognizable out of the general population. For instance, 40% among those who have less than a high school diploma, but only 2% among college graduates agree that, 'there is something about mental patients that makes it

Table 113. *Educational level and perception of mental patients – Border State* (Percentage who agree)

	Mental illness is an illness like any other	It is easy to recognize someone who once had a serious mental illness	Although patients discharged from mental hospitals may seem all right, they should not be allowed to marry
Some high school or less	75	36	40
Completed high school	65	16	12
Some college	89	16	14
Completed college	85	16	12

	There is something about mental patients that makes it easy to tell them from normal people	Many mental patients are capable of skilled labor, even though in some ways they are very disturbed mentally	People who were once patients in mental hospitals are no more dangerous than the average citizen
Some high school or less	40	88	69
Completed high school	14	89	72
Some college	13	92	70
Completed college	2	90	74

Table 114. *Educational level and perception of mental patients – Border State* (Percentage who agree)

	To become a patient in a mental hospital is to become a failure in life	Most women who were once patients in a mental hospital could be trusted as baby sitters	Although some mental patients seem all right, it is dangerous to forget for a moment that they are mentally ill
Some high school or less	17	35	61
Completed high school	5	60	40
Some college	2	64	33
Completed college	2	66	35

easy to tell them from normal people'. Correspondingly, 36% with less than a high school diploma agree that, 'it is easy to recognize someone who once had a serious mental illness'. Only 16% of respondents who are college graduates believe this.

Restrictive action toward mental patients is also differentially endorsed by respondents on the various educational levels. 40% of respondents with less than a high school diploma, and only 12% of respondents with a college education, agree that 'although patients discharged from mental hospitals may seem all right, they should not be allowed to marry'. Almost twice as large a proportion of college graduates as respondents with less than a high school diploma agree that 'most women who were once patients in a mental hospital could be trusted as baby sitters'. 17% of those who did not complete high school and 2% of college graduates believe that 'to become a patient in a mental hospital is to become a failure in life'. 61% of respondents with less than a high school diploma, and only 35% of college graduates believe that 'although some mental patients seem all right, it is dangerous to forget for a moment that they are mentally ill'.

The English sample

Tables 115 and 116 show the distributions of English respondents who agree with the following statements: 'Mental illness is an illness like any other', 'many mental patients are capable of skilled labor, even though in some ways they are very disturbed mentally', and 'people who were once patients in mental hospitals are no more dangerous than the average citizen'. The English distributions show the same trends as the border state sample.

However, in England, respondents who belong to the more educated groups are more likely than their U.S. mainland counterparts to believe that former mental patients may be differentiated from the general population, by agreeing with the statement that 'there is something about mental patients that makes it easy to tell them from normal people'. Also, when compared to U.S. mainland college graduates, the English respondents with university training are less likely to agree with the statement that, 'most women who were once patients in a mental hospital could be trusted as baby sitters'.

These results are consistent with the aforementioned findings on the English sample's relatively lower 'occupational trust' of mental patients.

Table 115. *Educational level and perception of mental patients – England* (Percentage who agree)

	Mental illness is an illness like any other	It is easy to recognize someone who once had a serious mental illness	Although patients discharged from mental hospitals may seem all right they should not be allowed to marry
Elementary	60	26	38
GCE to ordinary level	69	21	17
GCE to advanced level & some prof. or tech. training	76	21	22
Some university & completed prof. or tech. training	71	19	19
Completed university	73	13	0

	There is something about mental patients that makes it easy to tell them from normal people	Many mental patients are capable of skilled labor, even though in some ways they are very disturbed mentally	People who were once patients in mental hospitals are no more dangerous than the average citizen
Elementary	34	93	81
GCE to ordinary level	29	95	88
GCE to advanced level & some prof. or tech. training	29	91	86
Some university & completed prof. or tech. training	24	100	81
Completed university	27	100	93

Table 116. *Educational level and perception of mental patients – England* (Percentage who agree)

	To become a patient in a mental hospital is to become a failure in life	Most women who were once patients in a mental hospital could be trusted as baby sitters	Although some mental patients seem all right, it is dangerous to forget for a moment that they are mentally ill
Elementary	3	53	53
GCE to ordinary level	2	64	40
GCE to advanced level & some prof. or tech. training	2	66	35
Some university & compl. prof. or tech. training	–	48	33
Completed university	7	47	40

The Hawaiian sample

As Tables 117, 118 and 119 show, the results obtained in Hawaii reproduce the basic pattern which emerges from the U.S. mainland and English data. White and oriental respondents tend to display a more favorable perception if they have had more education. Differences between highly educated and less educated orientals are even more marked than differences between corresponding groups of white respondents on statements such as, 'although patients discharged from mental hospitals may seem all right, they should not be allowed to marry', 'to become a patient in a mental hospital is to become a failure in life', and 'although some mental patients seem all right, it is dangerous to forget for a moment thay they are mentally ill'. The findings on how education affects the perception of the mentally ill strongly suggest that amount of schooling overrides but does not eliminate cultural differences.

Table 117. *Education, ethnicity and perception of mental patients – Hawaii* (Percentage who agree)

	N	Mental illness is an illness like any other	It is easy to recognize someone who once had a serious mental illness	Although patients discharged from mental hospitals may seem all right, they should not be allowed to marry
White				
Some high school or less	18	61	50	39
Completed high school	39	74	10	28
Some college	38	90	13	10
Completed college	41	85	7	20
Oriental				
Some high school or less	46	60	34	51
Completed high school	89	69	30	33
Some college	35	86	25	28
Completed college	26	73	19	8

EDUCATION AND VIEWS ON WORK PERFORMANCE OF FORMER MENTAL PATIENTS

When we explore how people at various educational levels estimate the work performances of former mental patients we find interesting differences on a question dealing with ex-patients' intellectual capacity. The respondents are asked to judge the following statement as true or false:

'They (former mental patients) lack the intelligence with which to do the work.'

As Table 120 shows, in the border state sample 58% of respondents with less than a high school diploma say that the statement is never or rarely true, compared to 74% of college graduates who say this. In

Table 118. *Education, ethnicity and perception of mental patients – Hawaii* (Percentage who agree)

	N	There is something about mental patients that makes it easy to tell them from normal people	Many mental patients are capable of skilled labor, even though in some ways they are very disturbed mentally	People who were once patients in mental hospitals are no more dangerous than the average citizen
White				
Some high school or less	18	39	83	83
Completed high school	39	23	87	77
Some college	38	3	92	82
Completed college	41	5	95	81
Oriental				
Some high school or less	46	53	70	64
Completed high school	89	43	93	80
Some college	35	28	94	72
Completed college	26	15	96	73

the Hawaiian sample (Table 121) the differences between highly educated and least educated respondents are especially striking among whites. 17% of the least educated and 66% of college graduates think that ex-patients never or rarely lack the necessary intelligence to do the work. Among orientals, the same trend may be found to a lesser extent: In this group of respondents, 37% and 50% respectively state that ex-patients rarely or never lack the intelligence required to do the work. In all three samples, then, the more educated respondents more often than the less educated feel ex-mental patients do not lack the intelligence with which to do the work.

Some statements deal with other aspects of former mental patients' performance, such as:

(1) 'They require close supervision in their work',
(2) 'They are dangerous to those who work around them', and
(3) 'They are easily antagonized by their fellow workers'.
Responses to these items tend not to differ in terms of respondents' education.(See Tables 120, 121 and 122.)

Table 119. *Education, ethnicity and perception of mental patients – Hawaii* (Percentage who agree)

	N	To become a patient in a mental hospital is to become a failure in life	Most women who were once patients in a mental hospital could be trusted as baby sitters	Although some mental patients seem all right, it is dangerous to forget for a moment that they are mentally ill
White				
Some high school or less	18	33	44	50
Completed high school	39	8	54	31
Some college	38	3	79	26
Completed college	41	7	83	32
Oriental				
Some high school or less	46	23	36	60
Completed high school	89	6	52	49
Some college	35	3	44	47
Completed college	26	–	54	35

EDUCATION AND OPTIMISM ABOUT OUTCOME OF HOSPITALIZATION

We found that tolerance and a relatively favorable attitude toward mental illness are positively correlated with education in all three areas and that education overrides other variables such as cultural and ethnic affiliation. The same cannot be said about optimism about the curability of mental illness and about the final outcome of

Table 120. *Educational level and views on work performance of former mental patients – Border State* (In percentages)

	They require close supervision in their work (always, mostly)	They are dangerous to those who work around them (rarely, never)	They are easily antagonized by co-workers (rarely, never)
Some high school or less	35	68	18
Completed high school	25	82	8
Some college	25	77	15
Completed college	26	74	9

	They lack the intelligence with which to do the work (rarely, never)
Some high school or less	58
Completed high school	73
Some college	70
Completed college	74

hospitalization. Here the trend tends to be reversed: an increase in education goes with a decrease in optimism on the curability of mental illness.

Question 9 in the questionnaire asked: 'If a patient has been released from a mental hospital, when can you be sure that he is completely cured?' Table 123 shows the percentages of respondents agreeing with option (e): 'you can never be sure'. In the border state sample 58% of the college educated respondents and 55% of the least educated respondents agree that one can never be sure that a patient released from a mental hospital is completely cured. In Hawaii the trend is stronger; and in England 53% of respondents with an elementary education have doubts about a complete cure, compared to 69% with some university education.

Up to now the focus has been on what mental patients can do to fulfill external requirements. What happens when the focus is shifted to how family members should advise mental patients?

Table 121. *Education, ethnicity and views on work performance of former mental patients – Hawaii* (In percentages)

	N	They require close supervision in their work (always, mostly)	They are dangerous to those who work around them (rarely, never)	They are easily antagonized by co-workers (rarely, never)
White				
Some high school or less	18	44	44	28
Completed high school	39	38	77	13
Some college	38	31	77	16
Completed college	41	37	81	7
Oriental				
Some high school or less	46	49	49	30
Completed high school	89	37	64	20
Some college	35	36	70	26
Completed college	26	42	58	35

	N	They lack the intelligence with which to do the work (rarely, never)
White		
Some high school or less	18	17
Completed high school	39	67
Some college	38	74
Completed college	41	66
Oriental		
Some high school or less	46	37
Completed high school	89	52
Some college	35	49
Completed college	26	50

Table 122. *Educational level and views on work performance of former mental patients – England* (In percentages)

	They require close supervision in their work (always, mostly)	They are dangerous to those who work around them (rarely, never)	They are easily antagonized by co-workers (rarely, never)
Elementary	47	73	19
Ordinary level	31	81	14
Advanced level	31	79	11
Some university or more	42	69	11

	They lack the intelligence with which to do the work (rarely, never)
Elementary	47
Ordinary level	58
Advanced level	58
Some university or more	60

Table 123. *Educational level and belief that one can never be sure a patient released from a mental hospital is completely cured* (In percentages)

	N	*Border State*
Some high school or less	103	55
Completed high school	145	50
Some college	126	56
Completed college	106	58
	N	*Hawaii*
Some high school or less	93	61
Completed high school	153	52
Some college	84	55
Completed college	71	68
	N	*England*
Elementary	131	53
Ordinary level	57	47
Advanced level	57	53
Some university or more	36	69

EDUCATION AND LEVEL OF JOB RECOMMENDED FOR EX-MENTAL PATIENTS

The results shown in Table 124 suggest that in the three sample areas respondents who are highly educated are least likely to agree with this statement:

'When a patient is released from a mental hospital, his family should encourage him to take a job easier than the one he had before.'

Viewed across samples, American mainland respondents from all four educational groups seem most reluctant to advise a lowering of the job level of formerly hospitalized mental patients. At the opposite end of the distribution, the oriental respondents of the Hawaiian sample are those who consider it most advisable to suggest an easier occupation than the one held prior to hospitalization. It should be remembered that oriental respondents tended also to be more distrustful than other groups in restricting the number of occupations considered suitable for former mental patients.

Table 124. *Educational level and belief that when a patient is released from a mental hospital, his family should encourage him to take an easier job than before* (In percentages)

			N	*Border State*
Some high school or less			103	30
Completed high school			145	20
Some college			126	19
Completed college			106	14
			N	*England*
Elementary			131	37
Ordinary level			57	21
Advanced level			57	32
Some university			21	19
Completed university			15	27
	Hawaii			
	N	*White*	*N*	*Oriental*
Some high school or less	18	44	46	65
Completed high school	39	26	89	49
Some college	38	11	35	51
Completed college	41	27	26	35

EDUCATION AND IMPUTED MOTIVES FOR HIRING FORMER MENTAL PATIENTS

The same sharp distinction found in the imputed motive for hiring former mental patients by trustful and distrustful respondents turns up when people on different educational levels are compared. A content analysis was performed of answers to the following open ended question:

'When an employer knowingly hires a former mental patient, he does this because . . .'

Results of the content analysis are presented in Table 125. The two most frequent response categories were 'the ex-patient can do the job' and 'desire to help him'. The more educated the respondents are, the more often they think that an employer's reason for hiring a former mental patient may be the latter's ability to do the job. The connection between education and imputed motive is especially

Table 125. *When an employer knowingly hires a former mental patient, he does this because . . . By educational level* (In percentages)

	N	Desire to help him	The ex-patient can do the job
Border State			
Some high school or less	103	50	15
Completed high school	145	49	21
Some college	126	46	27
Completed college	106	27	42
Hawaii			
Some high school or less	94	51	12
Completed high school	154	40	26
Some college	85	34	45
Completed college	71	25	48
England			
Elementary	131	73	14
Ordinary level	57	63	16
Advanced level	57	60	33
Some university	21	62	14
Completed university	15	67	27

marked in the border state sample and in Hawaii. In these two areas, 50% of the replies given spontaneously by respondents with less than a high school diploma specify that a desire to be helpful or to do a good deed must have motivated the employer in his action. Half as many (27% and 25%) respondents with a college degree impute the same reason to an employer. The trend of replies given is exactly reversed when the category has to do with the fitness of the mental patient for the job. The border state and the Hawaiian sample distributions show that only 15% and 12% of respondents with less than a high school diploma mention spontaneously the ex-patients' fitness while almost one out of two of the college educated respondents express such a view, i.e., 42% and 48% in the border state and Hawaii respectively. These findings fit very well the picture obtained so far, that people with little education are more sensitive to the debilitating effect of mental illness than are highly educated people.

The results obtained with the English sample offer a somewhat different picture. Even though there is a stronger tendency for the highly educated respondents than for those with less education to think of a patient's fitness for the job as the reason for his employment, the differences between the two extremes of the English educational groups are not very striking (27% versus 14%). When all samples are considered, 'desire to help' and 'to accomplish a good deed' are more frequently imputed to the employer in England than in the border state and in Hawaii. This tendency is especially strong when we compare the most highly educated groups in the three areas: one out of four respondents with a college education imputes a charitable motive to the employer in the border state and in Hawaii, while in England two thirds (people with some university training) do so.

These findings confirm our initial evidence on the English respondents' relatively greater distrust and skepticism of the ability of a former mental patient to perform on the job and on their somewhat greater tolerance on the affective-conative dimension. Thus, of the three samples, the English display least dislike for various sorts of contact with former mental patients, but they do not show a corresponding trust in ex-patients' abilities.

SUMMARY

In this chapter, respondents' attitudes were related to their level of education. In all three samples, border state, Hawaii and England, the less educated the respondents were, the more likely they were to be very distrustful. This finding was related to relevant literature on social research.

In the present study, the relationship between education and the affective-conative dimension in the border state and the Hawaiian samples was similar to that found between education and the normative dimension. Reception of the mentally ill tended to be increasingly favorable as one ascends the respondents' educational ladder. In spite of this general trend, some variations were found among the three sample areas. The variations, which were described in detail, may be imputed to cultural characteristics.

In all three sample areas, the most highly educated respondents were least likely to feel that ex-patients should take easier jobs than they used to hold. The more educated the respondents were, the more often they believed the employer's reason for hiring ex-patients to be their ability to do the job.

To summarize the findings so far, in all three areas a favorable attitude toward mental patients tends to increase with education. This was most noticeable in the border state and the Hawaiian samples.

Even though occupational trust was positively linked to the respondents' education, the two variables were not overlapping; while some of the components of the attitudinal cluster were found to be related to the educational component, others were not. For instance, distrustful respondents tended to assume that a former mental patient needs more supervision and that he is more dangerous to those who work with him. However, it is not true that most respondents with little education thought so. As another example, distrustful respondents tended to be less optimistic about the complete curability of mental illness, but the least educated respondents were more optimistic on this score than the most educated ones.

Therefore, even though background variables such as education may on the whole be powerful predictors of people's attitudes, they cannot tell the entire story; there is still room for a psychological variable, which we may call a 'general orientation', to account for the consistency of various indicators.

CHAPTER 18

Occupation and attitudes

We will now see whether occupational level plays a role as a variable in affecting attitudes. To a certain extent, educational and occupational variables are overlapping; skills and education tend to increase together. However, within the blue collar category, further differentiations can be made. The views of unskilled and skilled workers and of foremen can be distinguished, even though all of them may be included in the low educational level.

Table 126* shows the relationship between respondent's occupational level and occupational trust of ex-mental patients. In all three sampling areas, unskilled workers tend to be more distrustful than management, clerical, or skilled workers. The unskilled workers' relative position on the index of occupational trust is similar in all three areas, but the absolute percentages obtained show regional differences. Among the unskilled workers 49% of the border state sample have a very low or low score on the index of occupational trust, whereas 67% of the Hawaiian and 64% of the corresponding English respondents have such scores. The distribution of scores among foremen is very similar in the three areas (50% in the border state, 52% in Hawaii, 55% in England) if we again combine the low and the very low scores of occupational trust. In other words, in all three areas blue collar workers tend to be distrustful of former mental patients.

Members of the management of large and medium sized companies in all three areas tend to exhibit more occupational trust. It was

* The sample distribution by occupational level was first shown in Table 92. For the sake of brevity, in the following tables 'large-medium managers' will stand for managers of large and medium companies, and 'small managers' will stand for managers of small companies.

Table 126. *Occupational level and occupational trust* (In percentages)

	Border State					Hawaii					England				
	Occupational trust					Occupational trust					Occupational trust				
	N	Very low	Low	Medi-um	High	N	Very low	Low	Med-ium	High	N	Very low	Low	Medi-um	High
Large-medium managers and professionals	116	7	19	47	28	112	17	22	40	21	41	12	20	51	17
Small managers	35	23	17	40	20	24	21	21	46	13	51	41	20	37	2
Clerical and low supervisory	213	11	19	44	26	135	18	22	48	12	89	18	20	35	26
Foremen	22	27	23	41	9	27	23	29	11	36	36	36	19	33	11
Skilled workers	46	11	15	52	22	39	26	31	41	3	29	14	28	48	10
Unskilled workers	47	21	28	45	6	67	45	22	25	7	39	41	23	23	13

previously established that when people are asked about their willingness to *work with* and to hire a former mental patient, a more favorable attitude is obtained on this affective-conative dimension than when they are asked to state in which occupations former mental patients should be *trusted* (occupational trust). However, interesting differences are obtained when occupational level as a variable is related to the affective-conative dimension.

As Table 127 shows, in the border state foremen and unskilled workers display least willingness to hire and to work with former mental patients. The great majority of unskilled workers are also unwilling to have a former mental patient as a boss. The attitudes of the other occupational categories are more favorable. In England a similar pattern is found among unskilled workers; this group tends to exhibit relatively less acceptance of former mental patients than any other occupational group. The foremen in England are more tolerant on the affective-conative dimension than their American counterparts.

In analyzing the Hawaiian data, we were obliged to condense the six occupational categories into four, because the sample had to be further subdivided by ethnic affiliation. The term 'managers' includes managers of companies of all sizes and professionals; 'white collar' refers to clerical and low supervisory personnel, and 'blue collar' includes both skilled and unskilled workers. Hawaiians, as an ethnic group distinct from the Caucasian and the oriental respondents, tended to fall into two occupational categories: white collar and blue collar workers. The Filipinos fitted only into one category, that of blue collar workers. The Filipino group comprised newly arrived immigrants, most of whom were unskilled.

Among the white respondents in Hawaii the same trend that was found in the border state is reproduced. In both areas unskilled workers and, to a certain extent, foremen are less favorable in their attitudes than the other occupational groups. The oriental respondents tend to be more homogeneous in their answers, since there is comparatively less acceptance of former mental patients in *all* the occupational categories described. The Filipinos, of all ethnic groups, are most unfavorable toward ex-mental patients. The ethnic Hawaiians sharply distinguish between the willingness to work with or hire (about which they show a relatively high tolerance) and the willingness 'to have as a boss' (about which they tend to exhibit very little tolerance).

Table 127. *Occupational level and affective-conative dimension* (in percentages)
In general, how would you feel about a person who has had a mental illness?

	N	Willing to take a job alongside such a person	Willing to have such a person as your boss	Willing to hire such a person	Willing to invite such a person to your home as a guest at a party	Willing to have such a person live next door	Willing to have such a person in the same household
Border State							
Large-medium managers & professionals	116	88	57	82	91	94	87
Small managers	35	83	52	83	97	98	92
Clerical and low supervisory	213	85	40	83	93	93	88
Foremen	22	64	41	55	78	86	77
Skilled workers	46	78	41	78	83	83	82
Unskilled workers	47	57	28	53	70	76	64
England							
Large-medium managers & professionals	41	88	39	80	94	100	91
Small managers	51	80	42	66	92	98	92
Clerical and low supervisory	89	89	41	82	95	96	90
Foremen	36	94	33	86	97	98	94
Skilled workers	29	90	45	90	93	100	93
Unskilled workers	39	77	26	77	85	90	80
Hawaii							
(White)							
Managers	77	91	47	90	96	96	93
Foremen	9	89	33	78	100	100	100
White collar	31	94	52	97	97	97	90
Blue collar	19	53	21	47	79	74	73
(Oriental)							
Managers	47	64	25	62	91	96	77
Foremen	13	69	23	62	85	85	69
White collar	81	75	22	65	84	88	82
Blue collar	55	67	20	57	80	78	67
(Hawaiian)							
White collar	15	80	20	74	86	86	87
Blue collar	11	73	9	82	82	73	63
(Filipino)							
Blue collar	19	42	27	37	68	58	42

OCCUPATION AND WILLINGNESS TO HAVE SOCIAL CONTACTS WITH EX-MENTAL PATIENTS

It may be remembered that the affective-conative dimension covered, in addition to work situations, also social contact situations. When we review the results obtained in each of the three areas studied (see Table 127) the pattern just outlined is repeated. In the border state there is a discrepancy in tolerance of social contact with former mental patients between (a) the respondents who occupy management and clerical positions, and (b) those who are foremen or occupy unskilled positions. In England, as we saw before, the expressed level of acceptance is relatively high on all occupational levels. In Hawaii, once more, white respondents closely reproduce the attitudinal pattern found on the American mainland: managers and white collar workers are more likely to be tolerant in their expressed feelings than unskilled workers. As was suggested before, the oriental respondents tend to be more homogeneous than the whites. They represent an intermediate position between the views of white management and those of white manual labor.

Ethnic Hawaiian respondents also differ in their views depending on whether they are white collar or blue collar workers with the former expressing more tolerance. The Filipinos, who are all blue collar workers, are most reluctant about having social contact with a former mental patient.

JOBS FOR WHICH EX-MENTAL PATIENTS ARE CONSIDERED FIT

It may be of special interest to see how the various occupational groups perceive the characteristics of jobs for which former mental patients may be considered fit. Table 128 shows that in the border state, management and white collar workers are more likely than either foremen or blue collar workers to accept the idea of hiring a former mental patient for positions of supervision. On all three questions, foremen are least favorable to ex-mental patients.

In Hawaii the views of white respondents differ strongly according to whether they are foremen and unskilled workers or are managers and white collar workers. Supervision and decision making jobs for ex-patients, interestingly, are more readily approved by managers and

Table 128. *If an employer knows that an applicant is a former patient, should he hire him for jobs . . .* (In percentages)

	In which he has to supervise other people	In which there are important decisions to make	With close personal contact with other people
Border state			
Large-medium managers & professionals	52	58	83
Small managers	46	49	83
Clerical & low supervisory	40	40	74
Foremen	36	36	50
Skilled workers	37	52	85
Unskilled workers	37	52	85
England			
Large-medium managers & professionals	53	43	95
Small managers	34	32	82
Clerical & low supervisory	33	63	74
Foremen	33	19	81
Skilled workers	38	28	83
Unskilled workers	26	26	85
Hawaii			
(White)			
Managers	45	43	82
Foremen	33	33	89
White collar	48	45	81
Blue collar	5	5	53
(Oriental)			
Managers	28	21	57
Foremen	23	23	54
White collar	26	19	60
Blue collar	22	20	69
(Hawaiian)			
White collar	33	7	60
Blue collar	0	0	64
(Filipino)			
Blue collar	26	32	37

white collar workers. Oriental respondents present a far greater homogeneity across occupations in their views than do the whites. Here as before, the result is a middle of the road position; the oriental managers are less tolerant than the white management members, but the oriental blue collar workers are more tolerant than their white counterparts. None of the blue collar ethnic Hawaiians approve of hiring former mental patients for positions of supervision and decision making, and only a small percentage of ethnic Hawaiian white collar workers do so. Quite unexpectedly, there is a relatively high approval among Hawaiians of hiring ex-patients for jobs that involve close contact with other people. Ethnic Hawaiians as a group are more likely to distrust former mental patients when they are asked to give an opinion on the level of performance which may be expected from them, but they are relatively willing to tolerate close contact with ex-patients.

OCCUPATION AND PERCEPTION OF MENTAL ILLNESS

We have reviewed before the general trends in the perception of mental illness in England, Hawaii and the border state. We will now briefly discuss the major differences which can be related to the occupational background of the respondents. The results obtained in the border state and England are reproduced in Tables 129 and 130. The Hawaiian results may be found in Tables 131, 132 and 133. In the border state unskilled workers sharply distinguish themselves from other occupational groups by expressing a more negative view of mental illness. The managers represent the opposite end. For example, 38% of unskilled workers and only 8% of the management believe that it 'is easy to recognize someone who once had a serious mental illness'; 38% of unskilled workers and only 10% of management agree that, 'although patients discharged from mental hospitals may seem all right, they should not be allowed to marry'. For these two statements, results obtained in England closely replicated the ones we just reviewed.

Only 3% of the border state managers and 45% of unskilled workers agree that 'there is something about mental patients that makes it easy to tell them from normal people'; in England the proportions are 31% for the managers and 49% for the unskilled workers. English and border state unskilled workers are also more

Table 129. *Occupational level and perception of mental patients – Border State and England* (Percentage who agree)

	There is something about mental patients that makes it easy to tell them from normal people		Many mental patients are capable of skilled labor, even though in some ways they are very disturbed mentally		People who were once patients in mental hospitals are no more dangerous than the average citizen	
	B.S.	England	B.S.	England	B.S.	England
Large-medium managers & professionals	3	31	93	98	73	93
Small managers	6	26	91	100	65	86
Clerical & low supervisory	17	37	89	94	74	87
Foremen	28	30	87	91	64	86
Skilled workers	26	14	91	97	68	86
Unskilled workers	45	49	83	92	53	79

Table 130. *Occupational level and perception of mental patients – Border State and England* (Percentage who agree)

	To become a patient in a mental hospital is to become a failure in life		Most women who were once patients in a mental hospital could be trusted as baby sitters		Although some mental patients seem all right, it is dangerous to forget for a moment that they are mentally ill	
	B.S.	England	B.S.	England	B.S.	England
Large-medium managers & professionals	2	2	73	65	41	44
Small managers	–	–	63	44	23	38
Clerical & low supervisory	5	4	59	77	38	41
Foremen	10	–	50	61	37	42
Skilled workers	6	3	61	66	35	52
Unskilled workers	18	6	42	47	75	57

Table 131. *Occupation, ethnicity and perception of mental patients – Hawaii* (Percentage who agree)

	N	Mental illness is an illness like any other	It is easy to recognize some-one who once had a serious mental illness	Although patients discharged from mental hospitals may seem all right, they should not be allowed to marry
White				
Managers	77	83	12	21
Foremen	9	89	33	22
White collar	31	87	3	13
Blue collar	19	58	42	42
Oriental				
Managers	47	81	26	21
Foremen	13	54	38	54
White collar	81	72	31	32
Blue collar	55	65	27	40
Hawaiian				
White collar	15	67	13	20
Blue collar	11	64	45	45
Filipino				
Blue collar	19	47	47	32

likely than managers to consider mental patients as dangerous and are less likely to trust them as baby sitters; they are more likely to consider them failures in life.

Data obtained in Hawaii once more fit the established pattern. The white respondents closely resemble those of the mainland; unskilled workers indicate a relatively negative view of mental illness and managers by comparison express a more favorable view. Correspondingly, the oriental group is more homogeneous in its view, management and blue collar workers agreeing more than their Caucasian counterparts in their perception of mental illness. As before, oriental

Table 132. *Occupation, ethnicity and perception of mental patients – Hawaii* (Percentage who agree)

	N	There is something about mental patients that makes it easy to tell them from normal people	Many mental patients are capable of skilled labor, even though in some ways they are very disturbed mentally	People who were once patients in mental hospitals are no more dangerous than the average citizen
White				
Managers	77	6	96	83
Foremen	9	11	89	67
White collar	31	6	84	77
Blue collar	19	58	84	84
Oriental				
Managers	47	32	91	74
Foremen	13	69	92	77
White collar	81	38	94	78
Blue collar	55	40	80	69
Hawaiian				
White collar	15	40	100	80
Blue collar	11	55	100	82
Filipino				
Blue collar	19	68	79	63

respondents may be thought of as being less favorable than the most favorable Caucasian group (managers) but as more favorable than the Caucasian white and blue collar respondents. The ethnic Hawaiians, like the whites, vary in their perception of mental illness according to whether they are blue collar or white collar workers. Among ethnic Hawaiians as among whites, increase of favorableness goes with increase on the occupational level. Filipinos, who in the sample are all blue collar workers, tend to be more negative in their perception of mental illness than the other blue collar groups.

Table 133. *Occupation, ethnicity and perception of mental patients – Hawaii* (Percentage who agree)

	N	To become a patient in a mental hospital is to become a failure in life	Most women who were once patients in a mental hospital could be trusted as baby sitters	Although some mental patients seem all right, it is dangerous to forget for a moment that they are mentally ill
White				
Managers	77	6	74	29
Foremen	9	11	56	44
White collar	31	6	77	23
Blue collar	19	26	42	58
Oriental				
Managers	47	2	43	43
Foremen	13	7	46	69
White collar	81	5	56	51
Blue collar	55	5	56	51
Hawaiian				
White collar	15	–	47	33
Blue collar	11	9	64	91
Filipino				
Blue collar	19	32	42	79

OCCUPATION AND VIEWS ON WORK PERFORMANCE OF FORMER MENTAL PATIENTS

How do people at various occupational levels differ in their evaluations of work performance of released mental patients? In the border state foremen and unskilled workers are more likely than managers, white collar and skilled workers to think that former mental patients require close supervision in their work (see Table 134). Foremen and unskilled workers are more likely to believe that ex-patients lack the intelligence with which to do the work. Specific fears of ex-patients as being dangerous and easily antagonized by their fellow workers emerge from the answers of unskilled workers. In England such a consistent pattern fails to appear.

Table 134. *Occupational level and views on work performance of former mental patients – Border State and England* (In percentages)

	They require close supervision in their work (always, mostly)		They are dangerous to those who work around them (rarely, never)		They are easily antagonized by co-workers (rarely, never)	
	B.S.	England	B.S.	England	B.S.	England
Large-medium managers & professionals	24	43	77	69	57	54
Small managers	31	46	72	74	75	54
Foremen	41	50	73	78	55	52
Clerical & low supervisory	27	34	82	79	70	51
Skilled workers	20	35	70	76	66	69
Unskilled workers	38	46	55	82	41	57

	They lack the intelligence with which to do the work (rarely, never)	
	B.S.	England
Large-medium managers & professionals	68	62
Small managers	75	48
Foremen	50	67
Clerical & low supervisory	79	64
Skilled workers	65	44
Unskilled workers	37	52

The results for Hawaii may be found in Table 135. In the white group there are no differences between management, foremen and blue collar workers when we compare their agreement with the statement that former mental patients require close supervision in their work. In contrast to this finding, striking differences emerge around the notion of danger. Only 33% of the foremen and 48% of unskilled workers, but as much as 79% of the management and even 90% of the white collar workers, agree with the statement that, 'former mental patients are "rarely or never" dangerous to those who work around them'.

Table 135. *Occupation, ethnicity and views on work performance of former mental patients – Hawaii* (In percentages)

	They require close supervision in their work (always, mostly)	They are dangerous to those who work around them (rarely, never)	They are easily antagonized by co-workers (rarely, never)
White			
Managers	40	79	65
Foremen	44	33	67
White collar	23	90	71
Blue collar	42	48	37
Oriental			
Managers	43	64	62
Foremen	61	77	61
White collar	41	61	49
Blue collar	32	57	47
Hawaiian			
White collar	60	60	47
Blue collar	45	82	36
Filipino			
Blue collar	53	32	42

In Hawaii as among border state respondents, the view that ex-patients are easily antagonized by co-workers was more widespread among blue collar workers than among any other occupational group. A similarity with the border state is also found in the belief that former mental patients 'lack the intelligence with which to do the work'. Foremen and blue collar workers agree with this statement more than any other group. Filipinos and ethnic Hawaiians also tend to express a negative view about the working performance of former mental patients. The pattern obtained with oriental respondents is less clearcut; oriental managers tend to be less favorable in estimating the working performance of ex-patients than white managers, but the differences among orientals by occupational categories do not follow a consistent trend.

	They lack the intelligence with which to do the work (rarely, never)
White	
Managers	66
Foremen	44
White collar	74
Blue collar	31
Oriental	
Managers	42
Foremen	62
White collar	51
Blue collar	44
Hawaiian	
White collar	73
Blue collar	54
Filipino	
Blue collar	37

OCCUPATION AND LEVEL OF JOB RECOMMENDED FOR EX-MENTAL PATIENTS

Table 136 shows that in the border state unskilled workers are the occupational group most likely to subscribe to the view that a family should encourage a former mental patient to take an easier job than he had before his illness. Managers are least likely to hold this view. Strangely enough, foremen, who have been so far close in their views to unskilled workers, are less inclined to suggest that it would be advisable for ex-mental patients to lower their vocational aspirations.

In England there are practically no differences on this issue according to occupational groups. In Hawaii, as Table 137 shows, the white managers once more share very much the opinions held by the managers in the continental United States. Only 17% of white managers as compared to 63% of blue collar workers subscribe to the view that his family should encourage a former mental patient to take an easier job than he had before his illness. In both sample areas,

Table 136. *Occupational level and belief that when a patient is released from a mental hospital, his family should encourage him to take an easier job than before* (In percentages)

	Border State	England
Large-medium managers & professionals	15	35
Small managers	20	34
Clerical & low supervisory	27	30
Foremen	16	31
Skilled workers	30	38
Unskilled workers	43	36

Table 137. *Ethnicity, occupation and belief that when a patient is released from a mental hospital, his family should encourage him to take an easier job than before* (In percentages)

	Hawaii
White	
Managers	17
Foremen	11
White collar	23
Blue collar	63
Oriental	
Managers	45
Foremen	62
White collar	49
Blue collar	58
Hawaiian	
White collar	40
Blue collar	58
Filipino	
Blue collar	95

therefore, white management members are less likely to suggest openly that mental illness should be considered an impairment; correspondingly, in both areas blue collar workers are more likely to agree to this view. On this issue foremen are more similar to management than to the blue collar workers, in contrast to their usual pattern.

The view that ex-patients' work activities should not be very demanding is relatively strongly endorsed by the entire oriental group, and especially so by foremen and blue collar workers. It is also relatively widespread among Hawaiians, particularly if they are blue collar workers. The Filipinos are almost unanimous in approving of it: 95% do so.

OCCUPATION AND IMPUTED MOTIVES FOR HIRING FORMER MENTAL PATIENTS

We have analyzed before in Chapter 17 how educational level and distrust affected the imputed motives behind an employer's decision to hire a former mental patient. Can the occupational variable add some information on this issue? Table 138 shows that in the border state foremen and unskilled workers are the groups most likely to

Table 138. *When an employer knowingly hires a former mental patient, he does this because . . . By occupational level* (In percentages)

	N	Willing to help him	The ex-patient can do the job
Border State			
Large-medium managers & professionals	82	51	49
Small managers	24	50	50
Clerical & low supervisory	151	66	34
Foremen	15	80	20
Skilled workers	36	64	36
Unskilled workers	27	81	19
Hawaii			
Large-medium managers & professionals	79	47	53
Small managers	15	47	53
Clerical & low supervisory	94	56	39
Foremen	15	73	27
Skilled workers	28	79	21
Unskilled workers	40	68	32
England			
Large-medium managers & professionals	41	68	32
Small managers	45	80	20
Clerical & low supervisory	79	79	11
Foremen	32	73	27
Skilled workers	22	87	13
Unskilled workers	35	91	9

give as an employer's motive his desire to help or to do a good deed. Very rarely do these respondents mention as a possible reason that a former mental patient can do the job. In England, too, unskilled workers are most likely to express the 'good deed' motive; this tendency is more widespread in England than in the border state on all but one occupational and educational level. In Hawaii, the trend closely resembles the mainland American one.

SUMMARY

In the current chapter, attitudes were seen in the light of different occupational levels. To a certain extent, educational and occupational variables were overlapping; skills and education tended to increase together.

In all three sample areas, the unskilled workers were more likely to show little occupational trust than management, clerical and skilled workers. Regional differences were discussed.

Majorities of all occupational groups were willing to have social contacts with ex-mental patients. Unskilled workers were relatively least willing to have such contacts or to accept ex-patients in supervisory and decision making jobs. Also the perception of former mental patients tended to become more favorable with the respondents' increasing occupational level.

In the border state sample, foremen and unskilled workers were most likely to think that ex-patients require close supervision in their work, that they lack the intelligence to do their work, and that they should be encouraged to take an easier job than they used to hold.

In all three samples, unskilled workers most frequently thought that ex-patients were hired because of the employer's humanitarianism rather than because of the patients' competence.

Thus, the general pattern found by analyzing the respondents' attitudes was that in the border state, according to various indicators, the foremen and unskilled workers tended to express the least favorable attitudes toward mental illness and former mental patients. In England a similar tendency emerged from the analysis of the data, but the pattern was less consistent.

The analysis of the results so far indicates a similarity in the orientation toward mental patients in the three areas sampled, even though differences in emphasis may be detected. In all three areas, education tended to be positively correlated with more favorable attitudes. The level of occupation was also a significant variable in locating attitudes in specific subgroups of respondents. Some cultural differences emerged: oriental respondents tended to be more homogeneous in their attitudes; level of education and type of occupation affected their general orientation toward mental illness less than they did among mainland American and English respondents. Among ethnic Hawaiians the differential pattern by education and occupation was present. It is difficult to estimate the views of the Filipinos as an ethnic group, since in the present sample they happened to be all blue collar workers.

CHAPTER 19

Perceived distinctions between nervous breakdown and mental illness

The results so far indicate that even though the severity and the type of mental illness were left unspecified, the respondents tended to select one portion of the continuum subsumed under the vague label of 'mental illness' and to organize several dimensions of their attitudes into a coherent cluster. However, the problem of cognitive evaluation of the phenomenon is still open. Do people have a notion of differences in type and degree of mental illness? A recurrent theme in the assessement of public opinion on mental illness has been that side by side with a strong rejection of mental illness, the public tends to deny pathological significance to clearcut symptoms of paranoia, schizophrenia and manic-depressive disorders. According to Star's findings, only the most extreme forms of mental illness, such as severe psychosis, are recognized as such by most people: 'The tendency is to resist calling anyone "mentally ill" and to do so more or less as a last resort' (Joint Commission, 1961, p. 75). Similar findings are reported by the Cummings (Cumming and Cumming, 1957) and Phillips (1967). The implication is that what may appear to mental health professionals as clearly pathological may be perceived by the general public as falling within the range of normality.*

In this context the present research has made it clear that there exists an intermediate step between what the popular mind defines as mental illness and what it defines as normal. This step corresponds to the popular notion of 'nervous breakdown'. According to our findings, this is the label reserved for the forms of emotional disturbance which do not exhibit the most severe symptoms.

* It may be mentioned, however, that some studies have reported an increase in the public's recognition of symptoms of mental illness, e.g. Lemkau and Crocetti (1962), Bentz, Edgerton and Kherlopian (1969).

The respondents were asked:

'Do you think that a nervous breakdown and mental illness are the same thing?'

Our results show that more than three fourths of the respondents in each of the areas sampled perceive mental illness as different from nervous breakdown. We then asked the respondents to describe what mental illness and what nervous breakdown consist of. The obtained descriptions show a remarkable consistency across the three sampling areas (see the excerpts from the questionnaires at the end of this Chapter). The English respondents tend to put greater emphasis on heredity as cause of mental illness than respondents in the border state and Hawaii. Nervous breakdown is perceived by the respondents as a disturbance, due to environmental pressure, which is temporary and curable and may require a short hospitalization. Mental illness, on the other hand, is generally considered to be incurable, an unchangeable component of personality requiring long hospitalization and affecting all spheres of functioning, as is the case in the most extreme forms of psychosis. As the excerpts from the questionnaires (below) show, even the minority who consider nervous breakdown and mental illness as the same thing often exhibit in their descriptions the same distinctions made by the majority, i.e., nervous breakdown is seen as a less serious disturbance.

Only a few consider the term nervous breakdown to be a polite word for mental illness. Thus, we may agree with Star and the Cummings that only the extreme forms of behavior are perceived as mental illness by most people, but we disagree with their implication that intermediate symptoms are viewed pretty much as ordinary behavior.

Nervous breakdown is the missing link between the most severe form of impairment and normality as seen by the general public. Nervous breakdown refers to emotional disturbances which would undoubtedly be included by any psychiatrist in the realm of mental illness. We may then conclude that various degrees and forms of emotional disturbances are classified differently by psychiatrists and by the general public. The latter see the less impairing, more curable forms of mental illness as a separate entity, different both qualitatively and semantically from more serious mental disorders. The experts, on the contrary, do not see a difference between a 'nervous breakdown' and a 'mental illness'.

The public was found to dissociate the label of mental illness from many symptoms of pathological states. This does not imply, as earlier researchers have argued, that the public considers such symptoms to lie within the limits of normality. Rather, one may understand these responses in the light of popular semantics as distinct from psychiatric semantics.

We may schematically illustrate the differences, as suggested by our empirical findings.

	Mental illness	*Nervous breakdown*
'Professional' View (Mental hygiene ideology)	Frequently curable; may be of short duration; may impair only part of person's functioning.	No precise medical meaning.
Popular view	Generally incurable; requires long hospitalization; due to inborn characteristics rather than external pressures; affects the total functioning of the person.	Curable; may be of short duration; requires short hospitalization; may be due to external pressures; impairs only part of person's functioning.

This cognitive distinction corresponds to an attitudinal distinction. The perception of nervous breakdown as an intermediate position between normality and mental illness is reflected in a greater tolerance toward people who are seen as having suffered the former type of disturbance.

The empirical evidence for this may be found by comparing results on the willingness to work, to hire and to have social contacts with someone who has had a mental illness (Table 99) with results on the same questions referring to someone who has had a nervous breakdown (see Table 139). The two tables show consistently more tolerance for persons suffering from 'nervous breakdown' in every instance, that is, for each of the six questions for all three samples. The only zone of relative resistance which persists has to do with accepting someone who has had a nervous breakdown as one's boss, though in England even in this point little discrimination is seen.

Table 139. *Nervous breakdown and the affective-conative dimension* (in percentages)
In general, how would you feel about a person who has had a nervous breakdown?

	Willing to take a job alongside such a person	Willing to have such a person as your boss	Willing to hire such a person
Border State	88	64	88
Hawaii	85	59	77
England	98	72	97

	Willing to invite such a person to your home as a guest at a party	Willing to have such a person live next door	Willing to have such a person in the same household
Border State	85	88	81
Hawaii	86	85	77
England	93	97	90

Table 139 shows that when the six questions are considered together, there is a tendency in Hawaii to be less tolerant. Further analysis of the data showed that these results are due to the responses of oriental and Filipino respondents, which are consistent with our previous findings. On the other hand, the English sample is the most tolerant on each of the six questions. In reference to 'mental illness' (see Table 99) the English sample was also most tolerant and the Hawaiian least tolerant.

Therefore, even though there appears to be more tolerance of 'nervous breakdown' than of 'mental illness', the relative position of the sample areas on the favorable-unfavorable continuum is not altered. Tables 140 and 141 show still more clearly that people who are more likely to be distrustful of ex-mental patients are also less tolerant of those who have had a nervous breakdown. However, when we compare their answers on the two issues we find these respondents are relatively more tolerant of those who suffered nervous breakdowns. A comparison of Tables 100 and 101 with Tables 140 and 141 shows the very clearcut greater tolerance for nervous breakdown over mental illness for all six questions across samples as well as across all degrees of occupational trust.

Table 140. *Occupational trust and willingness to accept at work someone who suffered a nervous breakdown* (In percentages)

Occupational trust	Willing to take a job alongside such a person			Willing to have such a person as your boss			Willing to hire such a person		
	B.S.	Haw.	Eng.	B.S.	Haw.	Eng.	B.S.	Haw.	Eng.
Very low	79	74	86	33	33	46	79	59	96
Low	87	89	98	56	60	68	87	80	93
Medium	93	94	90	72	68	73	93	86	89
High	89	96	100	84	89	98	87	94	100

Table 141. *Occupational trust and willingness to accept in a social context someone who suffered a nervous breakdown* (In percentages)

Occupational trust	Willing to invite such a person to your home as a guest at a party			Willing to have such a person live next door			Willing to hire such a person the same household		
	B.S.	Haw.	Eng.	B.S.	Haw.	Eng.	B.S.	Haw.	Eng.
Very low	69	69	86	78	71	94	71	55	84
Low	90	86	95	90	89	95	82	81	91
Medium	92	94	88	92	93	90	87	87	84
High	90	98	95	89	92	100	86	90	95

A few excerpts follow to exemplify how the respondents in the three sample areas describe 'nervous breakdown' and 'mental illness'. The first section will report descriptions of the majority, i.e., of respondents who consider 'mental illness' and 'nervous breakdown' to be different entities; the second section will give accounts by those who consider the two categories to represent the same entity.

Excerpts from the Questionnaires: respondents' descriptions of nervous breakdown and mental illness

NERVOUS BREAKDOWN AND MENTAL ILLNESS ARE DIFFERENT ENTITIES

Border state

Breakdown can be for short period of time. Mental illness usually requires more time for rehabilitation.

Nervous breakdown can be caused by overwork or worries. Mental illness generally runs in the family and is harder to cure.

Nervous breakdown is not as serious as the other and is more easily cured. Mental illness, being the opposite, offers a harder struggle to the patient to return to a normal life.

A nervous breakdown may come from overpressure in problems of life. Mental illness is really a disease of the mind, probably inherited.

Nervous breakdown – temporary, not seriously affecting reasoning. Mental illness – serious, affecting sanity and reasoning powers.

Nervous breakdown is a temporary illness caused by overload of work, family problems, etc. Mental illness is a long history of mental problems, heredity, etc.

Hawaii

Nervous breakdown may be due to emotional reactions and anxiety. Mental illness is usually from some mental defect, due to heredity, birth and prenatal period.

Nervous breakdown – temporary difficulty resulting from extreme anxiety – may be handled quickly with supportive therapy, or over long term period with psychiatric out-patient care. Mental illness – chronic disease – frequently requires hospitalization.

A breakdown is most usually brought on by pressure of overworking the mind. Mental illness is usually a weakness of the mind and an inability to cope with pressure of life.

Nervous breakdown is the overworking of the nervous system due to strain and tension. Mental illness is the disease of the nervous system.

Nervous breakdown – too much pressure, either from business or family. Mental illness has to do with the mind.

Nervous breakdown – due to pressure of work or surroundings. It happens to a lot of people and they can be cured faster. Mental illness – something that happens when a person can't face facts.

Nervous breakdown – more temporary. Mental illness, more permanent.

England

A nervous breakdown is usually brought about by overwork and worry. Mental illness is more serious.

A mentally ill patient is hardly ever properly cured. A nervous breakdown is not lasting, the patient always recovers. A mental patient remains as such.

A nervous breakdown is due to overworry, worry and an unhappy home life where nobody cares for you. A mental illness is something that runs in the family, it contains that certain grain of mentality that is never lost no matter how long the patient is treated for this complaint.

You would say mental illness would make a person unstable, eccentric, and to act in a way that is normally foreign to his nature. Nervous breakdown could be a general feeling of being run down, that you are unable to cope with your work, when this has previously been possible.

Nervous breakdown is mostly caused by worry. Mental illness is mostly caused at birth or family upset.

Nervous breakdown caused by overwork and worry. Mental illness is due to brain deficiency or shock.

Nervous breakdown is a temporary illness mainly due to anxiety. Mental illness: possibly hereditary or accidental through head injury.

A nervous breakdown is generally brought on by extra worry and strain. Mental illness is usually hereditary and is more severe than a nervous breakdown.

Nervous breakdown is caused by overwork and worry. Mental illness occurs when the brain has no control over its reactions.

Nervous breakdown is when a person has something on his mind. Mental illness is when a person has no control over his brain.

MENTAL ILLNESS AND NERVOUS BREAKDOWN ARE THE SAME ENTITY

Border state

I think that both are manifestations of the same tendency, although mental illness is far more general than nervous breakdown, so far as symptoms are concerned. The latter I think of as a withdrawal and inability to face normal situations, etc. Nervous breakdown short term. Mental illness long term.

Mental illness more severe. Nervous breakdown easier to recompose self, but nervous breakdown requires less time to regain confidence, I would think.

Hawaii

Nervous breakdown is a somewhat less intense manifestation of mental illness and could most likely be overcome with the removal of small but constant annoyances. Mental illness usually stems from deeper, perhaps longer, inflicted causes and because of the longer period of time involved in the latter, might take longer to cure.

Nervous breakdown – where specific recent events can be pointed out as being the pressures which caused the breakdown. Mental illness – precipitation of breakdown may or may not be as above, but underlying cause of breakdown goes deeper into past or to physical brain defects.

England
This is a matter of degree. A mental illness may develop from nervous breakdown if proper treatment is not available in the same way that a cold may develop into pneumonia.

A nervous breakdown is one where he suffers and can no longer cope with the normal mental stresses of every day life. Mental illness is a more complex and advanced stage of the same trouble.

Nervous breakdown can either be a mild relaxation of one's responsibilities, or it can be a nice way of describing mental illness. Generally, however, it connotes something less serious than mental illness. Mental illness is a very wide term and can cover many different types of mental abnormality. It can be harmless or violent, mild or severe. It may be noticeable at sight or only at intervals, or never be noticeable. Overwork can cause a nervous breakdown which is a mental disorder.

What starts as a breakdown by being depressed can if it is not treated and helped, then develop into mental illness.

They can be in stages. Mental illness can follow nervous breakdown.

Nervous breakdown seems to be a temporary illness caused by various day-to-day happenings. Mental illness suggests an ailment of the brain, embodying a nervous breakdown but also other causes, sometimes hereditary.

A nervous breakdown is a polite term for mental illness.

SUMMARY

The present research has made very clear that between popular definitions of mental illness and of normality there exists an intermediate stage corresponding to the popular notion of nervous breakdown. Nervous breakdown refers to those forms of emotional disturbance which do not exhibit the most severe symptoms. In all three sampling areas, nervous breakdowns tended to be perceived as disturbances due to environmental pressure, as temporary and curable, and as requiring only brief hospitalization. Mental illness, on the other hand, was generally seen as essentially incurable, as affecting all parts of the personality and as requiring long hospitalization.

This cognitive distinction corresponds to an attitudinal distinction. Persons who suffered from a 'nervous breakdown' were shown greater tolerance than were those who were 'mentally ill'. It was pointed out that in psychiatric language, the term 'nervous breakdown' has no precise meaning and the term 'mental illness' includes both the more and the less severe disorders. Practical implications will be discussed in Chapter 20.

CHAPTER 20

Recommendations for practical applications

In the preceding Chapter, we demonstrated the general distinction which is made by respondents in all three sample areas between 'mental illness' and 'nervous breakdown'. The practical implication of the findings will be obvious. An educational program to change the perception of ex-mental patients in the community need not create a new image but may utilize the existent concept of 'nervous breakdown', as this is considered not a permanent handicap but a curable, temporary condition.

Nunnally's study (1961) dealing with public views of mental illness shows that any attempt to change the connotations of words describing some aspect of it failed. It is not surprising that a concept which has a deeply rooted meaning could not be easily changed. Our data suggest an approach to create a more sympathetic appraisal of mental patients which partially bypasses the usual difficulty. We showed that among the general public there is a well structured concept which expresses precisely what the mental hygiene movement has been eager to find in order to minimize the stigma of mental illness. Persons involved in the rehabilitation of former mental patients should stress whenever possible the description of an individual hospitalization in terms of 'nervous breakdown' rather than of the more fearful 'mental illness'.

On the basis of our findings, it becomes a somewhat perplexing task to estimate the range of jobs available to a released mental patient. If we consider, for instance, an unskilled worker who was hospitalized for mental illness, we may expect he will find little resistance in obtaining employment, since the great majority of respondents agree that blue collar jobs may be entrusted to former mental patients. However, his potential co-workers, the unskilled section of the labor force, and the foremen who may be their direct recruiters, are precisely the groups which are most reluctant to work with him and to hire him.

On the other hand, a highly skilled person, professional or other, with a history of mental illness, even though he is likely to move in the more tolerant milieu of educated people, will encounter a limited range of openings, since positions of responsibility commensurate with his training may not be entrusted to him.

What practical implications have these two paradoxes for the rehabilitation of ex-mental patients? Our findings imply that for blue collar workers it is most important to create a sympathetic outlook toward mental patients in general, while on the most skilled level the need is greater for specific vocational information about the performance of ex-patients. A further practical recommendation may be made. If, as was shown, attitudes toward and perceptions of mental patients differ with the respondents' education, then different techniques will be required to change the attitudes of different educational groups, a process of some difficulty (see Cumming and Cumming, 1957; Rosen, 1970).

Another conclusion relevant for practical applications should be mentioned: The norms of duty toward people who are close to the respondents seem to override the intolerance they may have toward mental illness in general. Family ties and friendship make for a widespread readiness to help even among subgroups which were found to be generally distrustful of ex-mental patients. Therefore, when one has to assess the degree of acceptance the community is willing to extend to a former mental patient, special emphasis should be given to the immediate group around the ex-patient and to the feelings of duty toward him as a friend and relative.

As a consequence, it may be recommended that special counseling and advice on rehabilitation should be extended to the people who are in close contact with the ex-patient. Such people may be expected to be the best mediators between the patient and the community, and therefore their efforts should be made more effective.

APPENDIX I

Questionnaire for Professionals in the Mental Health Field

This questionnaire is part of a study being conducted by the World Federation for Mental Health. The purposes of this study are to learn what problems exist in the treatment of mental patients in different countries and to find new ways for helping mental patients. We feel we can learn most about mental health problems by asking professional workers like yourself how you feel about mental health problems and by benefiting from your experience. The information you give us will be extremely valuable in comparing mental health problems and practices in the United States and in other countries.

There are no 'right' or 'wrong' answers to the questions in this pamphlet. The only 'right' answers are those which best express *your* feelings and *your* experiences.

All your answers in this questionnaire will be held *strictly confidential.* You will not be asked to sign the questionnaire nor to mention any names. This study is not concerned with you personally nor with your institution but with the experiences and views of professional workers in the mental health field. Your replies to questions may be published only together with the replies of other professionals in the form of anonymous summaries.

Please be sure to answer all questions. Please work quickly and do not spend too much time on any question. Your *first impression* is the one we are interested in.

Thank you very much for your cooperation.

1. In your opinion, what is the most pressing need in the treatment of mental patients? (Comment *briefly*)

2. The best way to get along with mental patients is: (Check ONE)
   (a) by telling them what to do for their own good
   (b) by letting them do what they like as much as possible
   (c) by leaving them alone

3. The primary goal of the hospital staff should be (Check ONE)
   (a) to cure the patients of their illness
   (b) to rehabilitate the patients into society

4. In order to treat a mental patient, which one of the following do you consider most important? (Check ONE)
   (a) knowledge of his symptoms
   (b) knowledge of how his illness developed

5. What do you think is usually most important for a patient released from a mental hospital? (Check ONE)
   (a) to find a useful job
   (b) to be close to his family
   (c) to find happiness in normal society

6. Rank the following three statements. Put the number *1* behind the statement you think most important. Put the number *2* behind the statement you think next most important. Put the number *3* behind the statement you think least important.
   (a) Mental illness is due to a patient's heredity
   (b) Mental illness is due to a patient's environment
   (c) Mental illness is due to a patient's physical disease

7. Rank the following three statements. Put the number *1* behind the statement you think most important. Put the number *2* behind the statement you think next most important. Put the number *3* behind the statement you think least important.
   The chief function of a mental hospital is:
   (a) To safeguard society
   (b) To return the patients to society
   (c) To protect the patients

8. When former mental patients are readmitted to the hospital what are the *three* most important reasons? (Put the number *1* behind the reason you think most important, the number *2* behind the reason you think next most important, the number *3* behind the reason you think third most important).
   - (a) patient didn't try hard enough
   - (b) family didn't try hard enough
   - (c) employer or fellow workers didn't try hard enough
   - (d) community members didn't try hard enough
   - (e) public agencies didn't try hard enough
   - (f) patient was too used to being hospitalized
   - (g) patient was not well enough to be released

9. Staff members of mental hospitals hold different opinions on the use of open wards. (Please check *ALL* statements with which you agree:)
   - (a) patients escape more often from open wards than from closed wards
   - (b) open wards motivate patients in a hospital to improve
   - (c) closed wards are more efficient
   - (d) it is hard to maintain order and discipline in an open ward
   - (e) patients in open wards get cured faster
   - (f) closed wards are easier on the staff
   - (g) open wards often lead to trouble with the community

10. (Speaking very generally) what kind of treatment would you consider most promising for schizophrenic patients about age 30? (Check ONE)
    - (a) custodial care
    - (b) shock therapy
    - (c) psychotherapy
    - (d) staff members working as a team under a psychiatrist (milieu therapy)
    - (e) drug therapy
    - (f) don't know

11. Which of the following patients have you found it easiest to work with?
    - (a) male patients
    - (b) female patients

12. Which of the following patients have you found it easiest to work with?
    - (a) white collar workers
    - (b) blue collar workers

13. Which of the following patients have you found it easiest to work with?
    - (a) fee patients
    - (b) non-fee patients

14. Which of the following patients have you found it easiest to work with?
    - (a) Negro patients
    - (b) Oriental patients
    - (c) White patients

15. Do you think that persons who once have been mental patients could successfully work in *your* profession?
    - (a) always
    - (b) probably
    - (c) probably not
    - (d) never

16. In your opinion, about how many per cent of mental patients in your state *need* help in vocational rehabilitation? (Check ONE)
    - (a) very few (2% or less)
    - (b) few (about 15%)
    - (c) about a quarter (25%)
    - (d) about half (50%)
    - (e) most (more than 50%)
    - (f) all

17. In your opinion, about how many per cent of mental patients in your state have *received* help in vocational rehabilitation? (Check ONE)

(a) very few (2% or less)
(b) few (about 15%)
(c) about a quarter (25%)
(d) about half (50%)
(e) most (more than 50%)
(f) all

The questions on this page go together. Please give *two* answers to each question, one answer in each column:

(1) Check the kind of former mental patient you believe *most* likely to be successful in his job, and
(2) check the kind of former mental patient you believe *least* likely to be successful in his job.

	Most likely to be successful in his job	*Least* likely to be successfull in his job
18. Sex of former mental patient:		
(a) Male		
(b) Female		
19. Age of former mental patient:		
(a) below 20		
(b) 20 - 29		
(c) 30 - 39		
(d) 40 - 49		
(e) 50 - 59		
(f) above 59		
20. Ex-patients' new job mostly:		
(a) requires dealing with things		
(b) requires dealing with people		
21. Ex-patients' new job is:		
(a) white collar		
(b) blue collar		

	Most likely to be successful in his job	*Least* likely to be successful in his job
22. Ex-patient:		
(a) has to *compete* with his fellow workers		
(b) works independently		
23. Ex-patient in his new job:		
(a) supervises others		
(b) takes orders from others		
(c) neither supervises nor takes orders		
24. Ex-patient's yearly income *before* illness was:		
(a) below $4,000		
(b) 4,000 - 6,000		
(c) 6,000 - 8,000		
(d) above 8,000		
25. Ex-patient's yearly income *after* illness was:		
(a) below $4,000		
(b) 4,000 - 6,000		
(c) 6,000 - 8,000		
(d) above 8,000		
26. Ex-patient's ethnic background:		
(a) Negro		
(b) Oriental		
(c) White		

Please be sure you gave two answers to each question, one in each column.

27. When a former mental patient is applying for a job, shoud he tell the employer about his hospitalization?
    (a) Yes
    (b) No

    Explain *briefly* why you feel that way:

28. When should job planning for a mental patient best be started?
    (a) with his admission to the hospital
    (b) early in his treatment
    (c) late in his treatment
    (d) after his treatment has been completed

29. When a released mental patient asks for help in finding a job, it would be best: (Check ONE)
    (a) to return him to his old job
    (b) to find him first an easy job to get him used to regular work
    (c) to delay his getting a job until it is fairly certain he can keep it
    (d) to find him a new job as soon as possible
    (e) to find him a new permanent job

30. In your opinion, what are the *three* greatest difficulties in the vocational rehabilitation of former mental patients?

    Put the number *1* behind what you feel is the greatest difficulty.

    Put the number *2* behind what you feel is the second greatest difficulty.

    Put the number *3* behind what you feel is the third greatest difficulty.
    (a) weakness of the ex-patients
    (b) reluctance of employers to hire ex-mental patients
    (c) the patient's family doesn't understand him
    (d) lack of program in the hospital
    (e) lack of program among community mental health agencies
    (f) most people in the community don't understand the problems of former mental patients

31. Speaking quite generally of different racial groups you have known, and neither of the best nor of the worst members, would you like to have:

	as relatives by marriage	as church members	as neighbors in your street	in school with your children	as fellow workers	prefer not to have any close contact
(a) Negroes	1	2	3	4	5	6
(b) Orientals	1	2	3	4	5	6
(c) White	1	2	3	4	5	6

(Circle as many numbers on each line as apply)

The word pairs on the next three pages can describe different kinds of mental patients you have been working with. Each list contains 28 word pairs like this:

Manic _____ _____ _____ _____ _____ _____ _____ Depressive

You are asked to choose how well you feel these words describe certain patients. Here is an example:
Person to be rated:

MENTAL PATIENT I MOST ENJOY WORKING WITH

If you feel that one of the two words is *closely related* to the patient being rated, place your check mark next to this word as shown:

Hostile _____ _____ _____ _____ _____ _____ __V__ Friendly

If you feel that one of the two words is *somewhat related* to the patient being rated, place your check mark as follows:

Neat _____ __V__ _____ _____ _____ _____ _____ Untidy

If you feel that one of the two words is *slightly related* to the patient being rated, place your check mark like this:

Ugly ____ ____ ____ ____ _V_ ____ ____ Handsome

If you feel there is *no relationship* between the patient being rated and either of the two words, place your check mark in the center, as shown:

Short ____ ____ ____ _V_ ____ ____ ____ Tall

PLEASE NOTE:

(1) Place your check mark in the middle of the dash, not on the boundaries:

____ _V_ ____ ____ ____V____ ____

THIS NOT THIS

(2) Put only one check mark on each scale.

(3) Be sure you check each item, do not omit any.

Please do not look back and forth through the lists. Try to make each judgement independent of any other. Work quickly, and do not worry over details. Your *first impression* is the one we are interested in.

MENTAL PATIENT I *MOST* ENJOY WORKING WITH

1. Thoughtful __ __ __ __ __ __ __ Carefree
2. Excitable __ __ __ __ __ __ __ Calm
3. Trusting __ __ __ __ __ __ __ Suspicious
4. Unpredictable __ __ __ __ __ __ __ Predictable
5. Responsible __ __ __ __ __ __ __ Irresponsible
6. Changeable __ __ __ __ __ __ __ Stable
7. Outgoing __ __ __ __ __ __ __ Self-centered
8. Emotional __ __ __ __ __ __ __ Unemotional
9. Sociable __ __ __ __ __ __ __ Unsociable
10. Intelligent __ __ __ __ __ __ __ Stupid

11.	Unreliable	___ ___ ___ ___ ___ ___ ___	Reliable
12.	Old	___ ___ ___ ___ ___ ___ ___	Young
13.	City	___ ___ ___ ___ ___ ___ ___	Farm
14.	Violent	___ ___ ___ ___ ___ ___ ___	Gentle
15.	Interested	___ ___ ___ ___ ___ ___ ___	Apathetic
16.	Understandable	___ ___ ___ ___ ___ ___ ___	Obscure
17.	Low education	___ ___ ___ ___ ___ ___ ___	High education
18.	Cooperative	___ ___ ___ ___ ___ ___ ___	Uncooperative
19.	Shiftless	___ ___ ___ ___ ___ ___ ___	Steady
20.	Customary	___ ___ ___ ___ ___ ___ ___	Modern
21.	Verbal	___ ___ ___ ___ ___ ___ ___	Uncommunicative
22.	Highly insightful	___ ___ ___ ___ ___ ___ ___	Without insight
23.	Flexible	___ ___ ___ ___ ___ ___ ___	Compulsive
24.	Delusional	___ ___ ___ ___ ___ ___ ___	Reality oriented
25.	Aggressive	___ ___ ___ ___ ___ ___ ___	Submissive
26.	Independent	___ ___ ___ ___ ___ ___ ___	Dependent
27.	Rude	___ ___ ___ ___ ___ ___ ___	Polite
28.	Moral	___ ___ ___ ___ ___ ___ ___	Immoral

MENTAL PATIENT I *LEAST* ENJOY WORKING WITH

1.	Thoughtful	___ ___ ___ ___ ___ ___ ___	Carefree
2.	Excitable	___ ___ ___ ___ ___ ___ ___	Calm
3.	Trusting	___ ___ ___ ___ ___ ___ ___	Suspicious
4.	Unpredictable	___ ___ ___ ___ ___ ___ ___	Predictable
5.	Responsible	___ ___ ___ ___ ___ ___ ___	Irresponsible
6.	Changeable	___ ___ ___ ___ ___ ___ ___	Stable
7.	Outgoing	___ ___ ___ ___ ___ ___ ___	Self-centered
8.	Emotional	___ ___ ___ ___ ___ ___ ___	Unemotional
9.	Sociable	___ ___ ___ ___ ___ ___ ___	Unsociable
10.	Intelligent	___ ___ ___ ___ ___ ___ ___	Stupid
11.	Unreliable	___ ___ ___ ___ ___ ___ ___	Reliable
12.	Old	___ ___ ___ ___ ___ ___ ___	Young
13.	City	___ ___ ___ ___ ___ ___ ___	Farm
14.	Violent	___ ___ ___ ___ ___ ___ ___	Gentle
15.	Interested	___ ___ ___ ___ ___ ___ ___	Apathetic
16.	Understandable	___ ___ ___ ___ ___ ___ ___	Obscure
17.	Low education	___ ___ ___ ___ ___ ___ ___	High education
18.	Cooperative	___ ___ ___ ___ ___ ___ ___	Uncooperative

19.	Shiftless	_ _ _ _ _ _ _	Steady
20.	Customary	_ _ _ _ _ _ _	Modern
21.	Verbal	_ _ _ _ _ _ _	Uncommunicative
22.	Highly insightful	_ _ _ _ _ _ _	Without insight
23.	Flexible	_ _ _ _ _ _ _	Compulsive
24.	Delusional	_ _ _ _ _ _ _	Reality oriented
25.	Aggressive	_ _ _ _ _ _ _	Submissive
26.	Independent	_ _ _ _ _ _ _	Dependent
27.	Rude	_ _ _ _ _ _ _	Polite
28.	Moral	_ _ _ _ _ _ _	Immoral

There are many differences of opinion about mental illness. Many people agree with each of the following statements while many people disagree with each of these statements. We would like to know what *you* think about these statements. Each of them is followed by six choices:

strongly agree	agree	not sure but probably agree	not sure but probably disagree	disagree	strongly disagree

Please check (V) in the space provided, that choice which comes closest to saying how *you* feel about each statement. You can be sure that many people, including doctors, will agree with your choice. There are no right or wrong answers: We are interested only in *your opinion.* It is very important that you answer *every* item.

1. MENTAL ILLNESS IS AN ILLNESS LIKE ANY OTHER

strongly agree	agree	not sure but probably agree	not sure but probably disagree	disagree	strongly disagree

2. MOST PATIENTS IN MENTAL HOSPITALS ARE NOT DANGEROUS

strongly agree	agree	not sure but probably agree	not sure but probably disagree	disagree	strongly disagree

3. IT IS EASY TO RECOGNIZE SOMEONE WHO ONCE HAD A SERIOUS MENTAL ILLNESS

strongly agree	agree	not sure but probably agree	not sure but probably disagree	disagree	strongly disagree

4. ALTHOUGH PATIENTS DISCHARGED FROM MENTAL HOSPITALS MAY SEEM ALL RIGHT, THEY SHOULD NOT BE ALLOWED TO MARRY

strongly agree	agree	not sure but probably agree	not sure but probably disagree	disagree	strongly disagree

5. THERE IS SOMETHING ABOUT MENTAL PATIENTS THAT MAKES IT EASY TO TELL THEM FROM NORMAL PEOPLE

strongly agree	agree	not sure but probably agree	not sure but probably disagree	disagree	strongly disagree

6. IF OUR HOSPITALS HAD ENOUGH WELL TRAINED DOCTORS, NURSES, AND AIDES, MANY OF THE PATIENTS WOULD GET WELL ENOUGH TO LIVE OUTSIDE THE HOSPITAL

strongly agree	agree	not sure but probably agree	not sure but probably disagree	disagree	strongly disagree

7. MANY MENTAL PATIENTS ARE CAPABLE OF SKILLED LABOR, EVEN THOUGH IN SOME WAYS THEY ARE VERY DISTURBED MENTALLY

strongly agree	agree	not sure but probably agree	not sure but probably disagree	disagree	strongly disagree

8. PEOPLE WHO WERE ONCE PATIENTS IN MENTAL HOSPITALS ARE NO MORE DANGEROUS THAN THE AVERAGE CITIZEN

strongly agree	agree	not sure but probably agree	not sure but probably disagree	disagree	strongly disagree

9. TO BECOME A PATIENT IN A MENTAL HOSPITAL IS TO BECOME A FAILURE IN LIFE

strongly agree	agree	not sure but probably agree	not sure but probably disagree	disagree	strongly disagree

10. MOST WOMEN WHO WERE ONCE PATIENTS IN A MENTAL HOSPITAL COULD BE TRUSTED AS BABY SITTERS

strongly agree	agree	not sure but probably agree	not sure but probably disagree	disagree	strongly disagree

11. THE PATIENTS OF A MENTAL HOSPITAL SHOULD HAVE SOMETHING TO SAY ABOUT THE WAY THE HOSPITAL IS RUN

strongly agree	agree	not sure but probably agree	not sure but probably disagree	disagree	strongly disagree

12. PEOPLE WITH MENTAL ILLNESS SHOULD NEVER BE TREATED IN THE SAME HOSPITAL AS PEOPLE WITH PHYSICAL ILLNESS

strongly agree	agree	not sure but probably agree	not sure but probably disagree	disagree	strongly disagree

13. ALTHOUGH SOME MENTAL PATIENTS SEEM ALL RIGHT, IT IS DANGEROUS TO FORGET FOR A MOMENT THAT THEY ARE MENTALLY ILL

strongly agree	agree	not sure but probably agree	not sure but probably disagree	disagree	strongly disagree

14. SEX DELINQUENTS SHOULD BE SEVERELY PUNISHED

strongly agree	agree	not sure but probably agree	not sure but probably disagree	disagree	strongly disagree

15. PROFESSIONALS WHO WORK WITH MENTAL PATIENTS SHOULD TRY TO RAISE A PATIENT'S OPINION ABOUT HIMSELF

strongly agree	agree	not sure but probably agree	not sure but probably disagree	disagree	strongly disagree

The following questions are asked to help in the tabulation and in the statistical analysis of these questionnaires. They are *not* asked in order to pin you down as an individual. Please do *not* sign your name.

32. Sex:
    - (a) Male
    - (b) Female

33. Age:
    - (a) Under 20
    - (b) 20-29
    - (c) 30-39
    - (d) 40-49
    - (e) 50-59
    - (f) 60 and above

34. Marital status:
    - (a) Single
    - (b) Married
    - (c) Divorced
    - (d) Widowed
    - (e) Other (write in)

35. If you were asked to use one of these four names for your social class, which would you say you belonged in? (Check ONE).
    - (a) Middle class
    - (b) Lower class
    - (c) Working class
    - (d) Upper class

36. Education: (Check highest)
    - (a) Some grade school
    - (b) Completed grade school
    - (c) Some high school
    - (d) Completed high school
    - (e) Some college
    - (f) Completed college

37. If you attended college or professional schools please fill in the following:

Major field	*No. of yrs. studied in this field*	*Degree or Certificate if any*

38. What is your present occupation?
    - (a) Attendant
    - (b) Nurse
    - (c) Occupational therapist
    - (d) Physician (non-psychiatrist)
    - (e) Psychiatrist
    - (f) Psychologist (specify)
    - (g) Recreation therapist
    - (h) Rehabilitation counselor
    - (i) Social worker
    - (j) Other (write in)

39. How long have you worked in your present position? (Check ONE)
    (a) less than 3 months
    (b) 3 to 6 months
    (c) 6 months to 1 year
    (d) 1 to 2 years
    (e) 2 to 3 years
    (f) 3 to 5 years
    (g) more than 5 years

40. What other jobs have you held? (Please list earliest job first)

Occupation	*Type of employer*	*No. of yrs. employed*

41. Altogether, how many years have you worked with mental patients?
    (a) less than 3 months
    (b) 3 to 6 months
    (c) 6 months to 1 year
    (d) 1 to 2 years
    (e) 2 to 3 years
    (f) 3 to 5 years
    (g) 5 to 10 years
    (h) more than 10 years

42. On an average day, where do you work?
    (a) Open ward
    (b) Closed ward
    (c) Special service facility
    (d) Out patient facility
    (e) Outside of hospital (specify)
    (f) Other (write in)

43. What is your present total family income a year before taxes?
    (a) Up to $ 4,000
    (b) 4,000 - 6,000
    (c) 6,000 - 8,000
    (d) 8,000 - 10,000
    (e) 10,000 - 12,000
    (f) over 12,000

44. What is your religious preference?
    (a) Catholic
    (b) Jewish
    (c) Protestant
    (d) Other (write in)

45. What is your ethnic background:
    (a) Negro
    (b) Oriental
    (c) White

46. What was your father's last occupation?
    (a) Unskilled worker
    (b) Semi-skilled worker
    (c) Skilled manual worker
    (d) Office or sales worker
    (e) Small business owner or manager
    (f) Professional, big business executive or owner
    (g) Farm worker
    (h) Farm owner or manager

47. What was the highest school grade completed by your father? (Circle ONE)
    1 2 3 4 5 6 7 8 9 10 11 12 13 14 15 16 16+

Please make sure you have answered all questions.
Thank you again for your cooperation.

APPENDIX II

Community questionnaire

This questionnaire is part of a study being conducted by the World Federation for Mental Health in Hawaii, the United Kingdom and the United States. We are asking you, and a number of other people in this region, about the problems that may arise when patients leave a mental hospital. The purpose of this study is to compare your feelings on this matter with those of people in other countries. The information you give us will be extremely valuable in comparing the problems met by former mental patients and the people around them in different countries.

There are no 'right' or 'wrong' answers to the question in this pamphlet. The only 'right' answers are those which best express *your* feelings and *your* experiences.

All your answers in this questionnaire will be held strictly *confidential.* You will not be asked to sign the questionnaire nor to mention any names.

Please be sure to answer all questions. Please work quickly and do not spend too much time on any one question. Your *first* impression is the one in which we are interested.

All references to patients in the following pages refer to mental patients, and all references to hospitals to mental hospitals.

Thank you very much for your cooperation.

1. Would you say that most patients leaving a mental hospital are:
   (a) completely cured
   (b) not completely cured
   (c) as ill as before they entered the hospital
   (d) worse than before they entered the hospital

2. What do you think is most difficult for a patient leaving a mental hospital?
   (a) to find a good job
   (b) to get along well with his family
   (c) to have some good friends

3. Here are some statements about patients who have been released from mental hospitals. Please tell me for each statement whether it is *Always, Mostly, Sometimes, Rarely,* or *Never* True:

	Always	*Mostly*	*Sometimes*	*Rarely*	*Never*
They work as carefully as anybody else					
They require close supervision in their work					
They are dangerous to those who work around them					
They get along well with their co-workers					
They are easily antagonized by their fellow workers					
They are unable to stand the pressure of work					
They are stable in their work					
They lack the intelligence with which to do the work					
They antagonize their fellow workers					

4. Do you think that a patient released from a mental hospital, who had been properly trained, may be trusted in the following occupations?

	Yes	*No*	*Comments*
a medical doctor			
an actor			
a carpenter			
a policeman			
a doorman			
a bank cashier			
a judge			
a farmer			
a lawyer			
a bus driver			
a journalist			
a foreign service officer			
a general of the army			
a school teacher			
a clergyman			
a housekeeper			
a dentist			
a painter (artist)			
a scientist			
a groceryman			
a factory foreman			
a sales clerk			
a druggist			

5. If an employer knows that an applicant is a former mental patient, should he hire him for:

	Yes	*No*
(a) jobs in which he has to supervise other people		
(b) jobs in which there are important decisions to be made		
(c) jobs with close personal contact with other people		
(d) all types of jobs for which he has experience and training without restriction		

6. Do you think that when a patient is released from a mental hospital, his family should:

R PATIENTS COULD SUCCESSFULLY WORK IN MY OCCUPATION

agree	not sure but probably agree	not sure but probably disagree	disagree	strongly disagree

following questions are asked to help in the tabulation and e statistical analysis of these questionnaires. They are *not* in order to pin you down as an individual. Please *do not* our name.

a) Male
b) Female

) Under 20
) 20-29
) 30-39
) 40-49
50-59
60 or more

Status:
Single
Married
Divorced
Widowed
Separated
Religious Order
Other (write in)

re asked to use one of these four names for your social h would you say you belonged in?
Middle Class
Lower Class
Working Class
Upper Class

(a) encourage him to take a job easier than the one he had before
(b) encourage him to go back to his old work
(c) encourage him to take a more difficult job than he had before

7. When a former mental patient is applying for a job, should he tell the employer about his hospitalization?
   (a) Yes
   (b) No
   Why:

8. If you had to work closely with a former mental patient, would you want to have some specific information and assurances about him?
   (a) Yes
   (b) No
   If *Yes,* what kind of information and assurances would you want?

9. If a patient has been released from a mental hospital, when can you be sure that he is completely cured?
   (a) when he comes out of the hospital
   (b) after 6 months of regular work
   (c) after one year of work
   (d) after 5 years of work
   (e) you can never be sure

10. Do you think that a nervous breakdown and mental illness are the same thing?
    (a) Yes
    (b) No
    Please describe both:

11. What do you think happens to people who have *nervous breakdowns?*
    (a) They are usually sent for a long time to a mental hospital
    (b) They are usually sent for a few weeks to a mental hospital
    (c) They are hardly ever sent to a mental hospital

12. In general, how would you feel about a person who has had a:

	Nervous breakdown		*Mental illness*	
	Yes	*No*	*Yes*	*No*
Would you be willing to take a job alongside such a person?				
Would you be willing to have such a person as your boss?				
If you were the boss, would you be willing to hire such a person?				
Would you invite such a person to your home as a guest at a party?				
Would you be willing to have such a person live next door?				
Would you be willing to have such a person in the same household with you?				

13. What do you think an employer *generally does* when he knows that an applicant has been a patient in a mental hospital?
    (a) Hires him without difficulty
    (b) Hires him after obtaining some assurances from a doctor or former employer

21. Education (Check Highest):
    - (a) Some grade school
    - (b) Completed grade school
    - (c) Some high school
    - (d) Completed high school
    - (e) Some college
    - (f) Completed college

22. What is your religious preference?
    - (a) Catholic
    - (b) Jewish
    - (c) Protestant
    - (d) Buddhist
    - (e) Moslem
    - (f) Other (write in)

23. What is your ethnic background?
    - (a) Negro
    - (b) Oriental
    - (c) White
    - (d) Half-Oriental
    - (e) Hawaiian
    - (f) Part-Hawaiian
    - (g) Other (write in)

24. What is your current occupation?

    What kind of work does this involve?

25. Do you supervise anyone in your work?
    - (a) Yes
    - (b) No

    If *yes,* please indicate how many people you supervise

26. Do you participate in hiring new personnel in your work?
    (a) Yes
    (b) No

    If *yes*, please describe briefly:

27. What was your father's last occupation?

    What kind of work did this involve?

28. What was your father's education? (Check HIGHEST)
    (a) Some grade school
    (b) Completed grade school
    (c) Some high school
    (d) Completed high school
    (e) Some college
    (f) Completed college

29. How many people who are or have been in a mental hospital have you had contact with?
    (a) How many at work
    (b) How many as friends or relatives

30. Would you think of their troubles as due to nervous breakdown or mental illness?

Please make sure you have answered all questions.
Thank you again for your cooperation.

Bibliography

Adorno, T.W., Frenkel-Brunswik, E., Levinson, D.J., & Sanford, R.N. *The authoritarian personality.* New York: Harper, 1950.

Allen, Lucille. A study of community attitudes toward mental hygiene. *Ment. Hyg., N.Y.,* 1943, *27,* 248-254.

Allport, G. W. *The nature of prejudice.* Boston: Beacon Press, 1954.

Allport, G. W. The historical background of modern social psychology. In G. Lindzey & E. Aronson (Eds.), *The handbook of social psychology.* (2nd ed.) Vol. 1. Reading, Mass.: Addison-Wesley, 1968. Pp. 1-80.

Arieti, S. (Ed.). *American handbook of psychiatry.* New York: Basic Books, 1959-66, 3 vols.

Askenasy, A. R. Social workers' preferences among psychiatric patients. Paper presented at the 7th World Congress of Sociology, Varna, Bulgaria, September, 1970.

Baker, F., & Schulberg, H. C. The development of a community mental health ideology scale. *Comm. mental Health J.,* 1967, *3,* 216-225.

Barton, R. *Institutional neurosis.* (2nd ed.) Bristol: Wright, 1966.

Bennett, R.E. Clinical programs. *The Welfare Reporter,* 1959, *10* (1), 16-23.

Bentz, W. K., Edgerton, J. W., & Kherlopian, M. Perceptions of mental illness among people in a rural area. *Ment. Hyg.,* 1969, *53,* 459-465.

Bentz, W. K., & Edgerton, J. W. The consequences of labeling a person as mentally ill. *Social Psychiatry,* 1971, *6,* 29-33.

British psychiatry: A report. *The Welfare Reporter.* Trenton, N.J.: 1959, *10* (1).

Brown, G.W., Bone, M., Dalison, B., & Wing, J.K. *Schizophrenia and social care: A comparative follow-up study of 339 schizophrenic patients.* London: Oxford, 1966.

Burgess, E. W. Mental health in modern society. In A. M. Rose (Ed.), *Mental health and mental disorder.* New York: Norton, 1955. Pp. 3-17.

Carstairs, G. M. The social limits of eccentricity: an English study. In M. K. Opler (Ed.), *Culture and mental health.* New York: Macmillan, 1959. Pp. 373-390.

Carstairs, G. M., & Heron, A. The social environment of mental hospital patients: a measure of staff attitudes. In M. Greenblatt, D. J. Levinson, & R. H.

Williams (Eds.), *The patient and the mental hospital.* Glencoe, Ill.: Free Press, 1957. Pp. 218-227.

Christie, R. Authoritarianism re-examined. In R. Christie & Marie Jahoda (Eds.), *Studies in the scope and method of 'the authoritarian personality'.* Glencoe, Ill.: Free Press, 1954. Pp. 123-196.

Christie, R., & Merton, R. A sociological study of the value climate of medical schools. In *The ecology of the medical student,* Proceedings of the fifth annual conference, Evanston, Ill., Association of American Medical Colleges, 1958. Reprinted in *J. of medic. Educ.,* 1958, *33* (10), Part II.

Clark, A. W., & Binks, N. M. Relation of age and education to attitudes toward mental illness. *Psychol. Reports,* 1966, *19,* 649-650.

Cohen, J., & Struening, E. L. Factors underlying opinions about mental illness in the personnel of a large mental hospital. Paper read at Amer. Psychol. Ass., Cincinnati, September, 1959.

Cohen, J., & Struening, E. L. Attitudes toward the mentally ill of psychiatric hospital personnel as a function of occupation, education, sex and age. Paper read at Amer. Psychol. Ass., Chicago, September, 1960.

Cohen, J., & Struening, E. L. Opinions about mental illness in the personnel of two large mental hospitals. *J. abnormal soc. Psychol.,* 1962, *64,* 349-360.

Cohen, J., & Struening, E. L. Opinions about mental illness: mental hospital occupational profiles and profile clusters. *Psychol. Reports,* 1963, *12,* 111-124.

Cohen, J., & Struening, E.L. Opinions about mental illness: Hospital social atmosphere profiles and their relevance to effectiveness. *Journal of Consulting Psychology,* 1964, *28,* 291-298.

Cohen, J., & Struening, E.L. Opinions about mental illness: Hospital differences in attitude for eight occupational groups. *Psychological Reports,* 1965, *17,* 25-26.

Crocetti, G., Spiro, H. R., & Siassi, I. Are the ranks closed? Attitudinal social distance and mental illness. *Amer. J. Psychiat.,* 1971, *127,* 1121-1127.

Cumming, Elaine, & Cumming, J. *Closed ranks: an experiment in mental health education.* Cambridge: Harvard Univer. Press, 1957.

de Carozzo, Gladys Carbajal. Ein Versuch zur Erforschung der Einstellungen gegenüber psychisch Kranken. *Social Psychiatry,* 1971, *6,* 34-39.

Dightman, C.R., & Marks, J.B. Employer attitudes toward the employment of the ex-psychiatric patient. *Mental Hygiene,* 1968, *52,* 562-569.

Dohrenwend, B. P., & Chin-Shong, E. Social status and attitudes toward psychological disorder: the problem of tolerance of deviance. *Amer. Sociol. Rev.,* 1967, *32,* 417-433.

Edelman, A., Hammouri, Muneera, Maas, Sophie, & Tanenbaum, S. A study of the attitudes of social workers toward the vocational rehabilitation of mental patients. Unpublished masters' thesis, New York University, 1960.

Edwards, A. E. *Statistical methods for the behavioral sciences.* New York: Rinehart, 1954.

Ellenberger, H. A comparison of European and American psychiatry. *Bull. Menninger Clin.*, 1955, *19*, 43-52.

Ellenberger, H. Cultural aspects of mental illness. *Amer. J. Psychother.*, 1960, *14*, 158-173.

Enright, J.B., & Jaeckle, W.R. Psychiatric symptoms and diagnosis in two subcultures. *International Journal of Social Psychiatry*, 1963, *9*, 12-17.

Eysenck, H. J. *The psychology of politics.* London: Routledge, 1954.

Fairweather, G.W., Sanders, D.H., Maynard, H., Cressler, D.L., & Bleck, D.S. *Community life for the mentally ill.* Chicago: Aldine, 1969.

Ferguson, C. A. *The legacy of neglect.* Fort Worth, Texas: Industrial Mental Health Associates, 1965.

Foucault, M. *Madness and civilization: A history of insanity in the age of reason.* New York: Pantheon, 1965.

Frenkel-Brunswik, E. A study of prejudice in children. *Human Relations,* 1948, *1*, 295-306.

Giedt, F. H. Patterns of attitude similarity among psychiatric hospital staff. *Int. J. soc. Psychiat.*, 1959, *4*, 280-290.

Gilbert, Doris C., & Levinson, D. J. Ideology, personality and institutional policy in the mental hospital. *J. abnorm. soc. Psychology,* 1956, *53*, 263-271.

Gilbert, Doris C., & Levinson, D. J. 'Custodialism' and 'humanism' in mental hospital structure and in staff ideology. In M. Greenblatt, D.J. Levinson & R. H. Williams (Eds.), *The patient and the mental hospital.* Glencoe, Ill.: Free Press, 1957. Pp. 20-35 (a).

Gilbert, Doris C., & Levinson, D. J. Role performance, ideology, and personality in mental hospital aides. In M. Greenblatt, D.J. Levinson & R.H. Williams (Eds.), *The patient and the mental hospital.* Glencoe, Ill.: Free Press, 1957. Pp. 197-208 (b).

Giovannoni, J.M., & Ullmann, L.P. Conceptions of mental health held by psychiatric patients. *Journal of Clinical Psychology,* 1963, *19*, 398-400.

Goffman, E. *Asylums: essays on the social situation of mental patients and other inmates.* Garden City, N.Y.: Doubleday, 1961.

Greenblatt, M. Implications for psychiatry and hospital practice: the movement from custodial hospital to therapeutic community. In M. Greenblatt, D. J. Levinson & R. H. Williams (Eds.), *The patient and the mental hospital.* Glencoe, Ill.: Free Press, 1957. Pp. 611-619.

Greenblatt, M., Levinson, D. J., & Williams, R. H. (Eds.). *The patient and the mental hospital.* Glencoe, Ill.: Free Press, 1957.

Grob, Samuel, & Olshansky, Simon. Employer attitudes and practices in the hiring of ex-mental patients. *Mental Hygiene,* 1958, *42*, 391-401.

Halpert, H. P. Surveys of public opinions and attitudes about mental illness. Implications for communications activities. *Public Health Reports,* 1965, *80*, 589-597.

Halpert, H. P. Public acceptance of the mentally ill: an exploration of attitudes. *Public Health Reports,* 1969, *84*, 59-64.

Harmon, H. H. *Modern factor analysis.* Chicago: Univ. of Chicago Press, 1960.

Hoenig, J., & Hamilton, M.W. *The de-segregation of the mentally ill.* London: Routledge & Kegan Paul, 1969.

Hollingshead, A. B., & Redlich, F. C. *Social class and mental illness.* New York: Wiley, 1958.

Howard, T. W., & Sommer, R. A. A critical examination of ideology, personality, and institutional policy in the mental hospital. Unpublished manuscript. No date.

Hyman, H. H., & Sheatsley, P. B. 'The authoritarian personality' – a methodological critique. In R. Christie & Marie Jahoda (Eds.), *Studies in the scope and method of 'The authoritarian personality'.* Glencoe, Ill.: Free Press, 1954. Pp. 50-122.

Inkeles, A., & Levinson, D.J. National character: the study of modal personality and sociocultural systems. In G. Lindzey & E. Aronson (Eds.), *The handbook of social psychology.* (2nd ed.). Vol. 4. Reading, Mass.: Addison-Wesley, 1969. Pp. 418-506.

Jackson, D. N., & Messick, S. A note on ethnocentrism and acquiescent response sets. *J. abnorm. soc. Psychol.*, 1957, *54*, 132-134.

Jackson, D. N., & Messick, S. Content and style in personality assessment. *Psychol. Bull.*, 1958, *55*, 243-252.

Joint Commission on Mental Illness and Health. *Action for mental health.* New York: Science Editions, Inc., 1961.

Jones, Maxwell. *The therapeutic community.* New York: Basic Books, 1953.

Jones, Maxwell. Community psychiatry. In J.G. Howells (Ed.), *Modern perspectives in world psychiatry.* London: Oliver & Boyd, 1968.

Judd IV, G. P. *Hawaii, an informal history.* New York: Collier Books, 1961.

Klineberg, O. *Tensions affecting international understanding.* New York: Soc. Sci. Res. Council, 1950, Bull. 62.

Klineberg, O. *Social psychology.* (Revised ed.). New York: Holt, 1954.

Kraft, A. M. The therapeutic community. In S. Arieti (Ed.), *American handbook of psychiatry,* Vol. 3. New York: Basic Books, 1966.

Kramer, B. M. *Day hospital.* New York: Grune & Stratton, 1962.

Landy, D., & Greenblatt, M. *Halfway house.* Washington: Vocational Rehabilitation Administration, 1965.

Lawton, M. P. Personality and attitudinal correlates of psychiatric aide performance. *J. social Psychol.*, 1965, *66*, 215-226.

Lemkau, P.V., & Crocetti, G.M. An urban population's opinion and knowledge about mental illness. *Amer. J. Psychiatry,* 1962, *118*, 692-700.

Lewis, N. D. C. American psychiatry from its beginnings to World War II. In S. Arieti (Ed.), *American handbook of psychiatry.* New York: Basic Books, 1959. Vol. 1. Pp. 3-17.

Lind, A. W. *Hawaii's people.* Honolulu: Univ. of Hawaii Press, 1955.

Lindzey, G., & Aronson, E. (Eds.). *The handbook of social psychology* (2nd ed.). Reading, Mass.: Addison-Wesley, 1968-69. 5 vols.

Linn, L. Hospital psychiatry. In S. Arieti (Ed.), *American handbook of psychiatry.* New York: Basic Books, 1959. Vol. II. Pp. 1829-1839.

Lipset, S. M. Democracy and working-class authoritarianism. *American Sociological Review,* 1959, *24,* 482-501.

Lipset, S. M. *Political man.* New York: Doubleday, 1960.

Magee, H. S. The ancillary professions in British mental hospitals. *The Welfare Reporter,* 1959, *10* (1), 37-42.

Markwell, N. G. The teenager's conception of mental illness. Unpublished doctoral dissertation, Purdue Univer., 1959.

Meyer, J. K. Attitudes toward mental illness in a Maryland community. *Public Health Rep.,* 1964, *79,* 769-772.

Middleton, J. Prejudices and opinions of mental hospital employees regarding mental illness. *Amer. J. Psychiat.,* 1953, *110.*

Mora, G. *Recent American psychiatry.* New York: Basic Books, 1959. Pp. 18-57.

Morrissey, J. R. The case for the family care of the mentally ill. *Community Mental Health Journal Monograph,* 1967, No. 2.

Moscovici, S. *La psychanalyse, son image et son public.* Paris: Presses universitaires de France, 1960.

Myers, J.K., & Roberts, B.H. *Family and class dynamics in mental illness.* New York: Wiley, 1959, p. 286.

Nigrin, R. Similarity and differences in American and European psychiatry. *Neuropsychiatry,* 1959, *5,* 153-169.

Nunnally, J. C. The communication of mental health information: a comparison of opinions of experts and the public with mass media presentations. *Behav. Sci.,* 1957, *2,* 222-230.

Nunnally, J. C. Opinions of psychologists and psychiatrists about mental health problems. *J. consult. Psychol.,* 1958, *22,* 178-182.

Nunnally, J. C. *Popular conceptions of mental health.* New York: Holt, Rinehart & Winston, 1961.

Olshansky, S., Grob, S., & Ekdahl, Miriam. Survey of employment experiences of patients discharged from three state mental hospitals during period 1951-1953. *Mental Hygiene,* 1960, *44,* 519.

Opler, M. K. (Ed.). *Culture and mental health.* New York: Macmillan, 1959.

Osgood, C.E., Suci, G.J., & Tannenbaum, P.H. *The measurement of meaning.* Urbana, Ill.: Univ. of Illinois Press, 1957.

Parsons, T. Illness and the role of the physician: a sociological perspective. In C. Kluckhohn, H. Murray & D. M. Schneider (Eds.), *Personality in nature, society and culture.* (2nd ed.). New York: Knopf, 1953. Pp. 609-617.

Parsons, T. The mental hospital as a type of organization. In M. Greenblatt, D. J. Levinson & R.H. Williams (Eds.), *The patient and the mental hospital.* Glencoe, Ill.: Free Press, 1957. Pp. 108-129.

Peplau, Hildegard E. Principles of psychiatric nursing. In S. Arieti (Ed.), *American handbook of psychiatry.* New York: Basic Books, 1959. Vol. II. Pp. 1840-1856.

Phillips, D. L. Rejection of the mentally ill: the influence of behavior and sex. *Amer. sociol. Rev.*, 1964, *29*, 679-687.

Phillips, D. L. Public identification and acceptance of the mentally ill. *Amer. J. public Health*, 1966, *56*, 755-763.

Pine, F., & Levinson, D. J. Two patterns of ideology, role conception, and personality among hospital aides. In M. Greenblatt, D.J. Levinson & R. H. Williams (Eds.), *The patient and the mental hospital.* Glencoe, Ill.: Free Press, 1957. Pp. 208-217.

Polsky, H.W., Claster, D.S., & Goldberg, C. (Eds.). *Social system perspectives in residential institutions.* East Lansing: Michigan State University Press, 1970.

Pratt, S. Of myths and models: an agonizing reappraisal. Paper read at Amer. Psychol. Ass., New York, September, 1961.

Pratt, S., Giannitrapani, D., & Khanna, Prabha. Attitudes toward the mental hospital and selected population characteristics. *J. clin. Psychol.*, 1960, *16*, 214-218.

Pratt, S., Scott, G., Treesh, E., *et al.* The mental hospital and the 'treatment-field'. *J. psychol. Stud.*, 1960, *11*, Suppl. No. 8.

Querido, A. Experiment in public health. *Bulletin World Federation for Mental Health*, 1954, *6*, 203-216.

Rabkin, Judith G. Opinions about mental illness: a review of the literature. *Psychol. Bull.*, 1972, *77*, 153-171.

Rappaport, J., Chinsky, J.M., & Cowen, E.L. *Innovations in helping chronic patients.* New York: Academic Press, 1971.

Ray, I. Ideal character of the officers of a hospital for the insane. *Amer. J. Insanity*, 1873, *30*, 67.

Reiss, A. J., Jr., Duncan, O. D., Hatt, P. K., & North, C. C. *Occupations and social status.* New York: Free Press, 1961.

Rose, A. M. (Ed.). *Mental health & mental disorder: a sociological approach.* New York: Norton, 1955.

Rosen, A. C. Changes in the perception of mental illness and mental health. *Perceptual and motor skills*, 1970, *31*, 203-208.

Scheff, T. J. The role of the mentally ill and the dynamics of mental disorder: A research framework. *Sociometry*, 1963, *26*, 436-453.

Schermerhorn, R. A. Social psychiatry. In A. M. Rose (Ed.), *Mental health and mental disorder.* New York: Norton, 1955. Pp. 42-60.

Smith, H. L., & Levinson, D. J. The major aims and organizational characteristics of mental hospitals. In M. Greenblatt. D.J. Levinson & R.H. Williams (Eds.), *The patient and the mental hospital.* Glencoe, Ill.: Free Press, 1957. Pp. 3-8.

Snedecor, G.W. *Statistical methods* (5th ed.). Ames. Iowa: Iowa State College Press, 1956.

Stanton, A.H., & Schwartz, M.S. *The mental hospital.* New York: Basic Books, 1954.

Star, Shirley A. The public's ideas about mental illness. Paper read at Nat. Ass. Ment. Hlth, Indianapolis, 1955.

Star, Shirley A. Public attitudes – a measure of the difficulties. In American Psychiatric Association (Ed.), *Psychiatry, the press and the public.* Washington: Editors, 1956. Pp. 1-5.

Star, Shirley A. The place of psychiatry in popular thinking. Paper read at Amer. Ass. Publ. Opin. Res., Washington, 1957.

Stouffer, S. A. *Communism, conformity, and civil liberties.* New York: Doubleday, 1955.

Szasz, T. S. *The myth of mental illness: Foundations of a theory of personal conduct.* New York: Harper and Row, 1961.

Tannenbaum, G. The walk-in clinic. In S. Arieti (Ed.), *American handbook of psychiatry.* Vol. 3. New York: Basic Books, 1966.

Tereshima, S. The structure of rejecting attitudes toward the mentally ill in Japan. In W. Caudill & T. Y. Lin (Eds.), *Mental health research in Asia and the Pacific.* Honolulu: East-West Center Press, 1969. Pp. 195-215.

Thomas, W. I., & Znaniecki, F. *The Polish peasant in Europe and America.* 5 vols. Boston: Badger, 1918-1920.

Treesh, E. O., Struening, E. L., Pratt, S., *et al.* Attitudes of mental hospital employees toward mental patients, mental illness, and treatment. In progress. Reported in Health Information Foundation, An inventory of social and economic research in health (8th and 9th eds.). New York: Editors, 1959, 1960.

Tringo, J. L. The hierarchy of preference toward disability groups. *J. spec. Educ.,* 1970, *4,* 295-306.

Vernallis, F. F., & St. Pierre, R. G. Volunteer workers' opinions about mental illness. *J. clinical Psychol.,* 1964, *20,* 140-143.

Weber, M. *The religion of China.* Glencoe, Ill.: Free Press, 1951.

Wechsler, H., & Landy, D. (Eds.). New pathways from the mental hospital. *Journal of Social Issues,* 1960, *16* (2), 1-80.

Wing, J.K., & Brown, G.W. *Institutionalism and schizophrenia: A comparative study of three mental hospitals 1960-1968.* Cambridge: Cambridge University Press, 1970.

Woodward, J. L. Changing ideas on mental illness and treatment. *Amer. Sociol. Rev.,* 1951, *16,* 443-454.

Wright, F.H., & Klein, R. A. Attitudes of hospital personnel and the community regarding mental illness. *J. Counseling Psychol.,* 1966, *13,* 106-107.

Index of names

Index of subjects